高等院校旅游专业"互联网+"创新规划教材

旅游英语

（修订版）

主　编　于立新　蔡　宇

内 容 简 介

本次修订，本着"精讲多练""在用中学"的原则，减少了两个单元，增加了三个翻转课堂活动，充分利用网络教学资源，将视频、音频、团建、市场调研等融入旅游英语教学，营建旅游服务、景区规划、包容性与可持续性旅游发展等多维场景，既保持了原版的服务哲学、户外休闲、旅游业要素等核心内容，又在文旅融合、人地关系、全球化视角上进行了多方面拓展，力求在案例教学中提高学生的专业英语听说读写的应用能力。

本书可作为普通高校旅游管理相关专业英语教学之用，也可以为旅游和其他行业从业人员提供英语文化的学习平台。

图书在版编目(CIP)数据

旅游英语：修订版/于立新，蔡宇主编．—2 版．—北京：北京大学出版社，2023.1
高等院校旅游专业"互联网+"创新规划教材
ISBN 978-7-301-32785-2

Ⅰ.①旅⋯ Ⅱ.①于⋯ ②蔡⋯ Ⅲ.①旅游—英语—高等学校—教材 Ⅳ.①F59

中国版本图书馆 CIP 数据核字(2021)第 273679 号

书　　　名	旅游英语（修订版） LÜYOU YINGYU (XIUDING BAN)
著作责任者	于立新　蔡　宇　主编
策 划 编 辑	刘国明
责 任 编 辑	刘国明　罗丽丽
数 字 编 辑	金常伟
标 准 书 号	ISBN 978-7-301-32785-2
出 版 发 行	北京大学出版社
地　　　址	北京市海淀区成府路 205 号　100871
网　　　址	http://www.pup.cn　新浪微博：@北京大学出版社
编辑部邮箱	pup6@pup.cn
总编室邮箱	zpup@pup.cn
电　　　话	邮购部 010-62752015　发行部 010-62750672　编辑部 010-62750667
印 刷 者	河北滦县鑫华书刊印刷厂
经 销 者	新华书店
	787 毫米×1092 毫米　16 开本　13.25 印张　318 千字 2013 年 1 月第 1 版 2023 年 1 月第 2 版　2023 年 7 月第 2 次印刷
定　　　价	42.00 元

未经许可，不得以任何方式复制或抄袭本书之部分或全部内容。
版权所有，侵权必究
举报电话：010-62752024　电子信箱：fd@pup.pku.edu.cn
图书如有印装质量问题，请与出版部联系，电话：010-62756370

修订版前言

本书第一版问世至今已经九年了。九年来，国内外旅游业在变革中不断前行，业界和学界的焦点从相对主要关注经济问题转向更加多元化的视角。在"大众创业"的热潮中，旅游业因其门槛低的优势，成为不少年轻人创业的首选。自驾、体育、户外、游轮、主题乐园等旅游形式正逐渐成为大众旅游产品，旅游产业也日益成为地方经济的支柱产业；另外，慕课、微课、网络教学等新的教学方式使得学生比以往任何时候都更易获得学习素材，也更需要一部教材引导着他们在海量的资料中淘到对提高自己的专业英语水平最有价值的信息。在这样的背景下，本书进行了修订，一方面保留了原版对大旅游业全景式的通览，另一方面增加了学生的实训力度。同时，又对越来越成熟的旅游新业态和旅游界越来越关心的问题，在教材中予以了呼应。

本着上述原则，修订版将原来 16 个单元改为 14 个单元，适用于 64~96 课时的旅游专业英语教学，同时将课堂活动案例从 4 次大幅度增加为 7 次，其中两次是欣赏英文字幕的旅游题材的纪录片，教师引导课堂讨论；单元设计中，编者对传统的旅游业态进行了整合，新增了"生态旅游"和"旅游的影响"两个单元，并本着反映实践的发展和现场实景模拟的原则，用新的材料对各单元的对话、练习、专业词汇模块等进行了充分的修改，原有的"Tourism Link"因为实训强度一般，本次修订进行了删减，这样，每个单元从原版的 5 个部分修订为 4 个部分，同时增加了练习的强度。

编者希望本次修订能够为广大旅游管理和相关专业的师生提供一本反映旅游最新发展、实训旅游服务场景、接轨国外旅游管理、扩展专业外语能力的旅游英语教材。

除了文本部分，本书还有网络版资源，与正版教材配套使用，内容包括电子课件、与课堂案例和活动教学项目配合的视频材料和 PPT 形式的背景介绍、听力练习的音频材料、练习参考答案，编者多年来收集的多部英文字幕的英美旅游纪录片及其单词表也囊括在内，希望对拓展学生的国际视野有所裨益。作者团队将不定期更新网络版资源的内容，并展开与本教材使用者的网络互动，不断丰富网络版资源的内容；此外，各单元练习一的听力练习音频，除放在网络版资源中外，也同时以二维码的形式出现在教材相关位置。

本书由于立新教授、蔡宇副教授担任主编，修订中参考了诸多国内外学界前辈的成果，不胜感激，在此诚挚致谢。书中各种疏漏乃至错误之处，望各位不吝指正。

编　者

2022 年 5 月于西安

资源索引

初 版 前 言

本书是在旅游产业蓬勃发展、旅游学的学科地位持续提高的背景下推出的一本反映大旅游业前沿成果的专业英语教材，旨在培养学生运用专业英语从事旅游服务、旅游管理并进行初步的旅游研究的能力，适用于72~96课时的专业英语教学。全书的16个单元，从服务哲学入手，既涵盖了旅游业传统的交通、餐饮、住宿、景区、旅行社等业务领域和旅游产品、旅游营销等商业活动，又探讨了特种旅游、休闲娱乐、户外运动、节庆会展等旅游业的新兴话题，并从沟通、文化、可持续发展等视角对此进行了梳理，是一本体系完备、注重应用、对学生的英语和专业水平的提高均有帮助的旅游专业英语教材。

每个单元从结构上分5个部分：课文、对话、旅游业实用链接、专业英语词汇表和练习。课文由A、B两部分组成，围绕各单元的主题从不同角度加以阐述，教学中可被分别用作精读和泛读内容；不仅各单元的对话是单元主题在旅游交际中的具体应用，而且全书的对话整体上也演示了一次旅游活动的各个场景；旅游业实用链接部分使学生可直接接触行业实践中在用的单据、表格等文献，对行业有感性的认识；专业英语词汇表，一方面可模块式地扩大学生的专业词汇量，另一方面希望能够成为学生的专业英语手册，供其在职业生涯中查阅。

上述的5个部分，也体现了本教材较明显的阶梯性和层次性，英语基础较差的同学至少可以从对话、旅游业实用链接、专业英语词汇表的学习中掌握一些工作岗位有用的词汇和表达方式，从而与客人进行职业所需的必要交流；有一定英语基础的同学可以进一步掌握课文A，使自己的英语向使用专业英语、较灵活地与客人交流的方向迈进；英语基础较好的同学则可以要求他们掌握课文B，使自己的专业英语交流能力更上层楼。

除上述16个单元外，本书的一大特色就是设计了4个课堂案例和活动教学项目，经作者多年教学实践，对提高学生外语学习兴趣，培养团队合作和探索精神，提升口语水平、沟通技巧、思辨和研究能力，乃至了解客源国人们的思维方式，都有明显的作用。

本书的素材来自旅游实践活动中的各类实用材料，包括景区宣传册、国外旅游网站、原版专业文献等，确保其内容的真实性和表达方式的原汁原味，同时照顾国内学生实际，在词汇、句型等方面适当降低难度。

本书体例新颖、结构合理、知识面广、注重实践操作的相关知识和旅游业务的系统性，是旅游管理专业学生学习专业知识、提高专业英语能力不可多得的教科书。

本书参考了学界许多前辈的成果，在此诚挚致谢。由于时间仓促和水平所限，书中疏漏乃至错误之处在所难免，恳请各位专家和老师批评指正。

编 者

2012年11月于西安

目　　录

Unit 1　Service ··· 1
Unit 2　Tourism ·· 15
Activity 1：New Headline ·· 28
Unit 3　Hospitality Industry ··· 30
Unit 4　Tourism Attraction ··· 45
Activity 2：Incoming Tourists' Overall Impression on China ································· 57
Unit 5　Tourist Product ·· 60
Unit 6　Tourism Marketing ··· 76
Activity 3：Huizhou Trilogy ··· 88
Unit 7　Communication ·· 89
Unit 8　Special Interest Tours ··· 103
Activity 4：Freedom Trail ·· 115
Unit 9　Sports and Outdoor Activities ··· 116
Unit 10　Leisure and Recreation ··· 131
Activity 5：The Ski Resort ··· 145
Unit 11　Ecotourism ·· 147
Unit 12　Tourism Culture ··· 157
Activity 6：Museum Visitors' Survey ·· 173
Unit 13　Tourism Impact ·· 180
Unit 14　Tourism Sustainability ·· 192
Activity 7：Sherpa ·· 200
References ·· 202

Unit 1 Service

PART I TEXT

Text A What Are Services?

Put in the simplest terms, services are deeds, processes and performances provided or coproduced by one entity or person for another entity or person. The services offered by IBM are not tangible things that can be touched, seen, and felt, but rather are intangible deeds and performances provided and/or coproduced for its customers. To be concrete, IBM offers repair and maintenance service for its equipment, consulting services for IT and e-commerce applications, training service, web design and hosting, and other services. These services may include a final, tangible report, a website, or in the case of training, tangible instructional materials. But for the most part, the entire service is represented to the client through problem analysis activities, meetings with the client, follow-up calls, and reporting—a series of deeds, processes, and performances. Similarly, the core offering of hospitals, hotels, banks, and utilities are primarily deeds and actions performed for customers, or coproduced with them.

Although we will rely on the simple, broad definition of services, you should be aware that over time service and the service sector of the economy have been defined in subtly different ways. The variety of definition can often explain the confusion or disagreements people have when discussing services and when describing industries that comprise the service sector of the economy. Compatible with our simple, broad definition is one that defines services to include "all economic activities whose output is not a physical product or construction, is generally consumed at the time it is produced, and provides added value in forms (such as convenience, amusement, timeliness, comfort, or health) that are essentially intangible concerns of its first purchaser."

Service Industries, Service as Products, Customer Service, and Derived Service

As we begin our discussion of services marketing and management, it is important to draw distinctions between service industries and companies, services as products, customer service, and derived services. Sometimes when people think of service, they think only of customer service, but service can be divided into four distinct categories. The tool and strategies you will learn in this text can be applied to any of these categories.

Service industries and companies include those industries and companies typically classified within the service sector whose core product is a service. All of the following companies can be considered pure service companies: Marriott International[1] (lodging), American Airlines[2] (transportation), Charles Schwab[3] (financial service), Mayo Clinic[4] (health care).

Services as products represent a wide range of intangible product offerings that customers value and pay for in the marketplace. Service products are sold by service companies and by non-service companies such as manufacturers and technology companies. For example, IBM and Hewlet-Packard[5] offer information technology consulting services to the marketplace, competing with firms such as EDS[6] and Accenture[7] which are traditional pure service firms. Other industry examples included department stores, like Macy's that sell services such as gift wrapping and shipping, and pet stores like PetSmart that sell pet grooming and training services.

Customer service is also a critical aspect of what we mean by "service." Customer service is the service provided in support of a company's core products. Companies typically do not charge for customer service. Customer service can occur on-site (as when a retail employee helps a customer find a desired item or answers a question), or it can occur over the phone or via the internet (e.g. dell computer provides real-time chat sessions to help customers diagnose hardware problems). Many companies operate customer service call centers, often staffed around the clock. Quality customer service is essential to building customer relationships. It should not, however, be confused with the services provided for sale by the company.

Derived service is yet another way to look at what service means. In an award-winning article in the *Journal of Marketing*, Steve Vargo and Bob kusch argue for a new dominant logic for marketing that suggests that all products and physical goods are valued for the services they provide. Drawing on the work of respected economists, marketers, and philosophers, the two authors suggest that the value derived from physical goods is really the service provided by the good, not the good itself. For example, they suggest that a pharmaceutical provides medical services, a razor provides barbering services, and computers provide information and data manipulation services. Although this view is somewhat abstract, it suggests an even broader, more inclusive, view of the meaning of service.

Characteristics of Services Compared to Goods

There is a general agreement that differences between goods and services exist and that the distinctive characteristics discussed in this section result in challenges (as well as advantages) for managers of services. That is, services tend to be more heterogeneous, more intangible, more difficult to evaluate than goods, but the differences between goods and services are not black and white by any means.

Intangibility

The most basic distinguishing characteristic of services is intangibility. Because services are performances or actions rather than objects, they cannot be seen, felt, tasted, or touched in the same manner that you can sense tangible goods. For example, health care services are actions (such as surgery, diagnosis, examination, and treatment) performed by providers and directed toward patient, although the patient may be able to see and touch certain tangible components of the service (like the equipment or hospital room). In fact, many services such as health care are difficult for the consumer to grasp even mentally. Even after a diagnosis or surgery has been completed the patient may not fully comprehend the service performed, although tangible evidence of the service (e. g., incision, bandaging, pain) may be quite apparent.

Heterogeneity

Because services are performances, frequently produced by humans, no two services will be precisely alike. The employees delivering the service frequently are the service in the customer's eyes, and people may differ in their performance from day to day or even hour to hour. Heterogeneity also results because no two customers are precisely alike; each will have unique demands or experience the service in a unique way. Thus the heterogeneity connected with service is largely the result of human interactions (between and among employees and customers). For example, a tax accountant may provide a different service experience to two different customers on the same day depending on their individual needs and personalities and on whether the accountant is interviewing them when he or she is fresh in the morning or tired at the end of a long day of meetings.

Simultaneous Production and Consumption

Whereas most goods are produced first, then sold and consumed, most services are sold first and then produced and consumed simultaneously. For example, an automobile can be manufactured in Detroit, shipped to San Francisco, sold two months later, and consumed over a period of years. But restaurant services cannot be provided until they have been sold, and the dining experience is essentially produced and consumed at the same time. Frequently this situation also means that customers are present while the service is being produced and thus view and may even take part in the production process as co-producers or co-creators of the service. Simultaneity also means that customers will frequently interact with each other during the service production process and thus may affect each others' experiences. For example, strangers seated next to each other in airplane may well affect the nature of the service experience for each other. The fact passengers understand this is clearly apparent in the way business travelers will often go to great lengths to be sure they are not seated next to families with small children. Another outcome of simultaneous production and consumption is that service producers find themselves playing a role as part of product itself and as an essential ingredient in the service experience for the consumer.

Perishability

Perishability refers to the fact that services cannot be saved, stored, resold, or returned. A seat on an airplane or in a restaurant, an hour of lawyer's time, or telephone line capacity not used or purchased cannot be reclaimed and used or resold at a later time. Perishability is in contrast to goods that can be stored in inventory or resold another day, or even returned if the consumer is unhappy. Would it not be nice if a bad haircut could be returned or resold to another consumer? Perishability makes this action an unlikely possibility for most services.

Words and Expressions

amusement	[əˈmjuːzmənt]	n.	消遣，娱乐
articulate	[ɑːˈtɪkjulət]	v.	明确表达；adj. 善于表达的
barber	[ˈbɑːbə]	v.	为……理发；修整
bandage	[ˈbændɪdʒ]	v.	用绷带包扎
comprehend	[kɔmprɪˈhend]	v.	理解；包含
comprise	[kəmˈpraɪz]	v.	包含；由……组成
compatible	[kəmˈpætəbl]	a.	兼容的；能共处的
distinguish	[dɪsˈtɪŋgwɪʃ]	v.	区分；辨别
diagnosis	[daɪəgˈnəusɪs]	n.	诊断
deed	[diːd]	n.	行动
fluctuation	[flʌktjuˈeɪʃən]	n.	起伏，波动
follow-up	[ˈfɔləuʌp]	a.	后续的；增补的
framework	[ˈfreɪmwəːk]	n.	框架，结构
hosting	[ˈhəustɪŋ]	n.	待客，接待
heterogeneity	[ˌhetərədʒəˈniəti]	n.	[生物] 异质性；[化学] 不均匀性，多相性
illustrate	[ˈɪləstreɪt]	v.	阐明，举例说明
intangible	[ɪnˈtændʒəbl]	a.	无形的
incision	[ɪnˈsɪʒn]	n.	切口
insight	[ˈɪnsaɪt]	n.	洞察力；洞悉
inventory	[ˈɪnvəntri]	n.	存货，存货清单；详细目录
lodging	[ˈlɔdʒɪŋ]	n.	寄宿；寄宿处
manufacturer	[ˌmænjuˈfæktʃərə]	n.	制造商
manipulation	[məˌnɪpjuˈleɪʃn]	n.	操作；处理
navigation	[ˌnævɪˈgeɪʃn]	n.	航行；航海
on-site	[ɔnsaɪt]	a.	现场的
pharmaceutical	[ˌfɑːməˈsjuːtɪkl]	a.	制药（学）的；n. 药物
patent	[ˈpeɪtnt]	n.	专利权
resort	[rɪˈzɔːt]	n.	度假胜地
subtly	[ˈsʌtli]	a.	精细地
surgery	[ˈsəːdʒəri]	n.	外科；外科手术
tangible	[ˈtændʒəbl]	a.	有形的
year-round			整年的；一年到头的
customers service			客户服务；售后服务
derived services			派生服务
maintenance service			维护服务
to be concrete			具体地讲

Notes

（1）Marriott International：万豪国际集团是全球首屈一指的酒店管理公司。
（2）American Airlines：美国航空公司。
（3）Charles Schwab：嘉信理财是一家总部设在旧金山的金融服务公司，成立于1971年，如今已成为美国个人金融服务市场的领导者。
（4）Mayo Clinic：马约诊所，世界著名的医疗机构，总部位于美国明尼苏达州罗彻斯特。
（5）Hewlet-Packard：惠普公司。
（6）EDS：电子数据系统公司（Electronic Data Systems Corporation，EDS），是美国的一家全球信息技术服务公司。
（7）Accenture：埃森哲公司，是全球最大的管理咨询公司和技术服务供应商之一。

Text B　Service Level Agreement：Consequences for Non-performance

This article examines the ongoing challenge of establishing effective consequences for non-performance in Service Level Agreements (SLAs).

High Expectations

Like marriages, both parties generally enter SLAs with the best of intentions. Everyone anticipates a relationship that will be mutually beneficial, successful, and last a long while. The service provider expects to make a reasonable profit while satisfying the client. The customer expects that the service provided will meet their needs at an affordable price. If the service provider is an internal department, the expectations may he described differently, but they are basically the same.

For Better, but Not for Worse

Again, like a marriage, there is a nagging question[1] regarding SLAs—What happens when the expectations are not met? The answer is fairly simple when the expectations of an external service provider are not met. For example, if the customer does not pay, the provider simply discontinues the service. This alternative is not any more satisfactory than divorce. Although not quite as simple, the solution is similar for the customer of the external service provider. If the delivered service does not meet the level that has (hopefully) been specified in the contract, the customer can stop paying for the service.

Unfortunately, in either one of these scenarios, the result is reminiscent of an unsuccessful marriage—a divorce, with the terms of the separation determined through the intervention of lawyers and courts. It becomes a situation in which there are no real winners (except, perhaps, the attorneys). Of course, if the service provider and the client are part of the same company, the prospect of withholding service or payment is really not a viable option.

Can Punitive Penalties Motivate?

Thus, the question remains—What should a customer do when a service provider fails to meet service level guarantees? Popular thinking gravitates toward penalties[2]. The reasoning seems to be that if the service providers do not meet the commitment, then they deserve to be punished. The hope is that the threat of punishment will provide sufficient motivation to cause the provider to ensure that service level guarantees are met. In addition, <u>this punishment-oriented thinking purports that if the threat alone does not prevent service level violations, then the pain caused by the penalty will certainly deter future violations</u>. A corollary to this thinking is that the penalty can also serve as compensation for the losses resulting from substandard service. Sadly, this thinking is often misguided.

Monetary Penalties—A House of Cards

One key misstep in this trail of erroneous thinking is the belief that penalties must be monetary. To begin with, it is difficult to apply financial to in-house service providers. Granted, some financial penalties for in-house service providers[3] are possible—e. g., bonuses could be reduced.

Any type of penalty for nonperformance must be significant, whether for an in-house or an external group. And on the pragmatic side, a penalty to compensate the client for the impact of the substandard level of service is usually not workable. It is difficult to negotiate such agreements. Instead, the penalty must cause enough discomfort or pain to the service provider that avoiding it acts as an incentive to meet the service commitment. Although highly unethical, some service providers will make service level guarantees and then, subsequently, decide that it is cheaper to pay the penalty than to meet the service. Besides lacking ethics, this approach is likely to be detrimental to business since customer will almost certainly desert when contracts expire. It is clear that, often, financial penalties do not cause enough pain for the service provider.

Cutting Off Your Nose to Spite Your Face

Regardless of whether a service provider is in-house or external, it is unlikely that financial penalties can be large enough to fully compensate the client's company for the consequences of the degraded service. This cannot be stated too strongly. And, remember, agreeing to large financial penalties would quickly put external service providers out of business. Similarly, when it comes to internal SLAs, cutting the IT department's budget is a self-defeating strategy. Likewise, financial penalties applied directly to the IT staff (e. g., reduced bonuses) will quickly lead to disaffection and ultimately to desertion (yes, even in today's job market).

With both in-house and external service providers, if the financial penalty is material, the result will be to reduce their ability to deliver the required service. Clients must keep in mind that the goal is to motivate the provider to deliver the level of service that is necessary, not to hinder the group's ability to provide services in the future.

Other Kinds of Penalties

Which means that those negotiating SLAs may want to look at alternatives to financial penalties. The secret is to be creative. Many consequences for nonperformance—besides the sheer size of a penalty check—can cause amply pain. Consequences that embarrass are good candidates, as are those that force an escalation of problems in the service provider's hierarchy. While space does not allow a full exploration of many possibilities, this offers a basic starting point.

Considering Incentive-Based Agreements[4]

Behavioral psychologists have long known that positive reinforcement is far more effective in modifying behavior than negative reinforcement. This is worth considering when negotiating service level agreements. Consider rewards for meeting or exceeding guarantees, rather than penalties for nonperformance. Bonuses for in-house staff can be an option. More radical, but potentially very effective, are incentive payments to external service providers that deliver a high level of service.

Remember that in contemplating the creation of consequences for nonperformance, the most mutually beneficial relationship may be attained by staying creative and flexible. Think outside of the box. Consider both positive and negative alternatives and always remember that financial penalties may not be the best answer for many situations.

Words and Expressions

nag	[næg]	v.	抱怨；困扰；折磨
reminiscent	[ˌreməˈnɪsənt]	n.	回忆录；a. 怀旧的
attorney	[əˈtɜːrni]	n.	代理人；律师
withhold	[wɪðˈhoʊld]	v.	抑制（某事物）；克制
punitive	[ˈpjuːnətɪv]	a.	惩罚的；刑罚的
gravitate	[ˈɡrævɪteɪt]	v.	受重力作用；被吸引
purport	[pəˈpɔːt]	n.	意义，要旨；v. 声称，意味着
violation	[ˌvaɪəˈleɪʃən]	n.	违反；妨碍；侵犯
corollary	[ˈkɔrəleri]	n.	必然的结果；推论
erroneous	[ɪˈroʊnɪəs]	a.	错误的
degrade	[dɪˈɡreɪd]	v.	降低；（使）退化
negotiate	[nɪˈɡoʊʃieɪt]	v.	谈判；协商；交涉
exploration	[ˌekspləˈreɪʃn]	n.	勘探；探险；搜索；研究
psychologist	[saɪˈkɑlədʒɪst]	n.	心理学研究者；心理学家
potentially	[pəˈtenʃəli]	ad.	潜在地；可能地
contemplate	[ˈkɑntəmpleɪt]	v.	注视；凝视；深思熟虑

Notes

(1) nagging question：老生常谈的问题。

旅游英语（修订版）

（2）Popular thinking gravitates toward penalties. 一般人都是倾向于惩罚的。

（3）in-house service providers：组织内部的服务提供者。

（4）Incentive-Based Agreements：基于激励的服务合同。

PART Ⅱ   DIALOGUE

Dialogue 1   Applying for a Visa

Conversation 1

H：Hal；V：Visa Officer

H：I want to apply for a visa.

V：What's your purpose to Australia?

H：Just go sightseeing.

V：When do you prepare to depart?

H：I want to depart in a month, around the fifth of May.

V：Do you have a travel ticket to your final destination?

H：No, I haven't ordered the ticket. I want to do it after I get the visa.

V：Well, please give me your materials.

H：How long will it take to get the visa?

V：Please wait some days. We will inform you as soon as we get the result.

H：我想申请一个签证。

V：你去澳大利亚的目的是什么？

H：只是去旅游。

V：你准备什么时候出发？

H：我想在一个月之后，大约5月5日出发。

V：你有最终目的地的机票吗？

H：没有，我还没有订机票。我想拿到签证以后再去订。

V：好的，请把你的材料给我。

H：要多长时间能拿到签证？

V：请等几天。一出结果，我们就通知你。

Conversation 2

G：Gay；V：Visa Officer

G：Will you please tell me how to apply for a visa to Australia?

V：Are you proposing a trip to visit your relatives in Australia or to settle down there?

G：I will go to visit my relatives.

V：How long has it been since you last saw your relatives?

G：About 15 years.

V：Have you got any letter of invitation sent by your relatives in Australia?

8

G: Yes, I have.

V: Have you ever been to Australia before?

G: No, never.

V: How long do you intend to stay in Australia?

G: I intend to stay in Australia for 6 months.

V: All right. According to the regulations of our country, you must fill in an Application Form for an Entry Visa and prepare two photographs.

G: How long will it take to get an entry visa to Australia?

V: It won't be long, about one month.

G: 请告诉我怎样申请去澳大利亚的签证?

V: 你去澳大利亚是探亲还是定居?

G: 我是去探亲。

V: 你有多久没有见你的亲戚了?

G: 大约15年了。

V: 你有澳大利亚亲戚的邀请信吗?

G: 有的。

V: 你以前去过澳大利亚吗?

G: 不,从来没有。

V: 你准备在澳大利亚逗留多久?

G: 我打算在澳大利亚逗留6个月。

V: 好的。按我们国家的规定,你应该填写"入境签证申请表",并准备两张照片。

G: 需要等多久才能拿到入境签证?

V: 很快,大约一个月。

Dialogue 2   Booking Tickets

C: Clerk; J: John Smith

C: Good morning, China Eastern Airline. What can I do for you?

J: I'd like to make a reservation for two to Los Angeles, please.

C: For what day, sir?

J: Next Friday, if possible.

C: That's the 20th of July. Yes, we have flight at 10 a.m. and 6 p.m.

J: I prefer a morning flight. By the way, what type of aircraft is it?

C: Boeing 777. How do you wish to fly, sir, economy or first class?

J: First class and window seats, please.

C: All right. Will you pay in cash or by credit card, sir?

J: By credit card. By the way, is that a direct flight?

C: No. You'll have to make a stopover in Tokyo. It'll be a three-hour layover, and you're supposed to remain on board until the plane's off again.

J: Do you have a non-stop flight?

旅游英语(修订版)

C：I'm sorry. we don't have any direct flights on that day. We have Shanghai-Los Angeles non-stop flights only on Tuesday and Saturday. Will you change the date of your flight?

J：Oh, no. How long will the flight take? I mean the indirect flight.

C：It's about 16 hours, including the layover in Tokyo.

J：All right, then. Two tickets for that flight.

C：May I have your name please?

J：John Smith.

C：Thank you, Mr. Smith. I've booked the tickets for you on China Eastern Airlines, flight number MU192, leaving from Pudong International Airport, at 10 a.m. 20th of July. Please confirm your seats three days before departure.

J：I will. Thank you, Miss.

C：早上好！中国东方航空公司。我能为您效劳吗？

J：是的。我要预订两张去洛杉矶的机票。

C：请问要哪一天的？

J：如果可能的话，下星期五。

C：那是7月20日。我们有早上10点和下午6点的两次航班。

J：我要上午的航班。请问是什么机型？

C：波音777。先生，请问您要经济舱还是头等舱？

J：头等舱，靠窗的座位。

C：好的先生。请问您用现金支付，还是用信用卡支付？

J：信用卡。顺便问一下，是直飞航班吗？

C：不是。飞机要在日本东京作短暂停留，停留3个小时。旅客要留在机舱里直到飞机再次起飞。

J：有直飞的航班吗？

C：对不起，那天没有直飞的航班。上海至洛杉矶的直飞航班只在星期二和星期六有。请问您想更改飞行日期吗？

J：哦，不。请问多长时间能到洛杉矶？我是说中途停留的飞机。

C：大约16个小时，包括中途在东京停留的时间。

J：好吧，订两张这个航班的机票。

C：请问您的姓名？

J：约翰·史密斯。

C：谢谢。史密斯先生，我已经为您预订了东航飞往洛杉矶的MU192航班的机票。7月20日上午10点从浦东国际机场起飞。请在起飞前3天确认你们的座位。

J：我会的。谢谢你，小姐。

Word Service Station

on schedule   准时   cancellation   取消

PART Ⅲ GOOD TO KNOW: Transportation Terms

缆车	cable car	卧铺	sleeping car/ sleeper
月台/站台	platform	公交总站/航站楼	terminal
包厢	compartment	上（下/中）铺	upper (lower/middle) berth
交叉路口	intersection/crossroad	硬（软）座/卧	hard (soft) seat/berth
退票	refund a ticket	电车	trolley bus
包车	chartered bus	高速公路	expressway
立交桥	interchange/flyover	收费公路	tollway/toll road
颠簸	rocking/ bumping/ tossing	斑马线/人行横道	zebra crossing
计时停车	hourly/metered parking	单程/往返车票	one way/round trip ticket
地铁	metro/ subway/ underground		
高架铁路	elevated railway/railroad; overhead railway/railroad; aerial railway/railroad		

PART Ⅳ EXERCISES

Ⅰ. Listening comprehension.

Swiss Couple Keeps Rolling on 23-year Round-the-World Drive

1-听力资源

In 1984, Swiss couple Emil and Liliana Shemid traveled to the United States to get away from the monotony of office work. They became hooked on 1 _____ and haven't stopped since.

Now 23 years, 157 countries and 626,000 kilometers. Later Emil, 65, and Liliana, 66, have turned their Toyota Land Cruiser into their home and want to spend the 2 _____ of their life on the road, seeing nature, meeting interesting people and 3 _____ about different cultures.

The couple arrived in Taiwan in October. They 4 _____ across Taiwan's mountains and cities, stayed two nights at the plush Grand Hotel in Taipei as guests of the Taiwan Tourism Bureau, and made friends with many locals.

"Taiwan has a 5 _____ combination of natural scenery and city life. A few hours from cities, you are at the seaside or in tall mountains. And Taiwan has beautiful 6 _____ and rich culture." Emil said.

Over two decades ago, Emil, a computer 7 _____ engineer, and Liliana, a secretary, decided to go to the United States to 8 _____ for a year. However, 12 months proved not to be long enough. They now hope to visit every country in the world and have just 33 of the 194 states 9 _____ by the United Nations left on their list.

In 1997, they 10 _____ the Guinness Book of World Records as the "Longest Driven Journey", a record that almost certainly will hold for a one time to come.

Ⅱ. Put the following into Chinese.

1. tourist visa　　_____
2. entry visa　　_____
3. excursion　　_____
4. day tour　　_____
5. safari park　　_____
6. the World Tourism Organization（UNWTO）　　_____
7. visit friends and relatives（VFR）　　_____
8. natural heritage　　_____
9. electronic ticket　　_____
10. health care　　_____

Ⅲ. English sentences can be classified into seven basic types. They are SVC, SV, SVA, SVO, SVOA, SVOC, SVOO. Please determine the following sentences.

1. The car is mine.
2. Everybody laughed.
3. The plane is losing altitude.
4. Mary lent me her car.
5. They elected him president.
6. I live in Beijing.
7. I put the evidence in front of him.
8. He made himself a cup of tea.
9. We painted the wall white.
10. She speaks English fluently.

Ⅳ. Reading comprehension.

In sixteenth-century Italy and eighteenth-century France, waning prosperity and increasing social unrest led the ruling families to try to preserve their superiority by withdrawing from the lower and middle classes behind barriers of etiquette. In a prosperous community, on the other hand, polite society soon absorbs the newly rich, and in England there has never been any shortage of books on etiquette for teaching them the manners appropriate to their new way of life.

Every code of etiquette has contained three elements: basic moral duties; practical rules which promote efficiency; and artificial, optional graces such as formal compliments to, say, women on their beauty or superiors on their generosity and importance.

In the first category are consideration for weak and respect for age. Among the ancient Egyptians the young always stood in the presence of older people. Among the Mpongwe of Tanzania, the young men bow as they pass the huts of the elders. In England, until about a century ago, young children did not sit in their parents' presence without asking permission.

Unit 1
Service

Practical rules are helpful in such ordinary occurrences of social life as making proper introductions at parties of other functions so that people can be brought to know each other. Before the invention of the fork, etiquette directed that the fingers should be kept as clean as possible; before the handkerchief came into common use, etiquette suggested that after spitting, a person should rub the spit inconspicuously underfoot.

Extremely refined behavior, however, cultivated as an art of gracious living, has been characteristic only of societies with wealth and leisure, which admitted women as the social equals of men. After the fall of Rome, the first European society to regulate behavior in private life in accordance with a complicated code of etiquette was twelfth-century Provence, in France.

Provence had become wealthy. The lords had returned to their castles from the crusades, and there the ideals of chivalry grew up, which emphasized the virtue and gentleness of women and demanded that a knight should profess a pure and dedicated love to a lady who would be his inspiration, and to whom he would dedicate his valiant deeds, though he would never come physically close to her. This was the introduction of the concept of romantic love, which was to influence literature for many hundreds of years and which still lives on in a debased form in simple popular songs and cheap novels today.

1. In sixteenth-century Italy and eighteenth-century France, the ruling families _____.
   A. tired to destroy the lower and middle classes using etiquette
   B. discriminated against the lower class using etiquette
   C. tired to teach etiquette to the lower and middle classes
   D. put the middle and working classes into fenced enclosures

2. Every code of etiquette has contained three elements: _____.
   A. practical rules, optional moral duties and formal compliments
   B. formal compliments, basic moral duties and practical rule
   C. optional moral duties, optional practical rules and artificial graces
   D. rules, regulations and requirements

3. The custom of young men bowing to show respect when passing the dwellings of their elders was cited as a characteristic of _____.
   A. the ancient Egyptians
   B. parts of Tanzania
   C. England about a century ago
   D. all societies

4. Etiquette cultivated as art of gracious living _____.
   A. has been typical of rich and leisured societies
   B. advocates that women are the same as men
   C. began in nineteenth-century Provence
   D. looks down on extremely refined behavior

5. The ideals of chivalry demanded that _____.

A. a knight could have physical relationship with women
B. a knight should inspire his lady to valiant deeds
C. a knight should dedicate his valiant deeds to a woman
D. romantic people should influence literature

V. Translate the following sentences into Chinese.

1. Compatible with our simple, broad definition is one that defines services to include "all economic activities whose output is not a physical product or construction, is generally consumed at the time it is produced, and provides added value in forms (such as convenience, amusement, timeliness, comfort, or health) that are essentially intangible concerns of its first purchaser."

2. Frequently this situation also means that customers are present while the service is being produced and thus view and may even take part in the production process as co-producers or co-creators of the service.

3. If the customer does not pay, the provider simply discontinues the service. This alternative is not any more satisfactory than divorce.

4. A divorce, with the terms of the separation determined through the intervention of lawyers and courts. It becomes a situation in which there are no real winners (except, perhaps, the attorneys).

5. This punishment-oriented thinking purports that if the threat alone does not prevent service level violations, then the pain caused by the penalty will certainly deter future violations.

VI. Discussion and presentation.

Students are supposed to **share their holiday experiences** concerned with tourism. It's recommended that students, working as a team, do presentation via Power Point or/and photos that they have taken during the holiday.

Unit 2　Tourism

PART I　TEXT

Text A　Defining Tourism

　　As one of the world's largest industries, tourism is associated with many of the prime sectors of the world's economy. Any such phenomenon that is intricately interwoven into the fabric of life economically, socio-culturally, and environmentally and relies on primary, secondary, and tertiary levels of production and service, is difficult to define in simple terms. This difficulty is mirrored in a 1991 issue of *The Economy*:

*　　There is no accepted definition of what constitutes the [tourism] industry; any definition runs the risk of either overestimating or underestimating economic activity. At its simplest, the industry is one that gets people from their home to somewhere else (and back), and which provides lodging and food them while they are away. But that does not get you far. For example, if all the sales of restaurants were counted as travel and tourism, the figure would be artificially inflated by sales to locals. But to exclude all restaurant sales would be just as misleading.*

　　It is this complex integration within our socio-economic system, that complicates efforts to define tourism. Tourism studies are often placed poles apart in terms of philosophical approach, methodological orientation, or intent of the investigation. A variety of tourism definitions, each with disciplinary attributes, reflect research initiatives corresponding to various fields. For example, tourism shares strong fundamental characteristics and theoretical foundations with the recreation and leisure studies field and the terms "leisure","recreation" and "tourism" represent a type of loose, harmonious unity which focuses on the experiential and activity-based features that typify these terms. On the other hand, economic and technical/statistical definitions generally ignore the human experiential elements of the concept in favour of an approach based on the movement of people over political borders and the amount of money generated from this movement.

　　It is this relationship with other disciplines, e. g., psychology, sociology, anthropology, geography, economics, which seems to have defined the complexion of tourism. However, despite its strong reliance on such disciplines, other way in which we need to approach the tourism discipline should be built around the structure of the industry, which is an open system of five elements interacting with broader environments: (1) a dynamic human element, (2) a generating region, (3) a transit region, (4) a destination region, and (5) the tourist industry. This definition is to see tourism as comprising three basic elements: (1) a dynamic element, which involves travel to a selected destination; (2) a static element, which involves a stay at the destination, and (3) a consequential element, resulting from the above two, which is concerned with the effect, on the economic, social and, physical subsystems with which the tourist is directly or indirectly in contact. Others define tourism as a system of interrelated parts which is "like a spider's web—touch one part of it and reverberations will be felt throughout." Included in the tourism system are four component parts, which are market (reaching the marketplace), travel (the purchase of travel products), destination (the shape of travel demand), and marketing (the selling of travel).

In recognition of the difficulty in defining tourism, a more realistic solution is to accept the existence of a number of different definitions, each designed to serve different purposes. This may in fact prove to be the most practical of approaches to follow. In this article, tourism is defined as the interrelated system that includes tourists and the associated services that are provided and utilized (facilities, attractions, transportation, and accommodation) to aid in their movement, while a tourist, as established by the World Tourism Organization, is defined as a person travelling for pleasure for a period of at least one night, but not more than one year for international tourists and six months for persons travelling in their own countries, with the main purpose of the visit being other than to engage in activities for remuneration in the place(s) visited.

One of the most competing approaches to tourism development is mass and alternative paradigms. Tourism has been both lauded and denounced for its ability to develop and therefore transform regions into completely different settings. In the former case, tourism is seen to have provided the impetus for appropriate long-term development; in the latter the ecological and sociological disturbance to transformed regions can be overwhelming. While most of the documented cases of the negative impacts of tourism are in the developing world, the developed world is certainly not an exception, for example, documented the transformation of a small fishing farming community in Malta by graphically illustrating the extent to which tourism development—through an increasingly complex system of transportation, resort development, and social behavior—overwhelms such areas over time.

These days we are more prone to vilify or characterize conventional mass tourism[1] as a beast, a monstrosity which has few redeeming qualities for the destination region, their people and their natural resource base. Consequently, mass tourism has been criticized for the fact that it dominates tourism within a region owing to its non-local orientation, and the fact that very little money spent within the destination actually stays and generates more income. It is quite often the hotel or mega-resort that is the symbol of mass tourism's domination of a region, which are often created using non-local products, have little requirement for local food products, and are owned by metropolitan interests. Hotel marketing occurs on the basis of high volume, attracting as many people as possible, often over seasonal periods of time. The implications of this seasonality are such that local people are at times moved in and out of paid positions that are based solely on this volume of touristic traffic. Development exists as a means by which to concentrate people in very high densities, displacing local people from traditional subsistence-style livelihoods to ones that are subservience based. Finally, the attractions that lie in and around these massive developments are created and transformed to meet the expectations and demands of visitors. Emphasis is often on commercialization of natural and cultural resources, and the result is a contrived and inauthentic representation of, for example, a cultural theme or event that has been eroded into a distant memory.

Admittedly the picture of mass tourism painted above is outlined to illustrate the point that the tourism industry has not always operated with the interests of local people and the resource base in mind. This was most emphatically articulated through much of the tourism research that emerged in the 1980s, which argued for a new, more socially and ecologically benign alternative to mass tourism development. The philosophy behind alternative tourism[2] (AT)—forms of tourism that advocates an approach opposite to mass conventional tourism—was to ensure that tourism policies should no longer concentrate on economic and technical necessities alone, but rather emphasize the demand for an unspoiled environment and consideration of the needs of local people. This "softer" approach[3] places the natural and cultural resources at the forefront of planning and development, instead of as an afterthought. Also, as an inherent function, alternative forms of tourism provide the means for countries to eliminate outside influences, and to sanction projects themselves and to participate in their development—in essence, to win back the decision-making power in essential matters rather than conceding to outside people and institutions.

Words and Expressions

prime	[praɪm]	a.	最好的；首要的；基本的；n. 鼎盛时期
intricately	[ˈɪntrəkɪtli]	a.	杂乱地；复杂地；难懂地
interweave	[ˌɪntərˈwiːv]	v.	使交织；使混杂；织进
tertiary	[ˈtɜːrʃəri]	a.	第三的
artificially	[ˌɑːtɪˈfɪʃəli]	v.	人工地；不自然地
inflate	[ɪnˈfleɪt]	v.	膨胀；物价上涨；(使) 充气
methodological	[ˌmeθədəˈlɒdʒɪkl]	a.	方法的；方法论的；教学法的
orientation	[ˌɔːrɪenˈteɪʃn]	n.	方向；定位；新生（员工）培训
initiative	[ɪˈnɪʃətɪv]	n.	主动性；创造精神；倡议
anthropology	[ˌænθrəˈpɒlədʒi]	n.	人类学
reverberation	[rɪˌvɜːrbəˈreɪʃn]	n.	反响；反射；反射物
laud	[lɔːd]	v.	称赞；赞美
disturbance	[dɪˈstɜːbəns]	n.	打扰；骚乱
overwhelming	[ˌoʊvərˈwelmɪŋ]	a.	势不可当的；压倒一切的
conventional	[kənˈvenʃnl]	a.	传统的；平常的；依照惯例的
monstrosity	[mɒnˈstrɒsəti]	n.	庞然大物；怪物；巨兽
redeeming	[rɪˈdiːmɪŋ]	a.	补偿的；弥补的
subservience	[səbˈsɜːvɪrns]	n.	有益；从属（地位）；恭顺
commercialization	[kəˌmɜːʃəlaɪˈzeɪʃn]	n.	商业化；商品化

contrive	[kənˈtraɪv]	v.	设计；设法做到
inauthentic	[ˌɪnɔːˈθɛntɪk]	a.	不真实的；不可靠的
erode	[ɪˈrəʊd]	v.	侵蚀；腐蚀；削弱
sanction	[ˈsæŋkʃən]	v.	批准；鼓励，容忍
prone to vilify			容易被诽谤的

Notes

（1）mass tourism：大众旅游。

（2）alternative tourism：替代性旅游，也称"选择性旅游"，是一种其规划设计必须建立在保护当地生态环境的基础上，并使旅游生态原则贯穿其间的旅游方式。

（3）softer approach：指那种对旅游目的地扰动较少的旅游方式。

Text B Tourism, Good or Bad

Travel expenditures and receipts have widely different effects on the economy of a destination. There are a number of contributing factors: the relative importance of tourism in the economy, the linkages of the various parts of the economy with tourist expenditures, the percentage of tourism expenditures that soon leaves the economy, the saving habits of the residents, and the speed of expenditure within the economy. In Hawaii, for example, where tourism is by far the largest source of income, the rise and fall of tourist expenditures have immediate economic results. An economic model developed by the Bank of Hawaii has shown that a 10 percent drop in visitor arrivals will cause a $570 million decline in retail sales.

As soon as a tourist spends a dollar in a destination economy, it is received by someone, spent and re-spent. Some of the dollar may soon leave the destination ("a leakage") to pay for imported fuel, food, furniture, and other items that are not available locally, are not competitively priced, or are not of the desired quality. Some of the dollar may go abroad as interest payments or profits to nonresidential investors. Some goes for local and national taxes. The part that remains may be rapidly spent within the economy, invested, or saved. The spending that results within an economy "multiplies" its impact.

Tourist expenditures have direct, indirect, and induced effects on a destination economy. The direct effect is the change in sales, employment, and income that occurs as a direct result of purchases of goods and services by visitors. Examples are hotel room sales, restaurant sales, taxi fares, and airline ticket sales.

<u>Indirect effects are the changes in sales, employment, and income generated indirectly in other businesses that directly receive tourist dollars spent to buy material and service inputs to meet the demand created by direct sales to visitors.</u> Examples are sales by food vendors to restaurants, by linen vendors to hotels, and by gasoline dealers to taxi drivers.

The induced effect measures the further change in sales, employment, and income as employees and proprietors spend the salaries and income earned from their companies. An example is a hotel clerk's expenditures for food, clothing, and shelter.

These expenditures "multiply" their economic effects as they ripple through an economy. Tourist spending stimulates employment differently in the various components of a destination economy. The original tourist dollar may go directly to a hotel or restaurant employee or to a tour operator. That dollar is then recycled throughout the economy and provides work for other employees and proprietors.

International tourism has mostly developed since the 1960s, during a time when communication via education, television, and radio has burgeoned. Some of the changes blamed on tourism would have taken place without tourism. Tropical agriculture, mostly based on a single commodity such as cocoa, pineapples, sugar, palm nuts, coffee, coconuts, or bananas, has declined in value. Tourism is an economic alternative that provides many jobs that are better than those in agriculture. Which is the better choice: work in an air-conditioned hotel versus chopping sugar cane in the tropical sun? Tourism also creates new demands for foods that can be produced locally, such as fruits, seafood, vegetables, and eggs.

Tourism is surely an active agent in the process of bringing people and their different cultures together in a way that books and electronic media cannot. The outcomes of this convergence are not very predictable. Belief systems often clash rather than harmonize. Envy, greed, rivalry, fear and hate will continue to be part of the human race for a long time to come, and they are manifest in host/guest country relations, as they are in all human relations.

International travel removes "strangeness" and in most cases enhances "psychic affiliations" and provides for a salutary economic exchange between host and guest. International travel can become addictive; fortunately, it is a generally healthful addiction that is conductive to friendship.

The conditions of travel can affect the feelings visitors have for the destination. Each personal contact in the travel chain of events contributes toward a positive or less than positive feeling for the people of the destination. Advanced technology, efficient transport, minimal travel hassles, and improved safety can add up to liking and understanding the host people even before arrival in their country.

The attitudes visitors bring to a trip also color their experience. An impatient person has a hard time coping with immigration checks, airline schedule changes, and routine travel delays. A young backpacker doesn't mind sleeping on the ground; a more demanding traveler may require comfort and red-carpet treatment all the way. An open-minded, curious person of good will sees new countries and cultures quite differently from the person who is primarily interested in being courted, amused, and entertained.

Technology has changed travel and, with the exception of developing countries, put it within nearly everyone's reach. Travel, in turn, has changed what people think about and how they think.

Many destination areas have very high tourism density (the ratio of visitors to residents). Hawaii has several times as many visitors as there are residents. So do the Bahamas, the Cayman Islands, the Virgin Islands, Austria, and Switzerland[1]. Whether tourism density is a problem depends on the support services presented, the transportation systems, the disparity between the incomes of visitors and residents, the differences in culture and the history of relations between the host country and the visitors, the differences in religion and other belief systems, the attitudes of the visitors, and other factors.

Environmental concerns aroused by mass tourism have braked tourism development in some places and have colored resident opinion about the "benefits" of having thousands of visitors. One example, described by *The Wall Street Journal*[2], is what is happening in the Alpine ski areas of Europe. The Alps are blanketed by 40,000 ski runs and 14,000 ski lifts. Austria plans to limit mass resort development in favor of smaller but higher-quality resorts. Tigne, an alpine village in the French Alps, has a year-round population of 1,600 but is overwhelmed by 35,000 visitors during the ski season, and the infrastructure there cannot even handle the crush of skiers, and restaurants simply dump their garbage down the slopes.

The World Tourism Organization[3] has an optimistic slogan: *Tourism*: *Passport to Peace*. Of all human activities, tourism may hold that promise; reliance on world fellowship and religion to promote peace has had mixed results at best.

Words and Expressions

affiliation	[əˈfɪlɪˈeɪʃn]	n.	隶属（关系）；联系
addictive	[əˈdɪktɪv]	a.	使上瘾的
alternatives	[ɔːlˈtɜːnətɪvz]	n.	可供选择的事物；a. 备选的；另类的
ambassador	[æmˈbæsədə(r)]	n.	大使
aspiration	[ˌæspəˈreɪʃn]	n.	抱负；志向
backpacker	[ˈbækpækə(r)]	n.	背包客
burgeon	[ˈbɜːdʒən]	v.	发芽；急速发展
clash	[klæʃ]	n.	冲突
chop	[tʃɒp]	v.	剁碎；砍
convergence	[kənˈvɜːdʒəns]	n.	会聚；融合
court	[kɔːt]	v.	求爱；向……献殷勤
disparity	[dɪˈspærəti]	n.	悬殊；不一致
deferential	[ˌdefəˈrenʃl]	a.	恭顺的；表示敬意的
exotic	[ɪɡˈzɒtɪk]	a.	异国情调的；奇异的
expenditure	[ɪkˈspendɪtʃə(r)]	n.	费用；消费；开支
facilitate	[fəˈsɪlɪteɪt]	v.	使便利；促进
fellowship	[ˈfeləʊʃɪp]	n.	伙伴关系；团体；研究生奖学金
gasoline	[ˈɡæsəliːn]	n.	汽油
hassle	[ˈhæs(ə)l]	n.	争论；不断烦扰
induce	[ɪnˈdjuːs]	v.	促使；引起
infrastructure	[ˈɪnfrəstrʌktʃə(r)]	n.	基础设施；基础建设
jam	[dʒæm]	v.	挤满；堵塞
lavatory	[ˈlævətri]	n.	卫生间；洗手间

limousine	[ˈlɪməziːn]	n.	大型高级轿车
linen	[ˈlɪnɪn]	n.	亚麻布
linkage	[ˈlɪŋkɪdʒ]	n.	联合；关联
manifest	[ˈmænɪfest]	a.	明白的；明显的
multiply	[ˈmʌltɪplaɪ]	v.	增加；繁殖
predispose	[ˌpriːdɪˈspəʊz]	v.	使倾向于；伎易接受
proprietor	[prəˈpraɪətə(r)]	n.	所有者，业主
receipt	[rɪˈsiːt]	n.	收据；接收；收入
recycle	[ˌriːˈsaɪkl]	v.	回收再用
ripple	[ˈrɪpl]	v.	起伏；飘动；n. 涟漪；波纹
rivalry	[ˈraɪvlri]	n.	竞争；对抗；竞赛
salutary	[ˈsæljətri]	a.	有益的；效果好的
slogan	[ˈsləʊgən]	n.	口号
squeeze	[skwiːz]	v.	压榨
shelter	[ˈʃeltə(r)]	n.	庇护；避难所
vendor	[ˈvendə(r)]	n.	卖主；小贩
business-class seats			（飞机上的）商务舱
first-class seats			（飞机上的）头等舱
palm nut			棕榈果
population density			人口密度
red-carpet treatment			贵宾级的待遇
sugar cane			甘蔗
take sth. in stride			不费力地解决；轻松地胜任
via pre.			经由；经过

Notes

(1) Hawaii has several times as many... Austria, and Switzerland. 在夏威夷，游客要比当地居民的人数多好几倍。巴哈马群岛、开曼群岛、维京群岛、奥地利、瑞士等地的情况也是如此。The Bahamas Islands 巴哈马群岛，位于佛罗里达海峡口外的北大西洋上；the Cayman Islands 开曼群岛、Virgin Islands 维京群岛，均在加勒比地区。

(2) *The Wall Street Journal*：华尔街日报。

(3) The World Tourism Organization：世界旅游组织。

PART II DIALOGUE

Dialogue 1 Changing Foreign Currency

B：Bob；C：Clerk

B：Excuse me, is this the Banking Department?

C: Yes, it is. What can I do for you?

B: Can I exchange some foreign currency here?

C: I'm sorry. This counter is just for savings. You'd better go to No. 6 Counter. That's the Foreign Exchange Counter.

B: Thanks for your information.

(At No. 6 Counter)

B: Good morning! Is this the Exchange Counter?

C: Yes, it is.

B: I've got a note of 1,000 Euros, but I just want to change 500 Euros. Can you return me the remaining sum in the notes of 50 Euro?

C: I'll try my best. Please fill in this memo and show me your passport.

B: Here is my passport, and the memo has been filled out.

C: One moment, please. Your 500 Euros is changed into RMB 5,160 and the remaining 500 Euros are given back to you in eight notes of 50 Euro each and one note of 100 Euro. I'm sorry to say there are not enough 50 Euro notes.

B: It's just all right. Thanks a lot.

B: 劳驾, 这是业务部吗?

C: 是的, 这是。我能为您做点什么?

B: 我能在这儿兑换一些外汇吗?

C: 对不起, 这个柜台是储蓄部。您去6号柜台吧, 那是外汇兑换柜台。

B: 谢谢你的消息。

(在6号柜台)

B: 早上好! 这是兑换柜台吗?

C: 是的。

B: 我有一张面值为1000欧元的钞票, 但是我只想换500欧元, 剩下的500欧元能找给我10张50欧元的钞票吗?

C: 我会尽力的。请填写兑换水单并出示您的护照。

B: 这是我的护照。兑换水单已填好了。

C: 请稍候。您的500欧元兑换成了5160元人民币, 剩下的500欧元, 就给您8张面值为50欧元的钞票和1张面值100欧元的钞票。对不起, 50欧元面值的钞票不够了。

B: 没关系。非常感谢。

Word Service Station

sum	总数	exchange rate	汇率
memo	备忘录; 换汇水单	foreign currency	外汇
duplicate	复写; 复制品	sign	签名
column	栏	Foreign Exchange Certificates	外汇兑换券

Dialogue 2　Taking a Taxi

P：Passenger；D：Driver

P：Are you engaged?

D：No, madam. Can I help you?

P：I want to go to the airport.

D：Oh, hop in. When should we be there?

P：I've got to be there by 2:30. Can you make it?

D：OK, if there's no hold-ups.

P：Is this the right road?

D：Yes. This is the road without much traffic.

P：Can you hurry?

D：I won't exceed the speed limit. I have the pedal to the metal already!

P：Here we are. Just drop me here. How much do I owe you?

D：Ten dollars and fifty cents.

P：Here's fifteen dollars, and you can keep the change.

D：Thank you.

P：有人预定您的车吗？

D：没有，女士。我能帮助您吗？

P：我要去机场。

D：哦，上车吧。我们应该什么时候到？

P：我要在 2:30 之前赶到那儿。您能赶到吗？

D：可以，如果没有堵车的话。

P：我们的路线对吗？

D：对。这条路车少。

P：您能开快点吗？

D：我可不能超速行驶。我已经踩油门了。

P：我们到了。在这儿下车。我得给您多少钱？

D：10.5 美元。

P：给您 15 美元，零头不用找了。

D：谢谢

Word Service Station

| trunk | 后备厢 | rush hour | 高峰时段 |
| restrict | 限制，约束 | engage | 占用 |

PART Ⅲ　GOOD TO KNOW：At the Airport

机场费　　　airport fee　　　　国际/国内机场　international/domestic airport

航站楼	terminal	免税店	duty-free shop
不需报关	nothing to declare	海关	customs
登机口	departure gate	航班号	FLT NO.（flight number）
预计时间	scheduled time（SCHED）	实际/起飞时间	actual/departure time
已降落	landed	延误	delayed
中转/过境	transfer/ transit	登机牌	boarding pass（card）
行李领取处	luggage/baggage claim	办理登机手续	check-in
行李牌	luggage tag	登机柜台	check-in desk/counter
随身行李	carry-on luggage	托运行李	checked baggage
重量/大小限制	weight/size limits	超大/重行李	oversized/overweight baggage

PART Ⅳ   EXERCISES

Ⅰ. Listening comprehension.

When traveling by plane what makes our ears pop, and what is it exactly that pops? Most of us are familiar with this phenomenon of travel: it usually happens on takeoffs and 1 _____.

Our ears pop because of the change in air 2 _____ as the plane ascends or descends. At higher 3 _____ air pressure is lower, even though the plane is pressurized. Our ears are sealed off inside our heads, so as the plane ascends or descends the pressure outside and inside our ears is different. This difference in pressure can 4 _____ our ear drums and can be painful.

What needs to be done here is to equalize the pressure between our ears and the airplane cabin. Nature has provided the 5 _____ for this with a tube that runs from the middle ear to the nasopharynx（鼻咽部）—the open area behind our noses. It's called the Eustachian tube（咽鼓管）. Normally the Eustachian tube is closed; so in order to 6 _____ the pressure we need to open it. Seasoned travelers know that you can avoid the discomfort by swallowing or chewing 7 _____ when you feel the pressure change. The 8 _____ action when we chew gum or swallow opens the Eustachian tube, and allows the pressure to be equalized. The opening of the Eustachian tube is associated with the "pop" we hear.

Incidentally, babies often 9 _____ on takeoff and landing because they don't know to chew or 10 _____. Having them suck on something can open their Eustachian tubes and alleviate the pain—on their ears and the other passengers.

Ⅱ. Put the following into Chinese.

1. business visa   _____

2. visit visa   _____

3. transit visa   _____

4. the Tourist Society   _____

5. crew of airlines　_____
6. historical heritage　_____
7. foot massage　_____
8. time difference　_____
9. trade fair　_____
10. tour group　_____

III. Fill in each blank with the proper form of the given word.

1. Fifteen miles _____ (seem) like a long walk to me.
2. Neither Julia nor I _____ (be) going.
3. Both Paul and Bob _____ (have) gone fishing.
4. Ham and egg _____ (be) a good breakfast.
5. What I say and think _____ (be) no business of yours.
6. Many a man in this community _____ (find) himself in need.
7. One out of twenty _____ (be) badly damaged.
8. Thirty-five percent of the doctors _____ (be) women.
9. What caused the accident _____ (be) a complete mystery.
10. To eat well _____ (be) all he asks.
11. Joan is one of those people who never _____ (ask) for help.
12. He is the only one of those boys who _____ (be) willing to take on another task.

IV. Reading comprehension.

Tourism as a Global Industry

David Lodge, in his novel *Paradise News*, proclaims tourism half seriously as the new global religion. Using guidebooks as devotional aids, million of "pilgrims" tour to a galaxy of holy places every year from Disneyland to Delhi, from Cairo to coral reefs, from Harrods to the Himalayas.

Sitting on a lump of rock beside the Parthenon, watching the tourist milling about, clicking their cameras, talking to each other in different languages, it suddenly struck me: tourism is the new global religion. Catholics, Protestants, Hindus, Muslims, Buddhists, atheists—the one thing they have in common is they all believe in the importance of seeing the Parthenon, or the Sistine Chapel, or the Eiffel Tower.

What Lodge parodies is, of course, mass package tourism, the extreme form of the travel phenomenon, and the "phenomenon" is indeed, as it sweeps the world with seemingly unstoppable energy, like a tsunami. The numbers and growth rates are impressive: by the mid-1990s some 500 million travelers crossed international boundaries each year. In addition, throughout the world, domestic travel was growing as a component of social and economic changes. Despite indications of slowing down, travel and tourism remained, in the 1990s, one of the world's fastest growing industrial sectors, and was poised to become the world's leading industry, with six percent of global GDP and at least 13 percent of consumptive expenditure. Equally significant was the realization that, although over 60 percent of all travel still occurred between countries in North America and Europe, the highest growth rates were being recorded by newly industrialized countries (NICs) and less developed countries (LDCs). It must be remembered, too, that demand for, as well as supply of, tourism opportunities is becoming truly global, illustrated vividly by the rapid growth of high-spending tourists from Japan and the NICs of South-East Asia.

One of the most important characteristics of tourism is that it is, in essence, a fashion industry. The complex two-way relationship between demand and supply is based upon the dynamics of people's perceptions, experience, attitudes and values. Participation in tourism is, therefore, subject to powerful cultural filters, which may change over time. For example, the Japanese are well-known for their strongly developed work ethics, but this is changing, both organically in the way people think, and as an element of public policy, where the government is emphasizing the benefits of the leisure ethics. One result is the explosion in the Japanese demand for tourism experience. For instance, succeeding the well-publicized "sex tourism" packages to Bangkok for business executives, there is the rapidly growing Australian tour itinerary; Cairns-Barrier Reef-Ayers Rock-Sydney, which is causing concern over its carrying capacity, impacts and quality of experience.

1. Write T (true) or F (false) to each of the following statements.

(　　) (1) International tourism rush to tourist destinations in large numbers just like a tsunamisweeping in from the sea.

(　　) (2) Domestic tourism is developing rapidly over recent years and helps accelerate social and economic changes in many countries throughout the world.

(　　) (3) All industries, including the travel and tourism industry, were declining during the slowdown of world economic expansion in the 1990s.

(　　) (4) The travel and tourism industry took the largest percentage of global GDP and consumptive expenditure in the 1990s.

(　　) (5) The world's largest tourist-generating countries and tourist destination countries are in Europe and North America.

(　　) (6) International tourism has become a global industry for both industrialized countries and developing countries.

(　　) (7) Japan and South-East Asian countries have become very important tourist-generating regions in the world.

2. Write down your answer to each of the following questions.

(1) What is one of the most important characteristics of international tourism, according to the text?

Tourism is a _____.

(2) What did the Japanese used to be known for?

They used to be well-known for their _____.

(3) What is one of the results of the change in the ethics of the Japanese people?
They are demanding _____.
(4) In what way did Japanese executives change their interest in tourist destinations?
They used to favor _____, but now they prefer the popular Australian itinerary: _____.

V. Translate the following sentences into Chinese.

1. It is this complex integration within our socio-economic system that complicates efforts to define tourism. Tourism studies are often placed poles apart in terms of philosophical approach, methodological orientation, or intent of the investigation. A variety of tourism definitions, each with disciplinary attributes, reflect research initiatives corresponding to various fields.

2. Economic and technical/statistical definitions generally ignore the human experiential elements of the concept in favour of an approach based on the movement of people over political borders and the amount of money generated from this movement.

3. Indirect effects are the changes in sales, employment, and income generated indirectly in other businesses that directly receive tourist dollars spent to buy material and service inputs to meet the demand created by direct sales to visitors.

4. International travel removes "strangeness" and in most cases enhances "psychic affiliations" and provides for a salutary economic exchange between host and guest.

5. Environmental concerns aroused by mass tourism have braked tourism development in some places and have colored resident opinion about the "benefits" of having thousands of visitors.

VI. Writing.

Write an invitation to invite a friend to an informal lunch. The followings should be included.
1. The specific time and location of the lunch;
2. The main course of the lunch;
3. The guests participating in the lunch.

Activity 1: New Headline

Aim:

Based on teamwork, students are assigned to discuss the material and then share their decision with other teams; each team would select 1 − 2 students to report their viewpoints.

Agenda:

- Students should be grouped into several teams to do the class discussion.
- Total time – 20 minutes/each group in class.
- For each group, a preparation meeting would be held before class to discuss the situation in the future as described. In class, each group will come up with its decision and the reason. The presentation would last 15-20 minutes. The teacher would host the meeting and give comments on the performance of each group.
- The decision should be based on the sustainability of human race and human civilization;
- Suggested teaching arrangement: 2 class hours.

Workshop Material:

New Headline: Major Environmental Disaster Heralds End of the Human Race

In groups, come up with some disasters that could possibly destroy the Earth.

Now, imagine that this is a real headline from the future and that one of the disasters you have predicted is actually going to happen. There is a possibility however, that the human race will be saved.

Scientists working for the United Nations have discovered that a deserted island in the Pacific will not be affected by the disaster. There is enough water, vegetation and animal life on this island to sustain human life. The United Nations has decided to send a group of people to this island before the disaster strikes. This group of people will be all that's left of the human race and will have to start again. There is a helicopter waiting to take them to the island. However, time is running out and there has been a terrible mistake. The helicopter can only take 10 people, including the pilot (male, 32 years old). There are 14 people waiting to get on. The United Nations has appointed YOU to decide which 9 people are to be saved and which 5 must stay behind. You must come to an agreement on this.

    A Buddhist monk—male, 75

    An army officer—male, 54

    A doctor—female, 50

    A professor (broadly educated)—male, 48

New Headline — Activity 1

A lawyer—female, 45

A famous singer & actress—female, 32

A farmer—male, 30

An engineer—female, 29

A motor mechanic—male, 26

A medical student—female, 22

An Olympic swimmer—male, 20

A pregnant woman—19

A child—male, 15

A child—female, 6

Unit 3   Hospitality Industry

PART I   TEXT

Text A   You Are What You Eat

Over the last three decades, fast food has infiltrated every nook and cranny of American society. An industry that began with a handful of modest hot dog and hamburger stands in Southern California has spread to every corner of the nation, selling a broad range of foods wherever paying customers may be found. Fast food is now served at restaurants and drive-throughs, at stadiums, airports, zoos, high schools, elementary schools, and universities, on cruise ships, trains, and airplanes, at Wal-Marts, gas stations, and even at hospital cafeterias. In 1970, Americans spent about $6 billion on fast food; in 2000, Americans spent more than $110 billion. Americans now spend more money on fast food than on higher education, personal computers, computer software, or new cars. They spend more on fast food than on movies, books, magazines, newspapers, videos, and recorded music combined.

A nation's diet can be more revealing than its art or literature. On any given day in the United States about one-quarter of the adult population visits a fast food restaurant. During a relatively brief period of a time, the fast food industry has helped to transform not only the American diet, but also the landscape, economy, workforce, and popular culture. Fast food and its consequences have become inescapable, regardless of whether you eat it twice a day, try to avoid it, or have never taken a single bite.

The extraordinary growth of the fast food industry has been driven by fundamental changes in American society. Adjusted for inflation, the hourly wage of the average U.S. worker peaked in 1973 and then steadily declined for the next 25 years. During that period, women entered the workforce in record numbers, often motivated less by a feminist perspective than by a need to pay the bills. In 1975, about one-third of American mothers with young children worked outside the home; today almost two-thirds of such mothers are employed. The entry of so many women into the workforce has greatly increased demand for the types of services that housewives traditionally perform: cooking, cleaning, and child care. A generation ago, three-quarters of the money used to buy food in the United States was spent to prepare meals at home. Today about half of the money used to buy food is spent at restaurants—mainly at fast food restaurants.

The McDonald's Corporation has become a powerful symbol of America's service economy, which is now responsible for 90 percent of the country's new jobs. In 1968, McDonald's operated about 1,000 restaurants. Today it has about 28,000 restaurants worldwide and opens almost 2,000 new ones each year. An estimated one out of every eight workers in the United States has at some point been employed by McDonald's. The company annually hires about one million people, more than any other American organization, public or private. McDonald's is the nation's largest purchaser of beef, pork, and potatoes, and the second largest purchaser of chicken. The McDonald's Corporation is the largest owner of retail property in the world. <u>Indeed, the company earns the majority of its profits not from selling food but from collecting rent.</u> McDonald's spends more money on advertising and marketing than any other brand. As a result it has replaced Coca-Cola as the world's most famous brand. McDonald's operates more playgrounds than any other private entity in the United States. It is one of the nation's largest distributors of toys. A survey of American schoolchildren found that 96 percent could identify Ronald McDonald. The only fictional character with a higher degree of recognition was Santa Claus. The impact of McDonald's on the way we live today is hard to overstate. The Golden Arches are now more widely recognized than the Christian cross.

The key to a successful franchise, according to many texts on the subject, can be expressed in one word: uniformity. Franchises and chain stores strive to offer exactly the same product or service at numerous locations. Customers are drawn to familiar brand by an instinct to avoid the unknown. A brand offers a feeling of reassurance when its products are always and everywhere the same.

One of the ironies of America's fast food industry is that a business so dedicated to conformity was founded by iconoclasts and self-made men, by entrepreneurs willing to defy conventional opinion. Few of the people who built fast food empires ever attended college, let alone business school. They worked hard, took risks, and followed their own paths. <u>In many respects, the fast food industry embodies the best and the worst of American capitalism at the start of twenty-first century—its constant stream of new products and innovations, its widening gulf between rich and poor.</u> The industrialization of the restaurant kitchen has enabled the fast food chains to rely upon a low-paid and unskilled workforce. The only Americans who consistently earn a lower hourly wage are migrant farm workers.

A hamburger and French fries became the quintessential American meal in the 1950s, thanks to the promotional efforts of the fast food chains. The typical American now consumes approximately three hamburgers and four orders of French fries every week. But the steady barrage of fast food ads, full of thick juicy burgers and long golden fries, rarely mentions where these foods come from nowadays or what ingredients they contain.

Most fast food is delivered to the restaurant already frozen, canned, dehydrated, or freeze-dried. A fast food kitchen is merely the final stage in a vast and highly complex system of mass production. Foods that may look familiar have in fact been completely reformulated. What we eat has changed more in the last 40 years than in the previous 40,000.

The sociologist George Ritzer has attacked the fast food industry for celebrating a narrow measure of efficiency over every other human value. Others consider the fast food industry proof of the national great economic vitality, a beloved American institution that appeals overseas to millions who admire such a way of life. Indeed, the values, the culture, and the industrial arrangements are now being exported from the U. S. to the rest of the world. Fast food has joined Hollywood movies, blue jeans, and pop music as one of America's most prominent cultural exports. Unlike other commodities, however, fast food isn't viewed, read, played, or worn. It enters the body and becomes part of the consumer. No other industry offers, both literally and figuratively, so much insight into the nature of mass consumption.

Hundreds of millions of people buy fast food every day without giving it much thought, unaware of the subtle and not so subtle ramifications of their purchases. They rarely consider where this food came from, how it was made, what it is doing to the community around them. They just grab their tray off the counter, find a table, take a seat, unwrap the paper, and dig in. The whole experience is transitory and soon forgotten. But we should know what really lurks between those sesame-seed buns. As the old saying goes: you are what you eat.

Words and Expressions

adjust	[əˈdʒʌst]	v.	调整；适应；校准
aroma	[əˈrəumə]	n.	香气；香味
barrage	[ˈbɑːrɑːʒ]	n.	大量；压倒多数
bun	[bʌn]	n.	小甜圆面包
canned	[kænd]	a.	罐装的
conformity	[kənˈfɔːməti]	n.	一致；遵从
consistently	[kənˈsɪstəntli]	a.	一贯地；稳定地
cranny	[ˈkræni]	n.	裂隙，裂缝
cafeteria	[ˌkæfəˈtɪərɪə]	n.	自助餐厅
dehydrate	[ˌdiːˈhaɪdreɪt]	v.	（人体）脱水；使干燥
drive-through	[ˈdraɪvθruː]	n.	乘车穿过；免下车即可得到的服务
feminist	[ˈfemənɪst]	n.	女权主义者
fictional	[ˈfɪkʃənl]	a.	虚构的
figuratively	[ˈfɪgjurətɪvli]	a.	比喻地；象征性地
gulf	[gʌlf]	n.	海湾
handful	[ˈhændful]	n.	少数；一把
iconoclast	[aɪˈkɔnəuklæst]	n.	反对崇拜偶像者
inescapable	[ˌɪnɪˈskeɪpəbl]	a.	不可避免的
inflation	[ɪnˈfleɪʃn]	n.	膨胀；通货膨胀
infiltrate	[ˈɪnfɪltreɪt]	v.	潜入；渗透
ingredient	[ɪnˈgriːdɪənt]	n.	原料；成分
irony	[ˈaɪərəni]	n.	反语；讽刺
irrationally	[ɪˈræʃnəli]	a.	不合理地；无条理地
literally	[ˈlɪtərəli]	a.	照字面地
lurk	[lɜːk]	v.	藏匿；潜伏

motivate	[ˈməʊtɪveɪt]	v.	激发；刺激；诱导
nook	[nʊk]	n.	角落；隐匿处
overstate	[ˌəʊvəˈsteɪ]	v.	夸张；夸大的叙述
prominent	[ˈprɒmɪnənt]	a.	杰出的；广为人知的
purchaser	[ˈpɜːtʃəsə(r)]	n.	买方；购买者
quintessential	[ˌkwɪntɪˈsenʃl]	a.	典型的
ramification	[ˌræmɪfɪˈkeɪʃn]	n.	衍生物；分枝
sesame	[ˈsesəmi]	n.	芝麻
sociologist	[ˌsəʊsiˈɒlədʒɪst]	n.	社会学家
strive	[straɪv]	v.	努力
transform	[trænsˈfɔːm]	v.	改变
transitory	[ˈtrænsɪtri]	a.	短暂的
uniformity	[ˌjuːnɪˈfɔːməti]	n.	始终如一；保持一致
vitality	[vaɪˈtæləti]	n.	活力，生气
every nook and cranny			某地方的各处；到处
self-made man			白手起家的人
take a bite			吃饭；品尝

Text B Hostel

Hostels provide budget-oriented, sociable accommodation where guests can rent a bed, usually a bunk bed, in a dormitory and share a bathroom, lounge and sometimes a kitchen. Rooms can be mixed or single-sex, although private rooms may also be available. Hostels are generally cheaper for both the operator and the occupants; many hostels have long-term residents whom they employ as desk clerks or housekeeping staff in exchange for free accommodation.

In a few countries, such as the UK, Ireland, the Netherlands, India, and Australia, the word hostel sometimes also refers to establishments providing longer-term accommodation (often to specific classes of clientele such as nurses, students, drug addicts, or court defendants on bail) where the hostels are sometimes run by Housing Associations[1] and charities. In the rest of the world, the word hostel refers only to properties offering shared accommodation to travelers or

Aostel dormitory room

backpackers.

Within the "traveler" category, another distinction can be drawn between hostels which are members of Hostelling International[2] (HI), a UK-based, non-profit organization encouraging outdoor activities and cultural exchange for the young (formerly the IYHA[3]), and independently operated hostels. Hostels for travelers are sometimes called "backpackers" hostels, particularly in Australia and New Zealand (often abbreviated to just "backpackers").

History

In 1912, in Altena Castle[4] in Germany, Richard Schirrmann created the first permanent *Jugendherberge* or "Youth Hostel". These first Youth Hostels were an exponent of the ideology of the German Youth Movement[5] to let poor city youngsters breathe fresh air outdoors. The youths were supposed to manage the hostel themselves as much as possible, doing chores to keep the costs down and build character as well as being physically active outdoors. Because of this, many Youth Hostels closed during the middle part of the day. Very few hostels still require chores beyond washing up after self-catered meals or have a "lockout".

Communal Accommodation

There is less privacy in a hostel than in a hotel. Sharing sleeping accommodation in a dormitory is very different from staying in a private room in a hotel or bed and breakfast, and might not be comfortable for those requiring more privacy. The lessened privacy is also an advantage in some ways, because it encourages more social interaction between guests.

Theft can be a problem, since guests may share a common living space, but this can be avoided by securing guests belongings. Most hostels offer some sort of system for safely storing valuables, and an increasing number of hostels offer private lockers.

Noise can make sleeping difficult on occasions, whether from snoring, sexual activity, someone either returning late or leaving early or the proximity of so many people. This can be mitigated by carrying earplugs.

The ship Passat is a floating hostel and museum.

Types of Hostels

The traditional hostel format involved dormitory style accommodation. Some newer hostels also include en-suite accommodation[6] with single, double or quad occupancy rooms[7], though to be considered a hostel they must also provide dormitory accommodation. In recent years, the numbers of independent and "backpackers" hostels have increased greatly to cater for the greater numbers of overland, multi-destination travelers (such as gap-year travelers[8], and rail-trippers).

The quality of such places has also improved dramatically. While a few hostels do still insist on a curfew, daytime lockouts, and/or require occupants to do chores, this is becoming a rare exception rather than the rule, as hostels adapt to meet the changing expectations of guests.

Hostelling International (HI)

Richard Schirrmann's idea of hostels rapidly spread overseas and eventually resulted in Hostelling International, an organization composed of more than 90 different Youth Hostel associations representing over 4,500 Youth Hostels in over 80 countries.

Some HI Youth Hostels cater more to school-aged children (sometimes through school trips) and parents with their children, whereas others are more for travelers' intent on learning new cultures. However, while the exploration of different cultures and places is emphasized in many hostels, particularly in cities or popular tourist destinations, there are still many hostels providing accommodation for outdoor pursuits such as hillwalking, climbing and bicycle touring; these are often small friendly hostels retaining much of the original vision and often provide valuable access to more remote regions.

Despite their name, in most countries membership is not limited to youth.

Independent Hostels

Independent hostels are not necessarily affiliated with one of the national bodies of Hostelling International, Youth Hostel Association or any other licensing body. Often, the word *independent* is used to refer to non-HI hostels even when the hostels do belong to another hostelling organization.

The term "youth" is less often used with these properties. These non-HI hostels are often called backpackers' hostels. Unlike a hotel chain where everything is standardized, these hostels can be very diverse, typically not requiring a membership card.

Boutique Hostels

The general backpacking community is no longer exclusively typified by student travelers and extreme shoe string budgets. In response to demand, as well as increasing competition between the rapidly growing number of hostels, the overall quality of hostels has improved across the industry. In addition to the increase in quality, new styles of hostels have developed that have a focus on a more trendily-designed interior.

Hostels in Popular Culture

Motion pictures have portrayed hostels in two ways: as fun places for young people to stay (for example, *The Journey of Jared Price* [9] and *A Map for Saturday* [10]), or alternatively, as dangerous places where unsuspecting Americans face potential horrors in Eastern Europe (e.g. *Hostel* (2005 film) and *Hostel* 2 (2007 film)). There are some popular misconceptions that a hostel is a kind of a flophouse, homeless shelter, or halfway house, though this does not reflect the high quality and level of professionalism in many modern hostels.

Self Contained Facilities and Services

In attempts to attract more visitors, hostels nowadays provide additional services not previously available, such as airport shuttle transfers, internet cafes, swimming pools and spas, tour booking and car rentals.

Words and Expressions

abbreviate	[əˈbriːvieɪ]	v.	简短；缩略
bail	[beɪl]	n.	保释，保释人
Budapest	[ˈbuːdəpest]	n.	布达佩斯
communal	[ˈkɒmjunl]	a.	公共的；公社的
curfew	[ˈkɜːfjuː]	n.	宵禁；宵禁令
diverse	[daɪˈvɜːs]	a.	不同的；多种多样的
dramatically	[drəˈmætɪkəli]	a.	戏剧性地；引人注目地
defendant	[dɪˈfendənt]	n.	被告
earplug	[ˈɪəplʌg]	n.	耳塞
exponent	[ɪkˈspəʊnənt]	n.	[数] 指数；典型；说明者
exclusively	[ɪkˈskluːsɪvli]	a.	唯一地；专有地
formality	[fɔːˈmælɪti]	n.	礼节，正式手续
format	[ˈfɔːmæt]	n.	格式；版式
flophouse	[ˈflɒphaʊs]	n.	廉价旅馆
hostel	[ˈhɒstl]	n.	青年旅社
ideology	[ˌaɪdɪˈɒlədʒi]	n.	意识形态；思想意识
lounge	[laʊndʒ]	n.	休息室
lockout	[ˈlɒkaʊt]	n.	停工
mitigate	[ˈmɪtɪgeɪt]	v.	使缓和，使减轻
overland	[ˈəʊvəlænd]	a.	陆上的；经由陆路的
privacy	[ˈprɪvəsi]	n.	隐私；秘密
permanent	[ˈpɜːmənənt]	a.	永久的，永恒的

premise	[ˈpremɪz]	v. 引出，预先提出
proximity	[prɔkˈsɪməti]	n. 亲近，接近
socialize	[ˈsəʊʃəlaɪz]	v. 交际；参与社交
snore	[snɔː(r)]	v. 打鼾
scheme	[skiːm]	n. 计划；组合
sustain	[səˈsteɪn]	v. 维持；支撑
shuttle	[ˈʃʌtl]	n. 穿梭班机
spa	[spɑː]	n. 温泉浴场
tendency	[ˈtendənsi]	n. 倾向，趋势
bunk bed		架子床
multi-destination		多目标
washing up		洗餐具
budget oriented		预算导向型
boutique hostel		精品旅馆
self-catered		不包餐

Notes

（1）Housing Associations：住房协会。

（2）Hostelling International：国际青年旅舍。国际青年旅舍成立于1932年，是联合国教科文组织成员，总部目前设在英国，并注册为一家非营利机构。

（3）IYHA：国际青年旅舍联盟（International Youth Hostel Association，IYHA），成立于1932年，是联合国教科文组织成员，总部目前在英国，并注册为一家非营利机构。

（4）Altena Castle：阿尔特纳城堡。

（5）German Youth Movement：德国青年运动。

（6）en-suite accommodation：套间宿舍。

（7）double or quad occupancy rooms：双人间或四人间。

（8）gap-year travellers：空档年旅行者。

（9）*The Journey of Jared Price*：2000年上映的美国电影《发现爱的旅程》。

（10）*A Map for Saturday*：自助旅行的纪录片《星期六的地图》。讲述一个住在纽约HBO体育节目制作人突然决定离开工作，用一年的时间当背包客到世界各国自助旅行。

PART Ⅱ DIALOGUE

Dialogue 1 At the Information Desk

A：Clerk of the Airline；B：Guest

Scene 1

A：Good morning. Can I help you?

B: Yes, I'd like to know whether there is a flight to Frankfurt.

A: Yes, there is. Flight 217 departs at 10:30 a. m. and arrives in Frankfurt at 12:30 a. m.

B: How many flights do you have to Frankfurt every week?

A: Three flights, on Sunday, Tuesday and Friday.

B: OK. Thanks a lot.

A: 早上好。我能帮您做什么吗?

B: 好的,我想知道是否有飞往法兰克福的航班?

A: 是的,有。217 航班会在上午 10:30 起飞,上午 12:30 到达法兰克福。

B: 每周有多少次航班到法兰克福?

A: 三趟航班,分别在星期日、星期二和星期五。

B: 好。非常感谢。

Scene 2

A: Good afternoon, madam. May I help you?

B: Could you tell me where I check in for the Flight NH 203 to Tokyo?

A: Down to the far end of the lounge and you'll find the counter for flights to Tokyo.

B: I have a stopover in Chicago—do I need to pick up my luggage there?

A: No, it'll go straight through to Tokyo. Here is your boarding pass—your flight leaves from gate 15A and it'll begin boarding at 3:20p. m. Your seat number is 26E.

B: Can I have a seat by the window?

A: I'm sorry, all the window seats are fully taken. How about an aisle seat?

B: All right. Please mark this bag as "fragile". And, do you know when do they begin to check in?

A: Let me see. They will start in about an hour.

B: Thank you very much. By the way, where can I make a phone call?

A: You'll find phone booths upstairs, madam.

B: Thanks.

A: It's my pleasure.

A: 下午好,女士。我能为您做些什么?

B: 您能告诉我在哪里办理去东京的 NH 203 航班登机手续吗?

A: 到候机厅的尽头,您会找到飞往东京的航班的柜台。

B: 我在芝加哥转机,需要在那儿提取行李吗?

A: 不需要的,行李将直发东京。这是您的登机牌,您将在 15A 登机口登机,登机时间是下午 3:20,您的座位号是 26E。

B: 我想要个靠窗的座位。

A: 抱歉,所有靠窗的座位都满了。靠过道的行吗?

B: 好吧。请给这个行李贴上"易损"标志。还有,他们什么时候开始办理登机手续?

A：我看一下。他们将在大约一个小时内开始。

B：非常感谢你。顺便问一下，我在哪里可以打个电话？

A：可以在楼上找到电话亭，女士。

B：谢谢。

A：很乐意为您效劳。

Dialogue 2　Security Check

A：Security Inspector；B：Tourist

Scene 1

A：Good morning, sir. Do you have any unexposed films in this bag?

B：No, I haven't.

A：Will you please put your bag on the conveyer belt?

B：Sure.

A：Would you please put your watch, keys and other metal articles into this tray? Now, please walk through the gate and collect your bag and other personal belongings at the other side.

B：I see. Thank you.

A：早晨好，先生。您这个袋子里有任何未曝光的胶卷吗？

B：不，没有。

A：请把您的包放在传送带上好吗？

B：当然可以。

A：请把您的手表、钥匙和其他金属物品放进这个盘子里好吗？现在，请您走过安检门，在门那边取您的包和其他个人物品。

B：我明白了。谢谢。

Scene 2

A：Good evening, sir. Could you put that bag on the counter and open it, please? What is inside?

B：Some clothes, my shaving kit, a couple of books and some souvenirs.

A：Do you have anything else?

B：Let me see. Oh, yes, a pack of green tea and some bananas.

A：I'm sorry, sir. You are not supposed to bring fresh fruits into Germany. I'm going to confiscate them.

B：Oh, that's too bad. Can I leave now?

A：Well, you are in the clearance now. Sorry to have bothered you.

B：That's all right.

A：晚上好，先生。您能把那个包放在柜台上并打开它好吗？里面是什么？

B：一些衣服、我的剃须用具、几本书和一些纪念品。

A：还有别的吗？
B：我想一下。哦，对了，还有一包绿茶和一些香蕉。
A：对不起，先生。您不应该带新鲜的水果到德国，我要没收它们。
B：哦，真可惜。我现在可以离开吗？
A：嗯，您现在没问题了。抱歉，打扰您了。
B：好的。

PART Ⅲ　GOOD TO KNOW：In the Restaurant

按菜单点菜的	à la carte	酒，烈性酒	alcohol
有食欲的	appetizing	难吃的	awful taste
饮料	beverage	淡而无味的	bland
外卖	take-out/take-away	酒，烈性酒	booze
烤的	broiled	烧焦的	burnt
调味品	condiments	优惠券	coupon
刀叉	cutlery	镀银餐具	silverware
解冻，化冻	defrost	甜食	dessert
洗碗工，洗碗机	dishwasher	（拌沙拉的）酱料	dressing
主菜	entrée/main course	洗手间	rest-rooms
特价菜	special	油炸	fry
烧烤	grill	自制的	homemade
配料，成分	ingredient	微波炉	microwave
常客	regular	打包	pack up
生的，三成熟的	rare	辣的	spicy
油腻的	rich	调味汁，酱汁	sauce
自助的	self-served	摆放餐具	set table
酸的	sour	特制品，特产	specialty
甜的	sweet	男/女服务生	waiter/ waitress
全熟的	well-done	难吃的	yucky
加有冰激凌的	à la mode	开胃菜	appetizer
围裙	apron	烤肉	barbeque
苦的	bitter	煮	boil
（餐馆中的）高背椅	booth/ bench	裹面包屑后烹制的	breaded
自助餐	buffet	咸的	salty
（美）餐馆工	busboy	奶精	creamer
好吃的	yummy	配菜	side dish
油炸的	deep fried	美味的	delicious
客人使用过的餐具	dirty dish	食品袋	doggie bag
不加黄油（或果酱）的	dry	快餐	fast-food

Unit 3 Hospitality Industry

佐料，调味料	seasoning	小费	gratuity/ tip
餐馆中的儿童专用椅子	highchair	烫的，辣的	hot
菜谱	recipe	味道不重的，不辣的	mild
多收钱	overcharge	腌制的	pickled

PART Ⅳ EXERCISES

Ⅰ. Listening comprehension.

Zurich Ranks the Most Desirable Place to Live

Zurich has beaten its fellow Swiss rival Geneva to become the most desirable place to live in the world, according to a survey released on April 10th, 2006, measuring quality of life in more than 1 _____ cities worldwide.

Each city was judged on factors such as 2 _____, the environment and 3 _____ public services such as health, education and transport.

Zurich beat Geneva into second place, while Vancouver in Canada was third. The British Columbian city is consistently voted as one of the most desirable cities in the world to live. Surrounded by water on three sides and overlooked by mountains, it is a diverse city with a high standard of living, relatively 4 _____.

Zurich is situated where the river Limmat issues from the north-western end of Lake Zurich, about 30 km north of the 5 _____. Zurich is surrounded by wooded hills. The river Sihl meets with the Limmat at the end of Platzspitz, which borders the Swiss National Museum. The geographic and historic center of the city is the Lindeuhof, a small natural hill on the 6 _____ of the Limmat, about 700 meters north of where the river issues from Lake Zurich. Today the incorporated city stretches somewhat beyond 7 _____ confines of the hills and includes some neighborhoods to the northeast in the Glatt Valley and to the north in the Limmat Valley.

Ⅱ. Put the following into Chinese.

1. shopping paradise _____
2. specialty _____
3. blue and white porcelain _____
4. souvenir _____
5. embroidery _____
6. handicraft _____
7. lacquer ware _____
8. tea set _____
9. black tea _____
10. imitation/reproduction _____

III. Active voice & passive voice.

A. Fill in the blanks with the proper form of the given words.

1. I want you to watch carefully how the machine _____ (operate)?
2. I object to _____ (be kept) waiting.
3. He hopes to _____ (nominate).
4. This house is _____ (let).
5. Hundreds of people _____ (kill) in the crash.
6. It _____ (think) that he will come.

B. Translate the following sentences into English.

1. 城里又办起了一所大学。
2. 西红柿很容易碰伤。
3. 我的声音传不远。
4. 这火柴容易划着。
5. 这些土豆容易削皮。
6. 这个抽屉锁不上。
7. 牛奶容易变质。
8. 大家认为她已经康复。

IV. Reading comprehension.

Paris—A City of Restaurants

Food is more than just important to the French. It is a way of life, an art form, an indispensable part of being. In recent years the French Government has officially recognized the Art and Science of French Cuisine, and awarded a fairly large amount of money for its study, research, promotion, and practice.

There is a real embarrassment of riches from which to choose, from tiny, neighborhood cafes and bistros to the luxurious churches of gastronomic delight with just about everything in between: cuisine bourgeoisie, nouvelle cuisine, regional cuisine, even Burger King. If you are after a complete, formal dinner, then grand cuisine is the one. If you prefer a lighter touch, yet still with a recognizably traditional twist, try cuisine bourgeoisie. For an even lighter taste, with pure flavor, freshness, and an imaginative combination of ingredients (but often served in miniscule portions: it is said that this style means less on the plates but more on the check), go for nouvelle cuisine. Regional cuisine in Paris is similarly excellent, marked by an enormous variety of traditional and specially regional ingredients. There are also countless ethnic restaurants in the city, ranging from Chinese, Vietnamese, Japanese, Russian and Kosher, to Algerian, Moroccan, And Tunisian, with a few Indian and Indonesian restaurants thrown in for good measure.

Parisian restaurants still generally offer good value for money. Catering to such a large number of discriminating customers, the city's restaurants keep prices low and offer value for money. Most of the places that are recommended in city are not, therefore, too expensive. But always make a point of checking the menu posted outside before you go in. If you think it unreasonable, go elsewhere. You'd never have trouble finding a substitute: Paris is a city of restaurants. You should be sure to check the credit card stickers in the window. Don't assume that all the major cards in the world will be accepted here, even in the ritziest spots, because they won't be.

If you are watching your dollars carefully, then be sure to check out the set menus. Nearly all restaurants have several menus at different prices. Restaurants with especially interesting cuisine may have a gourmet (美食家) menu which will allow you to taste several of the chef's specialties at much less than if you had ordered them as separate dishes.

Paris restaurants have very variable opening times. A good many close for all or part of July and (especially) August. Similarly, a great many close on weekends, particularly Sundays and public holidays. Always check before turning up.

No guidebook could ever do justice to the restaurants of Paris. Even the most comprehensive books can present no more than tip of the iceberg. The restaurants listed in the City's Tour Guide are arranged by arrondissement and represent a mélange of the tried and the tested and the novel. But for every one they recommend there are probably another 20 just as good. Never be afraid to experiment. Bon Appétit!

1. Fill in the blanks to complete the following statements.

(1) To the French, food is a way of ＿＿＿＿＿＿, ＿＿＿＿＿＿, and an ＿＿＿＿＿＿.

(2) ＿＿＿＿＿＿ has been officially recognized by the French government in recent years.

(3) A fairly large amount of money has now been awarded for the ＿＿＿＿＿＿, ＿＿＿＿＿＿, ＿＿＿＿＿＿, and ＿＿＿＿＿＿ of French cuisine.

(4) There are different kinds of restaurants in Paris, ranging from ＿＿＿＿＿＿ to ＿＿＿＿＿＿.

(5) The cuisine that is mentioned in the text include ＿＿＿＿＿＿, ＿＿＿＿＿＿, ＿＿＿＿＿＿, ＿＿＿＿＿＿ and many foreign styles.

(6) Foreign style restaurants in Paris provide ＿＿＿＿＿＿, ＿＿＿＿＿＿, ＿＿＿＿＿＿, ＿＿＿＿＿＿, ＿＿＿＿＿＿, ＿＿＿＿＿＿, ＿＿＿＿＿＿, ＿＿＿＿＿＿ and ＿＿＿＿＿＿ food.

2. Read the following statements and decide which are true and which are false. Put a T for the true ones and an F for false ones.

(　　) (1) Paris is recognized as "a City of Restaurants" because French food is served in every restaurant in the city.

(　　) (2) French cuisine has never been so widely recognized and studied in French before.

(　　) (3) International visitors find it hard to choose an appropriate restaurant in Paris because there are too many of them.

(   ) (4) Restaurants in Paris keep prices low but offer good-value for money food and service.

(   ) (5) You can easily find a substitute in Paris if you don't like a specific restaurant.

(   ) (6) Major credit cards may not be accepted in most Parisian restaurants for no reason.

V. Translate the following sentences into Chinese. They are underlined in Text A.

1. They spend more on fast food than on movies, books, magazines, newspapers, videos, and recorded music combined.

2. During that period, women entered the workforce in record numbers, often motivated less by a feminist perspective than by a need to pay the bills.

3. Indeed, the company earns the majority of its profits not from selling food but from collecting rent.

4. In many respects, the fast food industry embodies the best and the worst of American capitalism at the start of twenty-first century—its constant stream of new products and innovations, its widening gulf between rich and poor.

5. No other industry offers, both literally and figuratively, so much insight into the nature of mass consumption.

VI. Writing.

Introduce a restaurant, and the followings should be considered:

1. The location and the environment, e.g., the size of the restaurant, and the decoration of the private room;

2. The special cuisine of the restaurant;

3. The service quality of the restaurant.

Unit 4   Tourism Attraction

PART I   TEXT

Text A   Touring round Banff

Your visit to the Canadian Rockies[1] would not be complete without taking a closer look at the surrounding wilderness. The Banff[2] and Lake Louise[3] Visitor Centers provide excellent brochures describing the geological and historical development of the area. For more than a century, many explorers have been dazzled by the magnificent Rocky Mountains, yet many of the summits and faces have only been challenged by mountain climbers in more recent decades. Nevertheless, even the occasional traveler can enjoy the beauty of the mountains from the valleys below. Here we begin our journey in the Banff vicinity, moving along the Trans-Canada Highway to Lake Louise. Most of the locals know the names of prominent peaks, mountain ranges, passes, lakes and rivers. We think you'll want to know a few too.

In and Around Banff

A few hours or a few days to spend? No matter. The sights, sounds and smells of the wilderness are at your doorstep. Watch for the elk that stroll through town parks and alleyways. South of the Bow River[4] bridge, behind the Park Administration Building, you'll find Mountain Avenue, the road to Sulphur Mountain. The paved road winds through dense forest for 4 km to the Upper Hot Spring Pool, on the right, and to the Sulphur Mountain Gondola lower terminal straight ahead. The pool is available for soaking, and the views from atop the gondola are sensational—mountain ranges and the entire Banff townsite and valley stretch before you. Bow Falls[5] has resulted from the Bow River flowing over the limestone bedrock between Mt. Rundle and Tunnel Mountain. The Spray River flows into the Bow at this point with the pounding water creating powerful rapids. The falls are accessible from the road to the Fairmont Banff Springs Golf Course.

Tunnel Mountain offers beautiful views of Banff, Mt. Rundle and the Bow Valley. This mountain, just east of the Banff townsite, was originally surveyed as the site for a railway tunnel. Plans were abandoned for a more economical line, which is the current route of the Trans-Canada Highway. Though the plans were changed, the original name for this mountain remained.

The native Indians believed the Hoodoos were nocturnal giants who awoke to pound the passerby with rocks hurled from the mountainside. Geologists believe the formations were cemented together with dissolving limestone over 20,000 years ago. Scientific analysis tells us the Hoodoos were pillars of glacial till. They are visible from the lookout point off Tunnel Mountain Road.

Mt. Rundle, named for Robert Rundle, the Wesleyan missionary who passed through the region in the 1840s, rises to 2,949 metres (9,700 feet). It is one of Banff's signature sights and is often seen on postcards or paintings with the town of Banff nestled just below it. Seven distinct high points along its ridge stretch southeast from Banff to the Whiteman's Gap. The 6.4 km (3.8 mile) drive to Mt. Norquay begins north of the Trans-Canada Highway from Banff, with a winding two-lane road providing striking views of Banff and the Vermilion Lakes. The elevation of Mt. Norquay is 2,522 meters (8,300 feet), and it is one of Banff's popular skiing areas in the winter.

The Vermilion Lakes are the most important wetlands for migratory birds in Banff National Park. Located near Banff, just south of the Trans-Canada Highway, the three lakes are connected by marshes and beaver dams. The varied lakeshore habitat makes this one of the richest bird and wildlife areas in the Park. Cascade Mountain, towers 2,998 metres (9,840 feet) north of the Banff townsite. Part of the Vermilion Range of mountains, Cascade's prominent waterfall can be viewed from the Trans-Canada Highway. The Lake Minnewanka loop road takes you to several popular sites for interpretive walking tours, picnicking, biking or fishing. Bankhead is 8 km (4.8 miles) northeast of Banff on the road to Lake Minnewanka. Watch for signs for Lower Bankhead, an abandoned coal mine, and Upper Bankhead, site of the previous coal mining community. The same forces that shaped the mountains also left exposed rich seams of coal on Cascade Mountain. In Banff's early days, these seams were mined to fuel the railway's ever-hungry steam engines. While industrial activities such as mining are no longer allowed in National Parks, visitors can walk through the scattered remains of the ghost coal town. Interpretive signs at the beginning of the self-guided trail will help you to discover Bankhead's story.

Two Jack Lake and Johnson Lake, the smallest of the three area lakes, are reachable from the Lake Minnewanka Drive via a loop. Both are popular spots for fishing, picnics and canoeing. You're likely to see Bighorn sheep[6] on your circuit. Lake Minnewanka is the largest lake in the Park, and the only one on which power boats are permitted. It is very popular with trout fishermen. Minnewanka, meaning "Lake of the Water Spirit" is also a popular family recreational family centre, with picnic areas, a snack shop, trails along the lake, boating and fishing.

The Bow Valley Parkway—Highway 1A

Although the Trans-Canada Highway is the better known route between Banff and Lake Louise, the Bow Valley Parkway (Highway 1A), which parallels the Trans-Canada, is very scenic and provides a more leisurely experience. Watch for interpretive signs, picnic areas and trail heads along the way. You can almost count on seeing wildlife from this road. Numerous campgrounds, too, are located on this route, which begins 6 km (3.6 miles) west of Banff, or 1 km (0.6 miles) from Lake Louise Village on the road to the ski area.

Johnston Canyon, 25 km (15.0 miles) northwest of Banff and accessible from the Bow Valley Parkway, boasts two magnificent waterfalls. The falls are a mere six meters (20 feet) across at some points along the trails and the Upper Falls, at 30 meters (more than 100 feet) high, are a real natural treat. Catwalks make access to the Lower Falls (1.1 km/0.7 miles) easy and the closeness to the pounding water magnificent. The Upper Falls (2.7 km/1.6 miles) are reached by a trail which winds through lodge pole pine, spruce and Douglas fir. The trail climbs above the falls another 3.2 km (1.9 miles) to the "Ink Pots" —brilliant blue and jade green springs whose constant temperature remains near 4℃. The pool's bottoms are composed of quicksand.

Castle Mountain, which at one time was named Mt. Eisenhower in honor of the American President, is nearly the mid-way point between Banff and Lake Louise. The Junction of Trans-Canada Highway and Highway 93 South to Radium Hot Springs in Kootenay National Park lies in the shadow of this mountain. Approximately 1 km west of this junction, stop and admire the views at the pull-off sign "Castle Cliffs".

In and Around Lake Louise

Lake Louise is the most famous glacial lake in the Canadian Rockies, and one of the most beautiful in the Western Hemisphere. The lake, named for Princess Louise Caroline Alberta[7], daughter of Queen Victoria, is 1,730 meters (5,680 ft.) above sea level. The world famous Chateau Lake Louise sits at the opposite end of the lake from Mt. Victoria and Victoria Glacier, named for the Queen. The nearest surrounding mountains, Mt. Lefroy and Mt. Fairview, add to the remarkable picture. <u>Melting glacier silt creates the striking turquoise color of the lake and keeps it at a frigid temperature year round!</u> Although swimming is impossible, you may rent a canoe and paddle the lake or simply enjoy the panoramic splendour of the glaciers and Lake Louise from across the valley at the Lake Louise Gondola.

Moraine Lake[8] is also quite famous, in that an image of the Valley of the Ten Peaks, surrounding the lake, appears on the back of older versions of the Canadian $20 bill. The highest peak is Deltaform at 3,424 meters (11,230 feet), and all the peaks—Fay, Little, Bowlen, Perren, Septa, Allen, Tuzo, Deltaform, Neptuak, and Wenkchemna—are whitecapped with what remains of the Wenkchemna Glacier. Views of these incredible mountains can be seen from the trails around the lake. Or, you can rent a canoe and paddle toward surrounding mountains. The huge mountain to the north, with the glacier on its summit, is Mount Temple, at 3,547 meters (11,636 feet), the third highest mountain in Banff National Park.

The Icefields Parkway

The Icefield Parkway (Highway 93 North) is often called the most scenic highway in the world! It is named for the tremendous glaciers which flank its westwardside; the 230 km (143 mile) Parkway weaves up and around mountains that separate Banff and Jasper National Parks. The drive provides breathtaking scenery along with dozens of picnic areas, campgrounds, interpretive viewpoints, and easy access hiking trails. Abundant with wildlife, you will likely have to slow down for mountain goats that often amble onto the highway—especially at dawn and dusk.

Although the route can be travelled safely in three and a half hours, most visitors take a full day or more to enjoy all of the many photo opportunities. Gas, accommodation and other services are available in only a few places along the way, so plan you route accordingly. And, be prepared for varied weather conditions. Snow can fall in the highest passes even in midsummer. Check your map for lakeshores most accessible from the highway. The largest include Herbert, Hector and Waterfowl Lakes. 36 km (22 miles) north of the Trans-Canada Highway, you'll encounter Bow Lake, sitting majestically below Crowfoot Mountain and Mt. Thompson.

The lake is surrounded by alpine fields of wildflowers at the edge of the timetable. Bow Summit, at an elevation of 2 068 meters (6,785 feet), is the highest point on the Parkway. Here the road crosses near the source of the Bow River before dropping into the Mistaya Valley. You can climb even higher than Bow Summit by following the short access road to an additional viewpoint overlooking Peyto Lake. Glaciers really can be seen nearly the entire length of the Parkway—with the renowned Columbia Icefield dominating the largest chain of glaciers along the Great Divide. It is one of the largest known accumulations of ice south of the Arctic Circle, and one of the most accessible in North America. The Icefield composed of a total of eight glaciers. Saskatchewan Glacier, the longest glacier in the Columbia Icefield, is located just inside the border to Banff National Park. <u>Source of the North Saskatchewan River system, the Glacier is best viewed from the alpine heights of Parker Ridge, a cold and treeless meadowland, easily attained after a short hike from the Icefields Parkway.</u> Athabasca, the Dome, and Stutfield Glaciers can be seen from the Parkway.

A short side trip from the highway actually takes you to the "toe" of Athabasca. Unguided travel any further onto the glacier is not recommended. Plan to include a visit to the world famous Columbia Icefield Centre, which is open from May to mid-October. The centre is a beautiful chalet-style stone building with all its services under one roof.

Words and Expressions

alleyway	[ˈælɪwei]	n. 小巷，背街，窄街
alpine	[ˈælpaɪn]	a. 高山的，阿尔卑斯山的；n. 高山植物
amble	[ˈæmbl]	n. 缓行慢步；v. 缓行
bankhead	[ˈbæŋkhed]	n. 横堤
catwalk	[ˈkætwɔːk]	n. 狭窄过道
cement	[sɪˈment]	v. 用水泥涂，巩固；n. 水泥
dazzle	[ˈdæzl]	v. 使眼花，使赞许；n. 光辉
dense	[dens]	a. 密集的，稠密的；n. 密集
doorstep	[ˈdɔːstep]	n. 门阶

elk	[elk]	n. 麋，驼鹿
glacial	['gleɪʃl]	a. 冰川（期）的，非常冷的
gondola	['gɔndələ]	n. 狭长小船，无盖货车，索道
hoodoo	['hu:du:]	n. 不祥的人和物；v. 使倒霉
icefield	['aɪsfi:ld]	n. 冰原
limestone	['laɪmstəun]	n. 石灰石
jade	[dʒeɪd]	n. 玉石，翡翠
jasper	['dʒæspə]	n. 碧玉
magnificent	[mæg'nɪfɪsnt]	a. 壮丽的，宏伟的
majestically	[mə'dʒestɪkli]	a. 威严地，雄伟地
marsh	[mɑ:ʃ]	n. 沼泽，湿地
meadowland	['medəulænd]	n. 草地
migratory	['maɪgrətri]	a. 迁徙的，流浪的
nestle	['nesl]	v. 依偎，（舒适地）安顿
nocturnal	[nɑ:k'tə:nl]	a. 在夜间的，（指生物）夜间活动的
panoramic	[ˌpænə'ræmik]	a. 全景的
pillar	['pɪlə]	n. 柱子，台柱
quicksand	['kwɪksænd]	n. 流沙，陷阱
splendor	['splendər]	n. 光彩，显赫，辉煌，壮丽
spruce	[spru:s]	n. 赤松
stroll	[strəul]	n. & v. 闲逛，漫步
summit	['sʌmɪt]	n. 顶点，最高阶层
turquoise	['tə:kwɔɪz]	n. 青松石，青绿色；adj. 青绿色的
valley	['væli]	n. 山谷，溪谷，流域
western hemisphere		西半球
Arctic Circle		北极圈
Douglas fir		绿松，花旗松，道格拉斯松
loop road		回旋路，环路
snack shop		小吃店

Notes

1. Canadian Rockies：加拿大落基山。加拿大境内的落基山脉国家公园群位于加拿大西南部的阿尔伯塔省和不列颠哥伦比亚省，面积2.3万平方千米，包括贾斯珀、班夫、约霍、库特奈等国家公园，以及汉帕、罗布森、阿西尼伯因等省立公园，是世界上面积最大的国家公园。

2. Banff：班夫国家公园，建于1885年，是加拿大历史最悠久的国家公园，坐落于落基山脉北段，距卡尔加里以西约110～180千米处。公园占地6641平方千米，遍布冰川、冰原、松林和高山。班夫镇成立于1883年，是班夫国家公园的主要商业中心，也是文化活动中心。

3. Lake Louise：路易斯湖，又称"翡翠湖"，位于加拿大落基山，班夫国家公园内，被称为"加拿大-落基山的宝石"。

4. Bow River：弓河，起源于加拿大落基山脉的弓河冰川和弓湖，向南流至路易斯湖，然后转向东，相继穿过班夫镇和坎莫尔，之后汇入科克伦上方的戈斯特湖水库，继续向东到达卡尔加里。弓河全长大约 600 千米，流域面积为 26 200 平方千米。弓河的名字取自印第安语，意为"取弓的地方"，那是因为印第安人猎弓最早取材于弓河沿岸的道格拉斯松木。

5. Bow Falls：弓河瀑布，是由弓河的断层所形成。由于弓河受大量冰河阻断改由山间穿过，与其支流泡沫河（Spray）交汇，由此而得名。瀑布落差不大，约为 10 米，虽然只是一个较小型的瀑布，但白浪翻腾，涛声阵阵，夺人心魄。

6. Bighorn sheep：大角羊，班夫的一种大型哺乳动物。

7. Louise Caroline Alberta：路易斯·卡罗琳·阿尔伯塔（1848 年 3 月 18 日－1939 年 12 月 3 日），英国维多利亚女王的四女，路易斯公主和她的驸马在 1878 至 1883 年期间担任加拿大总督和夫人。1884 年，为纪念她，加拿大的"翡翠湖"（Emerald Lake）改称为路易斯湖（Lake Louise）并一直沿用至今，阿尔伯塔省（Alberta）的名字也是取自这位公主。

8. Moraine Lake：梦莲湖，湖面呈宝石蓝色，晶莹剔透，被锯齿状的山谷拥环，像一块宝玉。这块"国宝"被印在加拿大旧版的 20 元纸币上。

Text B　Tourism Attraction

The tourism industry includes a number of key elements that tourists rely upon to achieve their general and specific goals and needs within a destination. Broadly categorized, they include facilities, accommodation, transportation, and attractions. Tourism attraction is a fundamental element of the tourist experience, which may be loosely categorized as cultural (e.g., history sites, museums), natural (e.g., parks, flora and fauna), events (e.g., cinemas), recreation (e.g., golf, hiking) and entertainment (e.g., theme parks, cinemas). Tourism attractions affect more on tourists than other components of the industry which represent the most important reasons for travel to destinations.

Tourism attractions may also be described as "empirical relationships between a tourist, a site and a marker"[1]. The tourist represents the human component, the site includes the actual destination or physical entity, and the marker represents some form of information that the tourist uses to identify and give meaning to a particular attraction; however, under the conditions of tourist-site-marker, virtually anything could become an attraction, including services and facilities. Thus, the objective and subjective characteristics of attractions ought to be concerned with three main areas of the attraction：

Ideographic. Describes the concrete uniqueness of a site. Sites are individually identified by name and usually associated with small regions. This is the most frequent form of attraction studied in tourism research.

Organizational. The focus is not on the attractions themselves, but rather on their spatial capacity and temporal nature. Scale continua are based on the size of the area which the attraction encompasses.[2]

Cognitive. A place that fosters the feeling of being a tourist. Attractions are places that elicit feelings related to "insider", "outsider", and the authenticity of front and back regions.

A tourist attraction is a systematic arrangement of three elements: a person with touristic needs, a nucleus (any feature or characteristic of a place they might visit) and at least one marker (information about the nucleus). There are three separate zones for a tourism attraction, including (1) the nuclei, or core of the attraction; (2) the inviolate belt, which is the space needed to set the nuclei in a context; and (3) the zone of closure, which includes desirable tourism infrastructure such as toilets and information.

Attractions occur on various hierarchies of scale, from very specific and small objects within a site to entire countries and continents. This scale variability further complicates the analysis of attractions as both sites and regions. Consequently, there exists a series of attraction cores and attraction peripheries, within different regions, between regions, and from the perspective of the types of tourists who visit them. Spatially, and with the influence of time, the number and type of attractions visited by tourists and tourist groups may create a niche; a role certain types of tourists occupy within a vacation destination. Through an analysis of space, time, and other behavioural factors, tourists can be fitted into a typology based on their utilization and travel between selected attractions. One could make the assumption that tourist groups differ on the basis of the type of attractions they choose to visit, and according to how much time they spend at them. The implications for the tourism industry are that often it must provide a broad range of experiences for tourists interested in different aspects of a region. A specific destination region, for example, may recognize the importance of providing a mix of touristic opportunities, from the very specific, to more general interest experiences for the tourists in search of cultural and natural experiences, in urban, rural and back-country settings.

Attractions have also been referred to as physical entities of a cultural or natural form. In their natural form, such attractions form the basis for distinctive types of tourism which are based predominantly on aspects of the natural world, such as wildlife tourism, and ecotourism. For example, to a birdwatcher individual species become attractions of the most specific and most sought-after kind. A case in point[3] is the annual return of a single albatross at the Hermaness National Nature Reserve in Unst, Shetland, Scotland. The arrival of this species prompts birdwatching tourists immediately to change their plans in an effort to travel to Hermaness. The albatross has become a major attraction for birder-tourists, while Hermaness, in a broader context, acts as medium (attraction cluster) by which to present the attraction (bird). Natural attractions can be transitory in space and time, and this time may be measured for particular species in seconds, hours, days, weeks, months, seasons, or years. For tourists who travel with the prime reason to experience these transitory attractions, their movement is a source of both challenge and frustration.

Words and Expressions

flora	[ˈflɔrə]	n.	植物群；植物志；植物区系
fauna	[ˈfɔnə]	n.	动物群；动物志
entity	[ˈentɪti]	n.	实体；实际存在物；本质
virtually	[ˈvɜːtʃuəli]	v.	实际上；实质上；无形中
ideographic	[ˌɪdɪrˈgræfɪk]	a.	表意的
spatial	[ˈspeʃl]	a.	空间的；受空间条件限制的
temporal	[ˈtempərəl]	a.	时间的；世俗的；暂存的
continua	[kənˈtɪnjʊ]	n.	连续统一体；连续统；闭联集
cognitive	[ˈkɑgnətɪv]	a.	认知的；认识的
foster	[ˈfɔstə(r)]	v.	培养；抚育
authenticity	[ˌɔːθenˈtɪsəti]	n.	可靠性；确实性；真实性
nucleus	[ˈnuklɪəs]	n.	中心；核心
inviolate	[ɪnˈvaɪəlɪt]	a.	不受侵犯的；未受损害的
variability	[ˌverɪəˈbɪləti]	n.	变化性；变化的倾向；变率
periphery	[pəˈrɪfəri]	n.	边缘；外围；边缘地带
typology	[taɪˈpɑlədʒi]	n.	象征主义；象征论
albatross	[ˈælbətrɔs]	n.	信天翁；沉重负担

Notes

（1）empirical relationships between a tourist, a site and a marker：旅游者、旅游区与旅游标志之间的空间关系。

（2）Scale continua are based on the size of the area which the attraction encompasses. 区域的连续性取决于旅游资源所涵盖的地理面积的情况。

（3）a case in point：关键之处在于。

PART II   DIALOGUE

Dialogue 1   Going Through Security

A：Security Inspector; D：Mr. Dan

A：Please lay your bags flat on the conveyor belt, and use the bins for small objects.

D：Do I need to take my laptop out of the bag?

A：Yes, you do. Take off your hat and your shoes, too.

(He walks through the metal detector.)

[BEEP BEEP BEEP BEEP]

A：Please step back. Do you have anything in your pockets—keys, cell phone, loose change?

Unit 4
Tourism Attraction

D: I don't think so. Let me try taking off my belt.

A: Okay, come through.

(He goes through the metal detector again.)

A: You're all set! Have a nice flight.

A: 请把您的包平放在传送带上，小件物品放在篮子里。

D: 我是否需要把笔记本电脑从背包里拿出来？

A: 是的。帽子和鞋也需要脱掉。

A: 请退回来。请问您口袋里有什么小东西？钥匙、手机、硬币？

D: 没有。让我脱掉皮带试试吧。

A: 好的。再走一遍试试。

A: 一切正常。祝您旅行愉快！

Dialogue 2   Announcements at the Gate

Here are a few announcements you might hear while you are at the gate, waiting for the plane to board. (下面是几句你在登机口候机时可能听到的通告)

"There has been a gate change. "（要更改登机口。）

"United Airlines flight 880 to Miami is now boarding. "（美联航飞往迈阿密的880次航班登机时间到了。）

"Please have your boarding pass and identification ready for boarding. "（请准备好各自的身份证明和登机卡等待登机。）

"We would like to invite our first- and business-class passengers to board. "（现在请头等舱和商务舱的乘客登机。）

"We are now inviting passengers with small children and any passengers requiring special assistance to begin boarding. "（现在请带小孩的和需要帮助的乘客登机。）

"We would now like to invite all passengers to board. "（现在请所有乘客登机。）

"This is the final boarding call for United Airlines flight 880 to Miami. "（现在是最后一次呼叫乘坐美联航880次班机飞往迈阿密的乘客登机。）

"Passenger John Smith, please proceed to the United Airlines desk at gate 12. "（约翰·史密斯旅客，请前往12号登机口的美联航柜台。）

PART Ⅲ   GOOD TO KNOW: The Types of Luggage

porter/red cap	搬运工人，行李员	valuable	贵重品
trolley	手推车	name tag	标有姓名的标签
trunk	大衣箱	suitcase	提箱
baggage elevator	行李电梯	traveling bag	旅行袋
storage room	行李仓	light luggage	轻便行李
shoulder bag	背包	purse	女士随身小手袋

PART IV   EXERCISES

I . Listening comprehension.

Chanel No. 5

• Chanel No. 5, a symbol of French style,

1. is _____ years since Chanel's original No. 5 first filtered through Paris society.

2. is a fragrance that used the best ingredients, including _____ and jasmine, which have been harvested from the same fields for generations.

3. is unique, and each bottle is _____, and sealed with a strip of ox bladder.

• The new version of No. 5 still has one of key codes of Mademoiselle Chanel, which is 4. _____. But the original version of No. 5 will continue its journey of 5. _____.

II . Put the following into Chinese.

1. Beijing's alleyways _____
2. waterway _____
3. pedicab _____
4. Ocean Park _____
5. Ghost City of Fengdu _____
6. credit card _____
7. statue _____
8. Temple of Heaven _____
9. Yangtze Cruise _____
10. cliff _____

III. Fill in each blank with the proper form of the given word.

Subjunctive Mood

1. The doctor insisted that he _____ (not eat) meat.
2. It is essential that all the facts _____ (exam) first.
3. Your advice that she _____ (wait) till next week is reasonable.
4. Though everyone _____ (desert) you, I will not.
5. Whatever _____ (be) his defense, we cannot tolerate this.
6. If the rumor _____ (be) true, everything is possible.
7. Long _____ (live) the People's Republic of China!
8. So _____ (be) it. (但愿如此，就这样吧)
9. If I _____ (be) you, I should wait till next week.
10. If only I _____ (be) not so nervous.

11. I wish it _____ (be) spring all the year round.

12. If you _____ (not watch) that late movie last night, you wouldn't be sleepy.

13. If Clara _____ (fail) this time, tell her to try again. (I know she works hard, and she will pass.)

14. I didn't know the extent of his difficulty, or else I _____ (promise) to help him.

15. I _____ (go) with you, but I was too tired.

16. I wish I _____ (not make) mistakes every day.

17. When he was asked why his friend had not accepted the offer, he suggested that his friend's pride _____ (prevent) his from accepting.

IV. Read the passage and answer the questions that follow.

Niagara Falls

Thundering just 90 miles (143 km) away from Lake Ontario, and carrying 34.5 million gallons (157 million liters) of water a minute in an awesome display of enormous raw power, Niagara Falls is known as one of the natural wonders of the world. It is the major falls at the site, 177 ft high and carrying 90 percent of the water (the others are Rainbow Falls on the US side of border and Bridal Veil Falls), and it is magnificent, no matter the viewpoint or the season. You can look down at it from towers go behind its downfall, approach it from below in what seems a very tiny boat or simply stand at the brink enjoying the sight and the sound. If the weather is pleasant, get some idea of the gorge from Rainbow Bridge to Table Rock, then gain entrance to the tunnels behind the falls through Table Rock House. For a small fee you are fitted out with raincoat and boots and take an elevator down 125 feet (38 m) to the first tunnel, which offers you three different views of the incredible wall of water. And "wall" is the word: "Curtain" has to frail a connotation to describe that mighty, battering, deafening downpour. After that, get another close-up view of the falls aboard the Maid of the Mist, which you will find at the end of a well-signposted trail down the gorge. Again you pay a small fee and wear raincoat and boots, but this time you see the downfall from the front, bobbing about like a frail cork on the surging sea (it operates from mid-May to late October).

Views from the look-out towers are scenic enough but they do not give you the vision of brute power you get, defened and drenched, at the base of the falls. The towers are a better choice at night when the falls are illuminated (approximately 9:00 p.m. to midnight in summer, 7:00 p.m. to 10:00 p.m. in winter). In addition, in winter, when ice formations and frozen spray can create a fairyland effects, citizens join the Niagara Park Commission, hotels and businesses in creating a Christmas-time effect with thousands of colored bulbs in a three-month (mid-November to mid-February) Festival of Lights. The town of Niagara Falls itself is very commercial but the falls, on Niagara Parks Commission land, make up for any gaudiness. The Parks Commission, incidentally, owns land rights along the 35-mile (56 km) length of border and its gardens are famous. Falls of Niagara-on-the-Lake. The falls can be reached from Toronto by car on the Queen Elizabeth Way as well as by bus, special coach tour, or train.

旅游英语（修订版）

Question

1. What is Niagara Falls known as?

2. How does Niagara Falls look when viewed from different viewpoints and in different seasons?

3. What are the five suggested ways that sightseers appreciate the grand views of the Falls?

4. What seems the best choice of site from where tourists can best enjoy the night view of the Falls in either summer or winter?

5. What activity is organized from mid-November to mid-February in the Niagara Park?

V. Translate the following sentences into Chinese. They are underlined in the texts.

1. The native Indians believed the Hoodoos were nocturnal giants who awoke to pound the passerby with rocks hurled from the mountainside.

2. Melting glacier silt creates the striking turquoise color of the lake and keeps it at a frigid temperature year round！

3. Source of the North Saskatchewan River system，the Glacier is best viewed from the alpine heights of Parker Ridge，a cold and treeless meadowland，easily attained after a short hike from the Icefields Parkway.

4. Spatially，and with the influence of time，the number and type of attractions visited by tourists and tourist groups may create a niche.

5. The implications for the tourism industry are that often it must provide a broad range of experiences for tourists interested in different aspects of a region.

VI. Write an itinerary according to the information given.

一个40人的新加坡代表团将于2022年12月22—25日到珠海考察。他们乘坐的航班将于12月22日上午10点到达珠海机场。在珠海期间，他们将考察高栏港经济区、航空产业园以及横琴新区的长隆海洋王国等项目。

Activity 2: Incoming Tourists' Overall Impression on China

Aim:

Based on team-work, each student team is required to collect at least 10 questionnaires; students are supposed to spend 10-15 minutes sharing their findings based on the statistics of the survey.

Agenda:

- Total time – 20 minutes/each group in class.
- For each group, do the on-site survey before the class presentation. Questionnaires would be sent to the incoming tourists in/around the tourist attractions like museums, scenic spots, restaurants, airports, etc.
- Based on the results of the collected questionnaires, each group should work out a report concerning the analysis of the questionnaires and suggestions to China's tourism, then share their findings through the class presentation; the presentation would last 10-15 minutes. The teacher would host the meeting and give comments on the performance of each group.
- Suggested layout of the questionnaire: printed on both sides of a paper in which way not to mix.
- Suggested teaching arrangement: 2 class hours.

The questionnaire is as shown in the next 2 pages.

QUESTIONNAIRE ON INCOMING TOURISTS' OVERALL IMPRESSION ON CHINA

Please take a few minutes to fill out this survey. Thank you for your time.

In what country do you reside? _____

What city? _____

Please indicate your perception of the similarity between your country and China on the following dimensions where **1 indicates very similar and 7 indicates not at all similar**:

	1 (very similar)	2	3	4	5	6	7 (not at all similar)
Education							
Family Life							
Religion							
Language							
Entertainment							
Aesthetics							
Food							
Hotels							
Automobiles							
Cleanliness							
Sports							
Economy							

On a scale of 1 (lowest) to 7 (highest), how important are the following values to you in everyday life? Please place a check mark of the one most important to you.

	1 (Not Important at all)	2	3	4	5	6	7 (Extremely Important)	Which is the most important value? (choose only one)
1. Sense of belonging								
2. Being well respected								
3. Security								
4. Self respect								
5. Warm relations with others								
6. Sense of accomplishment								
7. Self fullfilment								
8. Fun and enjoyment in life								

Incoming Tourists' Overall Impression on China — Activity 2

How would you rate the economic environment of your country?

Developed _____ Developing _____ Undeveloped _____

How would you rate the economic environment of China?

Developed _____ Developing _____ Undeveloped _____

What is the primary purpose of this visit to China?

Business _____ Pleasure _____ Education _____ Other _____

What is your overall impression of China?

 Very Favorable _____

 Somewhat Favorable _____

 Neither Favorable nor Unfavorable _____

 Somewhat Unfavorable _____

 Very Unfavorable _____

What have you liked most about China on this trip? _____

Is there anything that you have disliked? If so, please write it down here: _____

Have you visited China before? Yes _____ No _____

If yes, please list the year(s) and describe any changes that you have noticed.

_____

_____

What cities in China have you visited on this trip? _____

_____

What other cities in China will you Visit on this trip? _____

What other countrie(s) have you visited? _____

Please list the years in which you visited these countries and if your visit was for business or pleasure.

Age: _____ Gender: Male _____ Female _____

Occupation: _____

THANK YOU

Unit 5   Tourist Product

PART I   TEXT

Text A   The Silk Road, from Xi'an to Kashgar

Named in the 1870s by the German scholar, Baron Fredinand von Richthofen, the Silk Road—perhaps the greatest East-West trade route and vehicle for cross-cultural exchange—was first travelled by ambassador Zhang Qian in the second century BC while on a mission from Emperor Wudi (ruled 141 – 87 BC) of the Han dynasty (206 BC – AD 220). Zhang was sent to recruit the Yuezhi people, who had recently been defeated by the Xiongnus and driven to the western fringes of the Taklamakan Desert. Since the Warring States period (475 – 221 BC), the Huns had been launching aggressive raids into Chinese territory, which prompted Emperor Qin Shihuangdi of the Qin dynasty (221 – 207 BC) to build the Great Wall. Eager to defeat these powerful marauders, Wudi heard that the Yuezhi were seeking revenge on the Xiongnu and would welcome help with retaliation from any ally.

Zhang with a caravan of 100 men set out in 138 BC from the Chinese capital of Chang'an (present-day Xi'an) only to be soon captured by the Xiongnu as they passed through the Hexi Corridor in northwest Gansu. The surviving members of the caravan were treated well; Zhang married and had a son. After ten years, he had the remainder of the party managed to escape and continue their journey west along the northern Silk Road to Kashgar and Ferghana. Upon reaching the Yuezhi, Zhang found them to have settled prosperously in the various oases of Central Asia and to be no longer interested in avenging themselves of the Huns. Zhang stayed one year gathering valuable military, economic, political and geographical information and returned via the southern Silk Road, only to be captured again, this time by Tibetan tribes allied with the Xiongnu; once again he escaped. In 125 BC, 13 years later, he returned to Chang'an. Of the original party only he and one other completed the trail-blazing journey—the first land route between East and West and one that would eventually link Imperial China with Imperial Rome.

Zhang reported on some 36 kingdoms in the Western Regions, delighting Emperor Han Wudi with detailed accounts of the previously unknown kingdoms of Ferghana, Samarkand, Bokhara and others in what are now the Afghanistan, Pakistan and Persia (Iran) as well as the city of Li Kun, which was almost certainly Rome. Zhang recounted stories he had heard of the famous Ferghana horse, rumoured to be of "heavenly" stock. Tempted by this fast and powerful warhorse, seemingly far superior to the average steed and having the potential to defeat the marauding Xiongnu, Han Wudi dispatched successive missions to develop political contacts—the first of which Zhang led in 119 BC and return with foreign envoys, and of course horses, from the courts of Ferghana, Sogdiana, Bactria, Parthia and northern India. Now extinct, these horses were immortalized by artists of both the Han (206 BC-AD 220) and the Tang dynasties (AD 618 –907). Zhang continued seeking allies against the Xiongnu, travelling in 115 BC to the territory of the Wusun, a nomadic tribespeople who lived on the western frontier of the Huns, but again Zhang was unable to enlist support. Upon his return, Zhang died in 113 BC, bearing the Imperial Title of "Great Traveler".

Alexander the Great's[1] expansion into Central Asia stopped far short of Tarim Basin, and he appears to have gained little knowledge of the lands beyond. The Romans, with only a slightly better understanding, were convinced that the Seres (the Silk People, or the Chinese) harvested silk from trees, the "wool of the forests" according to Pliny. In 53 BC, the seven legions of Marcus Licinius Crassus were the first Romans to see silk in battle whilst pursuing the Parthians, a rough warlike tribe, across the Euphrates. They became the victims of the first "Parthian shot[2]", which broke the Romans' front line formation and was quickly followed by a tactic that both terrorized and amazed the Romans: the Parthians waved banners of a strange, shimmering material that towered above the defeated soldiers, blinding them in the brilliant heat of the desert. The Romans managed to obtain samples of this marvelous silk from the victorious Parthians, who had traded it for an ostrich egg and some conjurers with a member of Emperor Han Wudi's early trade missions.

The Parthians along with the Sogdians, Indians and Kushans soon became prominent middlemen in the trade of silk, reaping tremendous profits, bartering with Chinese traders who escorted their merchandise to Dunhuang and as far as Loulan, in the heart of the Lop Nor Desert beyond the Great Wall, and carrying the trade on to Persian, Syrian and Greek merchants. Each transaction increased the cost of the end product, which reached the Roman Emperor in the hands of Greek and Jewish entrepreneurs. Silk garments became all the rage in Roman society, so much so that in AD 14 men were no longer permitted to wear them, as they were perceived to contribute to an already decadent society. Despite the disapproval of the Empire's moral superiors and its high cost, silk was widely worn among even the lowest socio-economic classes. The silk trade flourished up until the second century AD, when it began to arrive in Rome via the sea trade routes.

Caravans and Trade Routes

Silk actually composed a relatively small portion of the trade along the Silk Road: eastbound caravans brought gold, precious metals and stones, textiles, ivory and coral, while westbound caravans transported furs, ceramics, cinnamon bark and rhubarb as well as bronze weapons. Very few caravans, including the people, animals and goods they transported, would complete the entire route that connected the capitals of these two great empires. The oasis towns that made the overland journey possible became important trading posts, commercial centers where caravans would take on fresh merchants, animals and good. The oasis towns prospered considerably, extracting large profits on the goods they bought and sold.

During the Han dynasty, the Chinese referred to the Taklamakan Desert as Liusha, or "moving sands", since the dunes are constantly moving, blown about by fierce winds. Geographers call it the Tarim Basin, after the glacier-fed Tarim River that flows east across the Taklamakan Desert to the Lop Nor Lake. The Taklamakan is bordered on three sides by some of the highest mountain ranges in the world: to the north, by the Heavenly Mountains (Tian Shan); to the west, by the Pamirs (Roof of the World); and to the south, by the Karakoram and Kunlun Mountains. To the east lie the Lop Nor and Gobi Deserts. The infamous Taklamakan— which in Turki means "go in and you will not come out"—has been feared and cursed by travelers for more than 2,000 years. Sir Clarmont Skrine, British consul-general at Kashgar in the 1920s, described it in his book *Chinese Central Asia*:

"*To the north in the clear dawn the view is inexpressively awe-inspiring and sinister. The yellow dunes of the Taklamakan, like the giant waves of a petrified ocean, extend in countless myriads to a far horizon with, here and there, an extra large sand-hill, a king dune as it were, towering above his fellows. They seem to clamour silently, those dunes, for travelers to engulf, for whole caravans to swallow up as they have swallowed up so many in the past.*"

The Fall of the Silk Road

Not coincidentally, the Silk Road flourished during the highly artistic and prosperous Tang dynasty. Chang'an, the capital, a large cosmopolitan centre, was the departure point and final destination for travelers on the Silk Road. The city in 742 was five by six miles in area and had a population of nearly two million, including over 5,000 foreigners. Numerous religions were represented and the city contained the temples, churches and synagogues of Nestorian Christians, Manicheans, Zoroastrians, Hindus, Buddhists and Jews, to name but a few. Foreigners from Byzantium, Iran, Arabia, Sogdia, Mongolia, America, India, Korea, Malaya and Japan lived in Chang'an. Some Tang tomb murals depict foreigners in the imperial court.

In addition to Western goods, religious thought and art, Chang'an received caravans from distant lands loaded with exotic treasures such as cosmetics, rare plants including saffron, medicines, perfumes, wines, spices, fragrant woods, books and woven rugs. Strange and unknown animals also arrived: peacocks, parrots, falcons, hunting dogs, lions, and a rare prize, the ostrich or "camel bird".

By the end of the eighth century, the sea routes from the southern coastal city of Canton (Guangzhou) to the Middle East were well developed, while the Tibetan occupation of the Tarim Basin from 790 until around 850 AD often disrupted the overland trade routes. The art of sericulture had been mastered by the Persians and Byzantines, and the heyday of the Silk Road was over. The Tang dynasty's downfall led to political chaos and an unstable economy less able to support extravagant foreign imports. At the same time, entire communities, active oasis towns, thriving monasteries and grottoes along the Silk Road were disappearing in the space of weeks, as the glacier-fed streams ran dry or changed course. Since the end of the Ice Age, shrinking glaciers have been consistently reducing the amount of water in the Tarim Basin. Only the most fertile and well-irrigated oasis towns have survived.

The rapid spread of Islam from the Middle East was one of the most critical factors in the disappearance of the Buddhist civilizations along the Silk Road, and perhaps the most destructive element in the loss of Serindian art. Only those caves and monasteries that had been swallowed by the sands centuries before were able to survive. Many of the Buddhist cave frescoes, silk paintings and statues had adopted the Gandharan figurative style, portraying "the almighty" in human form. By the late 15th century, Buddhist stupas and temples were either destroyed or left to crumble. At this time, the Ming dynasty (1368—1644) virtually shut China off from the outside world, effectively ending the centuries-old influx of foreign ideas and culture.

Words and Expressions

assimilate	[əˈsɪməleɪt]	v.	吸收；（使）同化
assortment	[əˈsɔːtmənt]	n.	各种各样分类；混合物
aggressive	[əˈgresɪv]	a.	侵略的；好斗的
ally	[ˈælaɪ]	n.	（尤指战时的）同盟国；伙伴
archeologist	[ˌɑːkɪˈɔlədʒɪst]	n.	考古学家
avenge	[əˈvendʒ]	v.	向……报仇
awe-inspiring	[ˈɔːɪnspaɪərɪŋ]	a.	使人敬佩的；令人惊叹的
Baghdad	[ˈbægdæd]	n.	巴格达（伊拉克首都）
Byzantium	[bɪˈzæntɪəm]	n.	拜占庭（今称伊斯坦布尔）
caravan	[ˈkærəvæn]	n.	大篷车；（尤指穿越沙漠的）旅行队
conjurer	[ˈkʌndʒərə(r)]	n.	魔术师；巫师
ceramic	[səˈræmɪk]	n.	制陶艺术，制陶业
clamour	[ˈklæmə(r)]	v.	吵闹；大声地要求
Canton	[ˈkæntɔn]	n.	广州（旧称）
crumble	[ˈkrʌmbl]	v.	崩溃；粉碎
coincidentally	[kəʊˌɪnsɪˈdentəli]	a.	巧合地；一致地
cosmopolitan	[ˌkɔzməˈpɔlɪtən]	n.	世界主义者；a. 世界性的
depiction	[dɪˈpɪkʃn]	n.	描写，叙述
doctrine	[ˈdɔktrɪn]	n.	主义；学说
dynasty	[ˈdɪnəsti]	n.	王朝，朝代
decadent	[ˈdekədənt]	n.	颓废者；a. 颓废的
dune	[djuːn]	n.	（风吹积成的）沙丘
detachment	[dɪˈtætʃmənt]	n.	分离；拆卸
disciple	[dɪˈsaɪpl]	n.	门徒；信徒
eastbound	[ˈiːstbaʊnd]	a.	往东的；向东旅行的
entrench	[ɪnˈtrentʃ]	v.	牢固确立
escapade	[ˌeskəˈpeɪd]	n.	（常指危险或愚蠢的）冒险行为

单词	音标	词性及释义
envoy	[ˈenvɔi]	n. 使者；全权公使
excavate	[ˈekskəveit]	v. 挖掘；开凿
engulf	[inˈgʌlf]	v. 吞没；吞食，狼吞虎咽
earthbound	[ˈɜːθbaund]	a. (只在)地球上的，陆地的，地面上的
enlist	[inˈlist]	v. (使)入伍；征募
Euphrates	[juːˈfreitiːz]	n. 幼发拉底河
fresco	[ˈfreskəu]	n. 湿壁画
fringe	[frindʒ]	n. (地区或群体)边缘；(某物的)穗
falcon	[ˈfɔːlkən]	n. [鸟]隼
fertile	[ˈfɜːtail]	a. 富饶的，肥沃的
garment	[ˈgɑːmənt]	n. 衣服，服装
grotto	[ˈgrɔtəu]	n. 洞穴
heyday	[ˈheidei]	n. 全盛期
immortalize	[iˈmɔːtəlaiz]	v. 使不朽；使名垂千古
indigenous	[inˈdidʒinəs]	a. 本地的；土生土长的
Kashgar	[ˈkæʃgɑː]	n. 喀什葛尔（中国新疆西部城市）
launch	[lɔːntʃ]	v. 发射；开始从事
legion	[ˈliːdʒən]	n. （尤指古罗马的）军团
maraud	[məˈrɔːd]	v. 掠夺；袭击
manuscript	[ˈmænjuskript]	n. 手稿；原稿
marvelous	[ˈmɑːvələs]	a. 不可思议的；惊人的
mural	[ˈmjuərəl]	n. 壁画；(美)壁饰
monastery	[ˈmɔnəstri]	n. 修道院；僧侣
Mahayana	[ˌmɑːhəˈjɑːnə]	n. 大乘佛教
nirvana	[ˌniəˈvɑːnə]	n. 涅槃；天堂
nomadic	[nəuˈmædik]	a. 游牧的；流浪的
oasis	[əuˈeisiːz]	n. 绿洲
ostrich	[ˈɔstritʃ]	n. 鸵鸟
Pamirs	[pəˈmiəz]	n. 帕米尔高原
petrified	[ˈpetrifaid]	a. 惊呆的；目瞪口呆的
pilgrim	[ˈpilgrim]	n. 朝觐者
pious	[ˈpaiəs]	a. 虔诚的；敬神的
persecute	[ˈpɜːsikjuːt]	v. （因种族、宗教或政治信仰）迫害；困扰
rage	[reidʒ]	n. 愤怒；狂怒
recount	[riˈkaunt]	v. 叙述（亲身经历）；重新清点
retaliation	[riˌtæliˈeiʃn]	n. 报复；反击
raid	[reid]	n. 袭击；突然袭击
recruit	[riˈkruːt]	v. 聘用；征募（新兵）
rhubarb	[ˈruːbɑːb]	n. 大黄

remnant	[ˈremnənt]	n.	剩余部分
relic	[ˈrelɪk]	n.	遗迹
Sakyamuni	[ˈsɑːkjəmuni]	n.	释迦牟尼
Sanskrit	[ˈsænskrɪt]	n.	梵语
Samarkand	[ˌsæməˈkænd]	n.	撒马尔罕（乌兹别克斯坦的一座城市）
shimmer	[ˈʃɪmə(r)]	v.	闪烁；发出微弱的闪
sinister	[ˈsɪnɪstə(r)]	a.	阴险的；有凶兆的；灾难性的
steed	[stiːd]	n.	战马，骏马
stupa	[ˈstuːpə]	n.	佛塔；舍利塔
statuary	[ˈstætʃuəri]	n.	雕像；雕像艺术
saffron	[ˈsæfrən]	n.	藏红花
sericulture	[ˈserɪˌkʌltʃə]	n.	养蚕；蚕丝业
synagogue	[ˈsɪnəgɒg]	n.	犹太教堂
sutra	[ˈsuːtrə]	n.	佛经
tempt	[tempt]	v.	诱惑；引诱
textile	[ˈtekstaɪl]	n.	纺织品；织物
Uygur	[ˈwiːgə]	n.	维吾尔族
Zoroastrian	[ˌzɔrəʊˈæstrɪən]	n.	琐罗亚斯德教（即拜火教）的教徒
Bokhara			布哈拉（中亚古国）
Tarim Basin			塔里木盆地（位于中国西部）
barter with			物物交换
cinnamon bark			肉桂皮
flowing robes			长袍
glacier-fed streams			冰川流
swallow up			淹没；吞下去；耗尽
woven rug			编织地毯
well-irrigated			灌溉良好的
Kushans			贵霜人
Lop Nor Desert			罗布泊沙漠
Seres			（希腊语）赛里斯（指中国人）
Sogdia			粟特文
Warring States period			战国时代
Yogachara			瑜伽行唯识学派

Notes

（1）Alexander the Great：亚历山大大帝。

（2）Parthian shot：安息回马枪，也叫帕提亚回马箭，属于骑兵的一种战术。在骑兵撤退或者诈逃时回射敌人，杀伤力大。1世纪时，安息帝国发展出当时世界最强的骑兵，分为轻骑兵和重骑兵。重骑兵结合冲锋骑兵和控铉骑兵，可使用冷兵器冲锋，也可以使用弓弩远程攻击。回马箭即由此引申而来。

Text B Banpo Museum

The Banpo Museum is the site of a matriarchal commune village that existed about 6,000 years ago. The site covers an area of 50,000 square metres, consisting of living quarters, a pottery-making centre and a graveyard. Through scientific excavation of the site, archaeologists have discovered over 10,000 tools and utensils of different kinds, the remains of 46 nearly intact houses, 200 storage pits, two pigsties, a surrounding moat and 73 children's burial urns.

Banpo men engaged predominantly in agriculture, hunting, fishing, animal husbandry and pottery. Banpo is a village of neolithic age, when tools were made by the technique of grinding and polishing to make them look shiny and smooth, with these stone tools people cleared up land, hewed trees and burnt down wild plants.

Harvesting tools unearthed at the village site include stone knives and sickles. Besides farming, hunting also played an important part in daily life. These stone spears and stone arrowheads were all hunting implements.

Fishing hooks and harpoons were invented and much improved at this time. There were no barbs on hooks or harpoons in the early days, so fish broke away easily after being caught. After repeated failure, people learned to make barbs on their fish hooks and harpoons.

Their pottery vessels may be divided into three categories: coarse-sand, fine-sand and fine clay. Coarse-sand pottery was used predominantly in cooking. Fine-clay utensils are smooth and beautiful. Some with exquisite designs show the relatively high level of ceramic technology to which the Banpo inhabitants had attained.

Like buckets in-use today, bottle with a pointed base was used to fetch water. Even though it looks clumsy, it applies the law of gravity.

The museum is a reconstruction of the Banpo primitive village. Around the village there is a moat about 300 metres long which served to protect the village against wild beasts and flooding. It was also used to prevent conflicts between different clans. The moat divided the whole village into three parts: the dwelling area enclosed by it, the kiln site to the east where pottery was made, to the north the communal burial ground. In the excavated site, the remains of 45 houses were discovered. A house of about 160 square meters was found in the centre of the village with smaller houses around it. The Banpo inhabitants probably met together at this place to discuss their communal affairs, plan their communal projects or settle their disputes. In the village site, several fireplaces were found which must have served to cook food collectively for the village members. This cross-section clearly shows us the structure of a house at that time. They first built up the wall by planting some posts in a circle and then daubing them with a layer of straw and mud.

The house faced south in order to avoid storms coming from the north. After entering the doorway, there was a small partition wall on either side. In the centre of the house there was a shallow round fireplace encircled by six posts. These served as the supports to the roof which contained a row of rafters with a framework of wooden planking above them and a layer of straw and mud on the top.

To bury dead children in urns was a burial custom of the Banpo inhabitants. When children died, family put their remains into burial urns and buried them either in groups, or singly within the dwelling area. Though each primitive clan had its own communal cemetery, children were not allowed to be buried there, simply because they were too young to live by themselves or they were not yet considered full members of the village. On the top of each jar, they made a little hole to allow the spirits of the children to come out to mingle with their parents. From scientific research we know that most of them were babies one or two years old.

The earliest writing found in China to date was the script on tortoise shells in the Shang Dynasty about 3,700 years ago. Here in Banpo, however, archeologists discovered carved and painted signs which have a history of 6,000 years. Comparing the signs with the script we may see that a few of them bear some resemblance to each other when we think of their location of discovery, since the tortoise shells scripts were unearthed in Anyang, Henan Province, and the signs discovered at Baopo were in Yellow River Valley, we find they are geographically connected as well. In this sense, we may say that the Banpo carved and painted signs were the predecessors of the script on the tortoise shells and the beginning of Chinese writing.

Through their long years of activity, Banpo inhabitants created many artistic objects such as paintings, sculptures and ornaments. The paintings on the pottery vessels might well represent the culture and art of that period. The main subjects of their painting were productive labour and daily life, like fish swimming in river, wild animals, mountains, grass and trees. Most Banpo paintings were of fish and deer.

This geometric pattern was found on one of the pottery vessels. Obviously, there was no such thing in nature but as Banpo men often went fishing, they developed a direct perception of fish and then, painted on the vessels lively and realistic pictures. Later, they painted two fish face-to-face and then separated the heads, bodies of the fish until finally an abstract geometric design was formed. This process of evolution is the very process of development from realistic painting to spontaneous expression and from concrete to conceptual.

The design of two fish painted on either side of the human face shows their wish to catch more fish.

Words and Expressions

matriarchal	[ˌmeɪtrɪˈɑːrkl]	a. 女家长的；母系氏族的
archaeologist	[ˌɑːrkɪˈɑlədʒɪst]	n. 考古学家
intact	[ɪnˈtækt]	a. 完整无缺的；未经触动的
moat	[moʊt]	n. 壕沟；护城河
urn	[ɜːrn]	n. 瓮；罐；骨灰盒
predominantly	[prɪˈdɑmɪnəntli]	a. 占主导地位地；显著地
neolithic	[ˌniəˈlɪθɪk]	n. 新石器时代的

hew	[hju]	v.	（用斧、刀等）砍、劈
sickle	['sɪkl]	n.	镰刀
implement	['ɪmpləmənt]	n.	工具；器械
harpoon	[hɑːˈpuːn]	n.	鱼叉
barb	[bɑːrb]	n.	（箭头、鱼钩等的）倒钩
clumsy	[ˈklʌmzi]	a.	复杂难懂的；笨拙的
clan	[klæn]	n.	宗族；氏族
kiln	[kɪln]	n.	大窑
daub	[dɔb]	v.	涂抹
partition	[pɑːrˈtɪʃn]	n.	划分；隔离物；隔墙
cemetery	[ˈsemətri]	n.	墓地，公墓
script	[skrɪpt]	n.	脚本；手迹；剧本
predecessor	[ˈpredəsesə(r)]	n.	原有事物；前身；前辈
ornament	[ˈɔrnəmənt]	n.	装饰；装饰物
geometric	[ˌdʒɪəˈmetrɪk]	a.	几何学的
perception	[pərˈsepʃn]	n.	知觉；觉察（力）
spontaneous	[spɑnˈteɪnɪəs]	a.	自发的；天然产生的
concrete	[ˈkɑːŋkriːt]	a.	具体的；有形的；实在的
conceptual	[kənˈseptʃuəl]	a.	观念的；概念的

PART Ⅱ　　DIALOGUE

Dialogue 1　On the Plane：Captain's Announcement

C：Captain；P1：Passenger 1；P2：Passenger 2

(After takeoff, Kathy and Evan are reading magazines when the pilot makes an announcement.)

C： Good evening, everyone. This is your captain speaking. I'm Captain Rogers and my crew and I will be piloting this 747 aircraft from New York to Amsterdam, the Netherlands.

P1： I can't believe we're on our way!

P2： Shh!

C： We're presently at an altitude of 28,000 feet ascending to our cruising altitude of 35,000 feet. The weather looks pretty good over the Atlantic, but we may experience some turbulence over the British Isles.

P1： Uh-oh. I hate choppy air!

P2： Shh!

C： You may have noticed that I turned off "fasten seat belt" sign a few moments ago. If you like, you may get up and move about the cabin. However, the crew and I advise you to keep that seat belt fastened in case of turbulence. We keep ours fastened, and we hope you will, too.

P1: That makes sense, doesn't it?

P2: Shh!

C: After we reach our cruising altitude, I'll give you the weather report for Amsterdam. Until then, sit back and relax and enjoy our famous KLM service. Thank you.

(起飞后,凯西和伊凡在阅读杂志时听到飞机驾驶员对大家广播。)

C: 各位晚上好。我是罗杰斯机长,我和本班全体机组人员将驾驶这架747客机从纽约飞往荷兰阿姆斯特丹。

P1: 真不敢相信我们已经在路上了!

P2: 嘘!

C: 我们现在的高度是28 000英尺,正往35 000英尺的飞行高度上升。大西洋上空的天气看起来相当不错,但是我们在经过不列颠群岛上空时可能会遇上湍流。

P1: 糟了。我讨厌不稳定的气流!

P2: 嘘!

C: 大家可能已注意到我在几分钟前关掉了"系好安全带"的指示灯。如果大家愿意的话,可以起身在机舱内走动。不过,我和全体机员都希望大家就座时系好安全带以免突然遇到湍流。我们自己随时系着安全带,希望大家也能这样做。

P1: 很有道理,不是吗?

P2: 嘘!

C: 在我们攀升至飞行高度时,我会向大家报告阿姆斯特丹的天气状况。在这之前,请坐好,放松自己,享受我们著名的荷兰皇家航空公司的服务。谢谢!

Dialogue 2   On the Plane: Having Meal

S: Stewardess; P: Passenger

(A stewardess comes by offering dinner.)

S: Would you put down your tray table, sir? Would you like chicken or beef?

P: Uh, I'll have the chicken. Thanks.

S: Anything to drink?

P: What kind of drink do you have?

S: Coke, Diet Coke, Sprite, Orange, and Dr. Pepper.

P: A Diet Coke, no ice, please.

S: Here you are. And the young lady?

(John looks over to see Helen sleeping.)

P: Oh! She's fallen asleep. Can I still take a dinner for her to eat a little later?

S: That would be all right. You'll have to lower her tray table, too, though.

P: No problem. Uh, she'll have the chicken, too.

S: Here you are. And would you like some wine with your meal?

P: Great. Thanks! Do you have white wine?

S：Sure. Here you are. I think we'd better wait for her to wake up before we give her a drink. She might spill it when she wakes up.

P：OK. I'll get her up in a minute.

S：By the way, we'll be coming around with coffee and tea in a moment, sir. Now, enjoy your meal.

（一位空姐走过来给大家送餐）

S：先生，请将您的餐板放下来好吗？您要吃鸡肉还是牛肉呢？

P：哦，我吃鸡肉好了，谢谢。

S：先生，喝点什么饮料？

P：你们有些什么饮料呢？

S：可乐、减肥可乐、雪碧、橙汁，还有 Dr. Pepper。

P：不加冰块的减肥可乐吧，谢谢。

S：鸡肉餐给你，那么这位年轻小姐呢？

（约翰转过头去看到海伦正在睡觉）

P：哦！她睡着了。我能不能先替她收一下，让她等一会儿再吃？

S：可以。但是，您还是得把她的餐板放下来。

P：没问题。嗯，她也吃鸡肉餐。

S：给您鸡肉餐。您用餐时要不要喝点酒呢？

P：很好，谢谢！有白葡萄酒吗？

S：有。酒来了。我想我们最好等她醒来再给她饮料。要不然她醒来时也许会把杯子打翻。

P：好的。我等一下会叫醒她。

S：哦，对了，我们等一下会送咖啡和茶过来，先生。现在，祝您用餐愉快。

Word Service Station

| overhead | 头顶上的 | bake | 烤 |
| sandwich | 三明治 | assistance | 帮助 |

PART Ⅲ GOOD TO KNOW：Maintenance and Safety

备用发动机	backup generator	木工活	carpentry
中央暖气系统	central heating system	灭火器	extinguisher
灭火系统	firefighting network	补偿，赔偿	indemnity
灯光装置	lighting fixtures	技术等级	mechanical rating
定期地	on a regular schedule	性能	performance
重新油漆	repainting	焊接	steel welding
磨损	wear	故障	breakdown
插销	deadbolt	消防通道	fire exit
室内陈设	furnishings	基础设施	infrastructure

润滑油，润滑	lubrication	微调	minor adjustment
管道系统	plumbing system	替换	replacement
不能使用	out of service	水电煤供给	utility
中央空调系统	central air conditioning system		
现有的标准	the established standards		

PART Ⅳ   EXERCISES

Ⅰ. Listening comprehension.

Hostel

For a hundred years after the first youth hostel was created, do such establishments have a part to play in the 21st century? After all, one of the 1 _____ images is of big draughty rooms that you have to share with snoring 2 _____, while being ordered to do the chores and forgo many of life's little luxuries.

A person who travels around and stays in 3 _____ hostels is a youth hosteller. Here's one youth hosteller with her reasons.

"It's good value as well, it's not just that they're 4 _____, although nowadays you're paying £10 to £15 most nights, it's hot showers, and good 5 _____ room facilities, good kitchen facilities. And most of the hostels I've stayed at have been very well kitted out."

Now this youth hosteller has been youth hostelling for 13 years. Her father did it before her and her 6 _____ did it before the Second World War.

"I've been hostelling, I think for about 13 years and my dad 7 _____ did it before that and my grandfather, he was certainly hostelling before the Second World War, back in the days when you weren't allowed to turn up any way other than on foot and by bike. There was no 8 _____ in the hostel and you had to do your chores before you were allowed out in the morning."

Here's another youth hosteller.

"There're a bit more switch to make to be than we viewed as chores and the wardens would make you clean the 9 _____, sweep the dormitories or whatever, and there's none of that anymore."

So youth hostels are changing. Here's Duncan Simpson from the YHA, the Youth Hostelling Association.

"If you look at the movement for society, people have looked for more and more 10 _____ and, to a degree, more comfort. And we need to reflect that and meet what people are looking for."

Ⅱ. Put the following into Chinese.

1. itinerary _____

2. travel arrangements _____
3. sightseeing tour _____
4. travel agency _____
5. package tour _____
6. place of interest _____
7. communication skills _____
8. Tian'anmen Square _____
9. Forbidden City _____
10. schedule _____

III. Fill in the blanks with the words given, and make changes if necessary.

Non-finite Verbs

1. The _____ (bore) lecture made the _____ (bore) audience want to leave.
2. Who is the boy _____ (watch) TV in the next room?
3. This is a letter _____ (write) in red ink.
4. The window is _____ (break).
5. The story is _____ (amuse).
6. The students were going to school _____ (laugh) and _____ (talk).
7. The old man got onto the bus _____ (support) by his son.
8. The door remains _____ (lock).
9. They found the guests _____ (go).
10. I have my hair _____ (cut) every ten days.
11. I have not any money _____ (leave).
12. I don't want you _____ (involve) in the scandal.
13. He won't like this question _____ (discuss) in the office.
14. _____ (sit) at the back as we are, we can't hear word.
15. He was hurt by a stone _____ (drop) from the roof.
16. Do you know anyone _____ (lose) a watch?
17. Did you see that boy _____ (question) by the police?
18. _____ (be) unable to help in any other way, I gave her some money.
19. _____ (see) these photos, I could not help thinking of my children days in Los Angeles.
20. _____ (frustrate), he went back to his home town.

IV. Reading comprehension.

"Green" Hotels and "Green" Hotels Association

Hotels are extremely large-volume users of water, detergent, cleanser and other chemicals that can be detrimental to our environment, and hotel managers must be aware of the hotel's impact on our life resource. "Green" Hotels are eco-friendly whose managers are eager to institute programs that save water, save energy and reduce solid waste while saving money to help PROTECT OUR ONE AND ONLY EARTH! These hotels include any hotels, motels, and inns, but have to be certified green by an independent third-party or by the state they are located in.

"Green" Hotels Association (GHA) is an organization that enjoys high reputation in the lodging industry, created by Patricia Griffin in 1993. The goal of this association is to reduce the amount of energy and water consumed by the lodging industry. GHA provides hotels around the world with easy access to environmentally friendly products and ideas. GHA is also interested in reducing the amount of solid waste produced by the lodging industry. Managers can add their hotel to the growing list of GHA's members by simply paying an annual membership fee of one dollar per room. Members receive a book consisting of over 85 pages listing different ways to save energy and cut back on waste. The eco-friendly products and ideas are always updated and informed by GHA. The hotel's name is also placed on GHA's website, www.greenhotels.com.

Two of the most popular products provided by GHA are the printed towel rack hanger and sheet-changing cards. The towel-rack hanger card encourages guests to use towels more than once, and says "Please decide for yourself." "Towels on the rack" means "I'll use it again." "Towels on the floor or in the tub" means "Please exchange." The sheet-changing card says, "Sheets are customarily changed daily, but if you feel that this is unnecessary, leave this card on your pillow in the morning, and your sheets will not be changed that day."

Hotels can save significantly by utilizing these cards. GHA reports that hotels can save approximately $1.50 per day per occupied room by using these two products. Guests who decide to use these cards help to reduce the amount of water, detergent, labor, and utilities used by a hotel in a given day. Many guests eagerly participate in their hotel's green program because they want to help protect the beautiful destination they are visiting. Very few people wash their linens and towels daily at home, and it is time that we recognize doing these in hotels is unnecessary and wasteful.

By using GHA's towel rack hangers and sheet-changing cards hoteliers are taking the first step toward keeping our earth green.

1. Test your vocabulary for "Green" Hotels. (Fill in the blanks with words from the box.)

bulk	recycler baskets	encourage	low-flow	sheets
lower	eco-friendly	recycling bins	turn off	unoccupied
leftover	towels	minimize	glass	replace

This passage lists sustainable practices that hotels can implement to keep hotels green.

(1) Start a linen (both ①_____ and ②_____) reuse program in all guest rooms.

(2) Install ③_____ showerheads that can save water.

(3) Whenever possible, buy food and guest amenities in ④_____ (i.e., use refillable hair and skin shampoo).

(4) Educate your staff to ⑤_____ lights and turn down heating/air conditioning when rooms are ⑥_____.

(5) Provide guestroom ⑦_____ for newspaper, white paper, glass, aluminum, cardboard, and plastic.

(6) Provide ⑧_____ both in public areas, in the kitchen, and in the back office to make recycling as easy as possible.

(7) Install window film to ⑨_____ heating and cooling loads and reduce glare in guestrooms.

(8) Use recycled paper products. ⑩_____ the amount of paper used for each guest (i.e., reduce paper size of invoices, etc.).

(9) Provide ⑪_____ cups and ceramic mugs (instead of plastic) for in-room beverages.

(10) Create an incentive program to ⑫_____ your staff to participate in and improve upon ⑬_____ practices.

(11) Donate ⑭_____ guest amenities, old furniture and appliances to charities.

(12) ⑮_____ regular light bulbs with energy-efficient bulbs.

2. Choose the best answer.

(1) If you've never been to this city, you should take a look at our _____.
A. menu   B. brochures   C. front desk   D. inn

(2) We do not have a _____ service. You'll have to park your car yourself.
A. room   B. dinner   C. laundry   D. valet

(3) The room has a pull _____ couch, so it will sleep an extra person.
A. off   B. over   C. out   D. on

(4) We don't have any vacancies. We are completely _____.
A. vacant   B. booked   C. complimentary   D. closed

(5) After your long conference you can relax in the _____.
A. kitchenette   B. parking lot   C. hot tub   D. front desk

(6) I'll call housekeeping and ask them to bring you some fresh _____.
A. milk   B. dinner   C. linen   D. ice

(7) If you need to do your workout we have a _____ on the third floor.
A. weight   B. restaurant   C. library   D. telephone

(8) I'll let you voice your complaint about the rate to the _____.
A. housekeeper   B. valet driver   C. hotel manager   D. chef

(9) Please put your used _____ in the basket and leave unused ones hanging on the rack.
A. dishes   B. towels   C. menus   D. keys

(10) If you need a midnight snack there's a _____ machine full of potato chips on your floor.
A. bellboy   B. kitchenette   C. cot   D. vending

V. Translate the following sentences into Chinese. They are underlined in the texts.

1. Of the original party only he and one other completed the trail-blazing journey—the first

land route between East and West and one that would eventually link Imperial China with Imperial Rome.

2. Numerous religions were represented and the city contained the temples, churches and synagogues of Nestorian Christians, Manicheans, Zoroastrians, Hindus, Buddhists and Jews, to name but a few.

3. At the same time, entire communities, active oasis towns, thriving monasteries and grottoes along the Silk Road were disappearing in the space of weeks, as the glacier-fed streams ran dry or changed course.

4. Banpo men engaged predominantly in agriculture, hunting, fishing, animal husbandry and pottery.

5. In the center of the house there was a shallow round fireplace encircled by six posts. These served as the supports to the roof which contained a row of rafters with a framework of wooden planking above them and a layer of straw and mud on the top.

VI. Discussion.

The ×××Vandalism Scandal

On May 24th, 2013, a Weibo user posted a picture of the engraving with the Chinese letters "×××到此一游" at the Luxor Temple in Egypt.

On May 25th, 2013, there were 11,000 comments and 83,000 reposts on the post. The boy, ×××, who scratched the Chinese characters was 15 and he and his parents publicly apologized on Weibo.

Discussion: What further measures and education processes could be put in place to make a positive change to the behaviour of Chinese tourists abroad?

Unit 6　Tourism Marketing

PART I　TEXT

Text A　Tourism Marketing

Tourism marketing fundamentally differs from the marketing of other types of products in three important ways: (1) tourism is primarily a service industry, where services are intangible, and quality control and evaluation of experiences are more difficult to envision; (2) instead of moving the product to the customer, the customer must travel to the product or resource; and (3) people usually participate in and visit more than one activity and facility while travelling. Therefore, tourism-related businesses and organizations need to cooperate to package and promote the tourism opportunities available in their areas.

The marketing of tourism products is strongly based on a firm understanding of the fact that the overall travel market is partitioned into selected market segments. Travel firms do not have the resources to tap the overall travel market, nor the inclination, owing to the magnitude of domestic and international travel. Instead, businesses target certain segments based on the product that they are selling and the needs and expectations of the group to which they wish to sell. Target marketing can occur in four main ways: (1) geographically, on the basis of geographical space; (2) demographically, based on age, gender, religion, race, etc.; (3) psychographically, based on individuals' lifestyles, attitudes, values, and personalities; and (4) benefits, which include an analysis of the benefits sought by tourists and the costs they avoid.

Marketers typically follow a systematic planning approach that enables them to focus on their organizational goals, and the specific needs of their clientele in association with various tourism products. The first stage of a typical marketing plan involves the identification of the direction of the agency or organization and the associated priorities that must be followed. This is followed by the definition of markets that will allow the organization to achieve its chosen goals. Upon the completion of this stage, the organization endeavours to examine fully the behaviour, needs, and characteristics of the market. Once the markets have been segmented, the organization can develop specific strategies which must be tailored to each segment. There follows the implementation of a monitoring and evaluation component, with subsequent modification in the future.

Demand is very much an integral part of the relationship between the tourism product and the market; in the future tourism marketers must be more sensitive to the changing composition of the tourist population. Owing to the changing lifestyles, economic conditions, and demographic

Unit 6 Tourism Marketing

structure of travelers, the market is shifting from manipulated, uncritical "old tourists" to mature, critical and emancipated "new tourists".

Two cornerstones to effective tourism marketing are the attraction for tourists, and tourism infrastructure to support the industry. <u>Given these criteria, agencies are free to undertake the necessary marketing requirements to attract clientele who are composed of "born" tourists (those who have a built-in predisposition towards travel), and "made" tourists (those who can be identified as representing latent demand or those who are unfamiliar with this or that form of tourism but who can be attracted through effective marketing).</u> A basic approach to marketing the tourism product is through (1) the identification of the characteristics of a desired group, (2) appropriate advertising, (3) careful crafting of the advertising message, and (4) the development of a mailing-list or internet-based promoting.

In Australia, the Office of National Tourism once undertook a market study of tourists in an attempt to understand the tourist market better and target tourism products more effectively, the conclusion they made might be illuminating:

1. Impulse. Characterized by nature-based day trips away from the main tourist destinations and mainly booked locally by both domestic and international tourists. The level of activity on these tours varies widely.

2. Active. Characterized by younger and middle-aged professionals who generally book in advance. There is a skew to domestic tourists, although there could well be potential for growth through international marketing, infrastructure, and product development.

3. Personalized. Essentially older professionals (or retired) who expect to be well looked after by the operator. This segment is skewed to international tourists who book overnight tours before arriving in Australia.

Words and Expressions

envision	[en'vɪʒən]	v.	想象；预见
magnitude	['mægnɪtud]	n.	量级；重大
psychographically	[ˌsaɪkəʊɡ'ræfɪkli]	ad.	心理图案地人格特性地
clientele	[ˌklaɪən'tel]	n.	顾客；客户
priority	[praɪ'ɔrəti]	n.	优先；优先权
endeavour	[en'devə]	v.	努力；竭力
segment	['seɡmənt]	v.	分割；划分
tailor	['telə]	v.	调整使适应；为……裁制衣服
modification	[ˌmɑdifɪ'keɪʃn]	n.	修改；改良
mature	[mə'tʊr]	a.	成熟的
emancipate	[ɪ'mænsəˌpet]	v.	解放；伎摆脱束缚
cornerstone	['knəstoʊn]	n.	奠基石；基础
latent	['letnt]	a.	潜在的；潜伏的
impulse	['ɪmpʌls]	n.	冲动；[电] 脉冲

skew   [skju]   v. 歪斜；斜交；偏离；曲线；使歪斜

Notes

（1）本文编自 David A. Fennell 教授的 *Ecotourism*：*An Introduction* 第二版，Routledge 出版社，2005 年。

Text B   Accor Launches Backpacker Brand

The new brand name has yet to be announced, but the backpackers' initiative will be rolled out over the next twelve months with a combination of new developments and management takeovers.

Accor[1] says it will enter the market with hostels that meet the four main criteria of backpacker travelers—prime locations, good-value prices, and high levels of safety and cleanliness[2].

The first hostel is being developed out of a heritage building located on Fort Street, Auckland in the heart of the city's backpacker and entertainment strip. The 435-bed hostel will have 40 en suite bedrooms and 355 beds in share-rooms of mainly four to six beds.

The hostel will also include a bar and café area with regular entertainment and activities, self-cooking facilities, and a travel centre, which will provide internet and job search facilities, as well as assistance for visa applications, banking, CVs, and other clerical services.

Advertisement

The hostel is scheduled to open in October 2002, in time for the Louis Vuitton Challenge and America's Cup.

The second hostel will be in Wellington in Cambridge Terrace, just off Courtney Place, in the heart of the city's most popular restaurant and entertainment area. The 298-beds hostel will be developed out of heritage-listed 1930s art deco building, the King George Building.[3]

A third hostel is being finalized in Rotorua. Final discussions are taking place, but the hostel is already operating as backpacker's accommodation and is regarded as the city's best located hostel.

Other key destinations in New Zealand for Accor's backpacker chain include Christchurch and Queenstown. Following the roll-out[4] of its New Zealand network, Accor plans to establish a similar network of hostels in Australia, as the two countries are usually incorporated in the same itinerary.

Commenting on the launch of the backpacker initiative, Accor Managing Director for Australia/New Zealand, Michael Issenberg, said that the backpacker sector had proved itself to be the most resilient in the market.

Unit 6 Tourism Marketing

"The backpacker travel experience is a very different one from that of the traditional tourist, who may book an all-inclusive holiday package and stay in hotels." he said.

"And all the evidence suggests that more and more travelers—irrespective of their financial status and even age—are choosing to travel this way because of the lifestyle aspects of the experience."

"Until now, most backpacker accommodation demand has been channelled into unbranded, low quality backpacker motels and hostels. Our aim is not to change the backpacker experience, but rather to make it better and more reliable."

Issenberg sees the backpacker market as a logical progression for Accor, as it already provides accommodation for the economy and budget sectors, and it recently entered the youth market with the first-ever Contiki Resort in Australia.

Words and Expressions

Auckland	[ˈɔːklənd]	n.	奥克兰（新西兰港市）
all-inclusive	[ˈɔːlɪnˈkluːsɪv]	a.	包括一切的
clerical	[ˈklerɪkəl]	a.	办事员的
comment	[ˈkɔment]	n.	评论；意见
Christchurch	[ˈkraɪstʃəːtʃ]	n.	克赖斯特彻奇（新西兰城市）
finalise	[ˈfaɪnəlaɪz]	v.	使……结束
itinerary	[aɪˈtɪn(ə)(rə)rɪ;ɪ-]	n.	旅程，路线
irrespective	[ɪrɪˈspektɪv]	a.	无关的
resilient	[rɪˈzɪlɪənt]	a.	有复原的，有弹力的
strip	[strɪp]	n.	带；条
status	[ˈsteɪtəs]	n.	地位；状态
takeover	[ˈteɪkəuvə]	n.	接管；验收
Wellington	[ˈwelɪŋtən]	n.	惠灵顿（新西兰首都）
America's Cup			美洲杯
Cambridge Terrace			剑桥台地
Fort Street			堡垒街

Notes

（1）Accor：法国雅高集团，经营旅馆业。

（2）Accor says it will enter the market with hostels that meet the four main criteria of backpacker travelers—prime locations, good-value prices, and high levels of safety and cleanliness.

雅高集团说他们进入市场后提供的青年旅舍会达到背包客们的四个主要标准，即黄金地段、超值价格、高水平的安全和清洁。

（3）The 298-beds hostel will be developed out of heritage-listed 1930s art deco building, the King George Building.

这家有 298 个床位的青年旅舍将会建在已被列为世界遗产名录的具有 20 世纪 30 年代

旅游英语(修订版)

的艺术装饰的英皇佐治大厦中。

(4) roll-out 初次公开展出。

PART Ⅱ　DIALOGUE

Dialogue 1　Immigration Formalities

A：Immigration Officer；B：Tourist

A：Good morning. Please show your ticket, passport and immigration/arrival card.

B：Here you are.

A：What's the purpose of your visit in this country? On business or for pleasure?

B：On business. I have several places to visit.

A：How long will you be staying in New Zealand?

B：5 days. I will be leaving on May 25th.

A：Where do you intend to stay while in the country?

B：In the hotels.

A：How much money have you got?

B：I have 2,000 US dollars in cash.

A：Do you have a return ticket?

B：Yes, here you are. Can I leave now?

A：Just a second. Do you remember when you got your last vaccination?

B：Three days ago, just before I came here. You may check my health certification.

A：OK. I think you are cleared. Thank you for your cooperation.

A：早上好。请出示您的机票、护照和入境卡。

B：给您。

A：您在这个国家的访问的目的是什么？是为了业务还是为了娱乐？

B：为了业务，我有几个地方要参观。

A：您将在新西兰待多长时间？

B：5天，我将在5月25日离开。

A：您打算在哪里住？

B：在宾馆。

A：您带有多少钱？

B：我有2 000美元现金。

A：您有返程票吗？

B：当然，给您。我现在可以离开吗？

A：稍等一下。您还记得你最后一次接种疫苗的时间吗？

B：三天前，就在我来这里之前，您可以检查我的健康证。

A：好的。我想您没问题了。谢谢合作。

Dialogue 2 Luggage Claiming

A：Clerk of the Airport；B：Passenger

A：Good morning. What can I do for you?
B：Yes. I came from Hangzhou by CA 558. Where can I get my luggage?
A：The luggage claim area is downstairs.
B：Which carousel is for the luggage from Hangzhou?
A：The one on the left, No. 2.
B：Excuse me. I can't find my baggage, they haven't yet shown up. Here is my claim tag.
A：Don't worry, ma'am. Can you describe your baggage?
B：One is medium-sized Polo, and it's gray. The other is a larger leather suitcase with my name tag. It's dark blue.
A：Are those yours, ma'am? I'm afraid you've come to the wrong place.
B：Oh, they are mine. Thank you very much. But the handle of my suitcase is broken. Where can I go to report it?
A：Please go to the Luggage Service over there. The clerks there will help you.
B：I see.
A：早上好。我能为您做点什么？
B：是的。我乘 CA558 航班从杭州来，在哪能找到我的行李？
A：行李认领区在楼下。
B：哪条旋转传送带是从杭州来的行李？
A：左边的那个，第 2 号。
B：打扰一下，我找不到我的行李了，到现在还没出来呢。这是我的行李票。
A：别担心，女士，您能描述一下您的行李吗？
B：一个是中等大小的 POLO，它是灰色的。还有一个更大的皮制的手提箱，上面有我名字标签，深蓝色的。
A：这些是您的行李吗，女士？恐怕您刚才是走错地方了。
B：哦，它们是我的。非常感谢您，但我的手提箱的把手坏了，我应该去哪里报告呢？
B：请去那边的行李服务处，那里的服务人员会帮助您的。
A：我明白了。

PART Ⅲ GOOD TO KNOW：Housekeeping

ashtray	烟灰缸	bedside lamp	床头灯
floor lamp	落地灯	wall lamp	壁灯
pillowcase	枕套	quilt	被子
pillow	枕头	vacuum cleaner	吸尘器
toilet	马桶	wash basin	盥洗池
bath tub	浴盆	detergent	清洁剂

hair-dryer	电吹风	clothes-hange	衣架
electric iron	电熨斗	rollaway	折叠床
transformer	变压器	public area	公共区域
baby-sitting service	照看婴儿服务	complimentary	免费的
valet service	洗烫服务	outside call	外线电话
room service	客房送餐服务	laundry section	洗衣部
Occupied Dirty	占用脏房	Out of Order	坏房
Vacant Dirty	空脏房	Vacant Ready	空净房
Occupied Room	占用房		

PART Ⅳ EXERCISES

Ⅰ. Listening comprehension.

Business-Hospitality: Stay with Me

As online rivals whizz ahead, hotels try to be both big and nimble. Hotel companies check out well just now. On May 3rd Hyatt became the latest chain to report sunny results—profits were up by 55% over the same quarter in 2015. In America RevPAR (revenue divided by rooms available in a given period) has risen for the past six years, according to STR, a data outfit.

Analysts debate when fortunes will change. Americas market has been buoyed by a 1 _____ of slow-growing supply and robust demand. In the long term, however, the greatest uncertainty is not cyclical, but 2 _____ as online firms change the industry's shape. Neither Airbnb, a room-sharing site, nor online travel agents are hotels' obvious adversaries. Big hotel chains subsist on 3 _____; Airbnb does not. Yet the growing popularity of the platform, now valued at around $25 billion, means it may siphon more guests from hotels in future.

Booking sites help hotels but chomp into their margins with fees of up to 25%. Last year they accounted for nearly one in five bookings in America, up from one in ten in 2006, according to Focusright, a research firm. In Europe, where the hotel market is 4 _____ online agents account for one in four. For hotel firms, one solution is to get bigger. After a bidding war with Anbang, a Chinese insurer, Marriott agreed to buy Starwood for more than $13 billion last month. The result will be a 1.1 million room behemoth. Other firms are bulking up, too. Last year saw $67 billion of hotel mergers, according to Dealogic, a research firm—the highest level since 2007. Scale will help hotels battle their 5 _____ other hotels. But the recent spate of deals is also a response to challengers online. A bigger hotel firm can seek 6 _____ from online travel agents. Investments in technology can be deployed across more rooms. And the more hotels a firm manages, the more credibly it can urge travellers to bypass 7 _____ and look for rooms on its own site, as Hilton, InterContinental Hotels and others are doing. Hotels are also finding new partners or acquiring firms outright.

On April 5th Accor Hotels, a French firm, said it would buy Onefinestay, an upscale rival to Airbnb. InterContinental, which was due to hold its annual meeting on May 6th, is partnering with a company called Amadeus to launch a new, 8 _____ system that gives more personalised service. Despite such efforts, it will be difficult for hotel firms to keep up. They cannot beat online firms' reach. Airbnb has more rooms than even the combined Marriott and Starwood; online travel agents' inventory is broader still. Expedia's scale is particularly worrisome for hotel companies.

Its sites include not just Expedia. com but Travelocity, Hotwire, Hotels. com and Orbitz an acquisition regulators declined to challenge in September to the dismay of hotel chains. Less than two months later, Expedia said it would pay $3.9 billion to buy HomeAway, which helps 9 _____ rent their houses to those who want them for a holiday. Matching online firms' agility will be equally challenging. Airbnb is trying to attract business types by helping them find homes with 10 _____ 24-hour access and a desk. Expedia plans to offer more listings than show hotel rooms beside houses and flats. Such a move could make both Airbnb and hoteliers bristle.

II. Put the following into Chinese.

1. egg-shell china _____
2. four treasures of the study _____
3. cloisonné enamel _____
4. oolong tea _____
5. silk product _____
6. minority peoples _____
7. Dali Batik _____
8. Zisha teapot _____
9. tri-colored glazed pottery _____
10. papercut _____

III. Identify the using of "it" in each sentence is Empty it ("虚义" it), Anticipatory it ("先行" it) or Cleft sentence defined ("分裂句引导词" it).

1. **It** is very warm.
2. **It** is two miles to the post office.
3. **It** is awful.
4. **It** is my turn.
5. You will catch **it** (will be scolded) for breaking the glasses.
6. **It** is illegal to drive without a license.
7. **It** was pleasant meeting you in London that day.
8. He made **it** clear that he didn't want to speak to me.
9. **It** was not known whether there was gold left in the mine.
10. **It** was John that/who gave Mary that book yesterday.
11. **It** was Mary that John gave a book to.

12. **It** was a book that John gave to Mary.

13. **It** was yesterday that John gave Mary a book.

IV. Reading comprehension.

How to Choose the Right Conference Call Service

There are several different types of conference calling service available for all types of businesses, whether they are large corporations or small to medium sized businesses.

Audio Conferencing

This conference call service has been available for quite a long time. It is very popular due to its cost effectiveness and allowing communication from all over the world.

All that is required for an audio conference is a telephone for each person attending the conference.

Those in the call are able to hear each other instantly, as if they were all in the same room.

One of the main problems with an audio conference call is not being able to see the other people you are talking to or to be able instantly to share images or information directly related to the business.

Video Conferencing

It's a conference call service that has been available to businesses for around ten years. Due to the cost of equipment, only larger companies used video conferencing.

Recently, due to changes in technology and cheaper equipment, video conferencing is now readily available to smaller businesses.

The equipment needed for a video conference is a camera and television on each end of the conference. This allows all of the participants in the conference call to hear and see each other.

Video conferencing is very effective and is ideal for those wishing to have conferences on a regular basis, although it is quite difficult to set and trouble shoot the equipment. Regular maintenance by a professional is required to keep video conferencing equippment working correctly.

Web Conferencing

Web conferencing is the newest of the three types of conference calling services. This new technology uses the Internet to hold the conference or meeting.

The real bonus with web conferencing is that those attending can share files, visual aids and text messages instantly.

Web conferencing has all of the benefits of a traditional audio or video conference meeting. Those attending can still hear and see each other in real time over the Internet, without the need for overly expensive equipment.

The best way to choose a conference call service provider is to stop around and find the package that best suits your needs. For example, if your budget is low and you only require verbal communication to communicate, audio is most probably the best option.

If you require whiteboard sharing and face to face meetings, video is ideal. Web conference calling services are the most expensive of all of the services, but will allow you to share files and communicate on a much higher level with those included in the business conference hall.

1. Test your vocabulary of Meeting Service. (Fill in the blanks with words from the box.)

theater style	conference or boardroom style	lectern	poster projector
screen	U-shape recorders	banner	classroom style	microphone
tier	wireless microphone			

Conference Room Set-up

A conference room set-up should be carefully designed so that the message may reach everybody.

(1) _____: Seats or chairs in rows facing a stage area, head table, or speaker (with no conference table). This is the most efficient set-up when the attendees act as an audience. This set-up is not recommended for food events or if note taking is required.

(2) _____: A series of conference tables set in the shape of the letter U, with chairs around the outside. This layout style is often used for meetings where there is a speaker, audio-visual presentation or other focal point.

(3) _____: Rows of conference tables with chairs facing the front of a room (and usually a speaker), providing writing space for each person. This room set-up is ideal for note taking, meetings requiring multiple handouts or reference materials, or other tools such as laptop computers. This is the most comfortable set-up for long sessions and allows refreshments to be placed within reach of each attendee.

(4) _____: A rectangular or oval table set-up with chairs around all sides and ends. Used for this table layout is often used for Board of Director meetings, committee meetings, or discussion groups.

Sound/Audio Visual

Usually on the wall of the Convention Center is (5) _____, a flat vertical surface on which pictures or words are shown; and in front of it is a(an) (6) _____, a machine that projects films or slides onto a screen or wall. In addition, Convention Centers also provide the basic equipment such as a(an) (7) _____: a machine for recording sound or pictures or both; a(an) (8) _____ which is used for making your voice louder when you are speaking to an audience. If you want to interact with the audience, you can use (9) _____, which is free from cables.

Miscellaneous Equipment

A (10) _____ is usually put in the lobby of the hotel, which is large, usually printed notice, or announcement to advertise or publicize something. In the convention hall, guests can see some (11) _____, a piece of cloth bearing a name, motto or slogan, as of a meeting. The speaker will stand behind a (12) _____, which is a stand that serves as a support for the notes or books of a speaker. In some grand convention halls, the center stage can be raised or lowered in (13) _____.

2. Choose the best answer.

(1) The hotel provides you _____ all conferencing services available for your business or family needs.

A. with　　　　B. to　　　　C. by　　　　D. at

(2) This conference technology with Internet enables you to easily and instantly _____ information with your associates.

A. tell　　　　B. exchange　　　　C. say　　　　D. spread

(3) Video and web conferencing services are usually more _____ solutions.

A. expensive　　B. cheap　　　　C. so so　　　　D. accepted

(4) We are going to _____ a news press next week.

A. make　　　　B. show　　　　C. hold　　　　D. rent

(5) Would you please come with me to the _____ to arrange the guest-rooms for you?

A. Room Service　　　　　　B. Laundry
C. Recreation Center　　　　D. Front Desk

(6) I want to reserve rooms for the guests _____ the meeting.

A. making　　　B. coming　　　C. going　　　D. attending

(7) We need an auditorium that can _____ 100 guests.

A. accommodate　B. make　　　C. attend　　　D. put

(8) Could you give me more _____ about your requirements for the meeting?

A. details　　　B. news　　　　C. things　　　D. informations

(9) A _____ is designed to hold activities of various kinds, such as performance shows, exhibitions, large and small size business meetings, seminar and press meeting.

A. multi-function hall　　　B. convention hall
C. meeting room　　　　　　D. auditorium

(10) _____ is mainly required for a conference. While a speaker is making a speech, the interpreter interprets the speaker's speech into a specified language, which will be transferred to the other attendees via earphone.

A. Interpreter　　　　　　B. Simultaneous
C. Translator　　　　　　 D. Software

V. Translate the following sentences into Chinese.

1. Therefore, tourism-related businesses and organizations need to cooperate to package and promote the tourism opportunities available in their areas.

2. The marketing of tourism products is strongly based on a firm understanding of the fact that the overall travel market is partitioned into selected market segments.

3. The first stage of a typical marketing plan involves the identification of the direction of the agency or organization and the associated priorities that must be followed.

4. Given these criteria, agencies are free to undertake the necessary marketing requirements to attract clientele who are composed of "born" tourists (those who have a built-in predisposition

towards travel), and "made" tourists (those who can be identified as representing latent demand or those who are unfamiliar with this or that form of tourism but who can be attracted through effective marketing).

5. Until now, most backpacker accommodation demand has been channelled into unbranded, low quality backpacker motels and hostels. Our aim is not to change the backpacker experience, but rather to make it better and more reliable.

VI. Writing.

Write an event planning. The followings should be included:
1. the purpose of the event;
2. the time, location organizer, participator of the event;
3. the envisagement of the event.

Activity 3: Huizhou Trilogy

Aim:

After watching the distinguished documentary film maker—Professor Carma Hinton's *Huizhou Trilogy*, students are supposed to understand the traditional Huizhou architecture, Huizhou's marriage customs and Spring Festival customs, and pick out their commons and differences between traditional and more recent practices. What's more, the tourism development of the Huizhou villages of Xidi, Hongcun, Huangling, among many others, would be discussed. Students need to present their own opinion on what the aforementioned Huizhou cultures have been applied in the tourism practices of the villages, and how. Whether they have been presented to tourists authentically should be considered, too.

Agenda:

- Total time – 100 minutes in class;
- First 10 minutes, the teacher would lead the students to sweep the tourism development practices in the Huizhou region, focused on the villages of Xidi, Hongcun, Huangling, among many others;
- The following 60 minutes, the teacher would guide the students to watch the films—*Yin Yu Tang*, *Guo Nian* and *Guo Men*, which could be downloaded at...
- The last 30 minutes, discussions on, but not limited to the questions in the above paragraph.

Unit 7 Communication

PART I TEXT

Text A Developing Interpersonal Skills

Would it surprise you to know that more managers are probably fired because of poor interpersonal skills than a lack of technical ability? Moreover, a survey of top executives at *Fortune* 500 companies found that interpersonal skills were the most important consideration in hiring senior-level employees. Because managers ultimately get things done through others, competencies in leadership, communication, and other interpersonal skills are prerequisites to managerial effectiveness. Therefore, here are some key interpersonal skills that every manager needs.

Why Are Active Listening Skills Important?

The ability to listen is too often taken for granted because we tend to confuse hearing with listening. Listening require paying attention, interpreting, and remembering sound stimuli.

Effective listening is active rather passive. In passive listening, you resemble a tape recorder. You absorb and remember the words spoken. If the speaker provides you with a clear message and makes his or her delivery interesting enough to keep your attention, you'll probably hear most of what the speaker is trying to communicate. Active listening requires you to get inside the speaker's mind to understand the communication from his or her point of view. As you will see, active listening is a hard work. You have to concentrate and fully understand what a speaker is saying. Students who use active listening techniques for an entire 75-minute lecture are as tired as their instructor when the lecture is over, because they have put as much energy into listening as the instructor put into speaking.

Active listening requires four essential elements: (1) intensity, (2) empathy, (3) acceptance, (4) a willingness to take responsibility for completeness. As noted, the human brain is capable of handling a speaking rate that is about six times as fast as that of the average speaker, leaving a lot of time for day-dreaming. The active listener concentrates *intensely* on what the speaker is saying and tunes out the thousands of miscellaneous thoughts (about money, sex, vacation, parties, exams, and so on) that create distractions. What do active listeners do with their idle brain time? They summarize and integrate what has been said. They put each new bit of information into the context of what preceded it.

Empathy requires you to put yourself into the speaker's shoes. You try to understand what the speaker wants to communicate rather than what you want to hear. Notice that empathy demands both knowledge of the speaker and flexibility on your part. You need to suspend your own thoughts and feelings and adjust what you see and feel to your speaker's world. In that way, you increase likelihood that you'll interpret the message in the way the speaker intended.

An active listener demonstrates acceptance. He or she listens objectively without judging content, which is not an easy task. It's natural to be distracted by what a speaker says, especially when we disagree with it. When we hear something we disagree with, we have a tendency to begin formulating our arguments to counter what is being said. Of course, in doing so, we miss the rest of the message. The challenge for the active listener is to absorb what's being said and withhold judgment on content until the speaker is finished.

The final ingredient of active listening is taking *responsibility for completeness*. That is, the listener does whatever is necessary to get the full intended meaning from the speaker's communication. Two widely used active listening techniques are listening for feeling as well as for content and asking questions to ensure understanding.

Just how, though, can you develop effective listening skills? The literature on active listening emphasizes eight specific behaviors. As you review these behaviors, ask yourself whether they describe your listening practices. If you're not currently using these techniques, there's no better time than right now to begin developing them.

Why Are Feedback Skills Important?

Ask a manager about the feedback he or she gives to employees, and you're likely to get a qualified answer. If the feedback is positive, it's likely to be given promptly and enthusiastically. Negative feedback is often treated differently. Like most of us, managers don't particularly enjoy communicating bad news. They fear offending the receiver or having to deal with his or her emotions. The result is that negative feedback is often avoided, delayed, or substantially distorted. The purposes of this section are to show you the importance of providing both positive and negative feedback and to identify specific techniques to help make your feedback more effective.

What is the diffrence between positive and negative feedback? We know that managers treat positive and negative feedback differently, so, too, receivers. You need to understand this fact and adjust your feedback style accordingly.

Positive feedback is more readily and accurately perceived than negative feedback. Furthermore, whereas positive feedback is almost always accepted, negative feedback often meets resistance. Why? The logical answer appears to be that people want to hear good news and block out the rest. Positive feedback fits what most people wish to hear and already believe about themselves. Does this mean, then, that you should avoid giving negative feedback? No! <u>What it means is that you need to be aware of potential resistance and learn to use negative feedback in situations which are most likely to be accepted.</u> What are those situations? Research indicates that negative feedback is most likely to be accepted when it comes from a credible source or if it's objective. Subjective impressions carry weight only when they come from a person with high status and credibility. In other words, negative feedback that is supported by hard data—numbers, specific examples, and the like—is more likely to be accepted. Negative feedback that is subjective can be a meaningful tool for experienced managers, particularly those in upper levels of the organization who have built the trust and earned the respect of their employees. From less experienced managers, those in the lower ranks of the organization, and those whose reputations have not yet been established, negative feedback that is subjective in nature is not likely to be well received.

How do you give effective feedback? Six specific suggestions can help you become more effective in providing feedback.

- **Focus on specific behaviors**. Feedback should be specific rather than general. Avoid statements such as "You have a bad attitude." or "I'm really impressed with the good job you did." They are vague, and, although they provide information, they do not tell the receiver enough so that he or she can correct the "bad attitude," or on what basis you concluded that a good job has been done so the person knows what behaviors to repeat.
- **Keep feedback impersonal**. Feedback, particularly the negative kind, should be descriptive rather than judgmental or evaluative. No matter how upset you are, keep the feedback focused on joy-related behaviours and never criticize someone personally because of an inappropriate action. Telling people they are incompetent, lazy, or the like is almost always counterproductive. It provokes such an emotional reaction that the performance deviation itself is apt to be overlooked. When you are criticizing, remember that you are censuring job-related behavior, not the person. You might be tempted to tell someone he or she is rude and insensitive (which might just be true); however, that is hardly impersonal. It's better to say something more specific, such as "You've interrupted me three times with questions that weren't urgent when you knew I was talking long distance to a customer in Brazil."
- **Keep feedback goal oriented**. Feedback should not be given primarily to "dump" or "unload" on another person. If you have to say something negative, make sure it is directed toward the receiver's goals. Ask yourself whom the feedback is supposed to help. If the answer is essentially ("I've got something I just want to get off my chest"), you bite your tongue and hold the comment. Such feedback undermines your credibility and lessens the meaning and influence of future feedback sessions.
- **Make feedback well timed**. Feedback is most meaningful to a receiver when only a short interval elapses between his or her behavior and the receipt of feedback about that behavior. For example a new employee who makes a mistake is more likely to respond to his or her manager's suggestions for improving right after the mistake or at the end of the work day rather than during a performance review session six months from now. If you have to spend time recreating a situation and refreshing someone's memory of it, the feedback you are providing is likely to be ineffective. Moreover, if you are particularly concerned

with changing behavior, delays in providing timely feedback on the undesirable actions lessen the likelihood that the feedback will bring about the desired change. Of course, making feedback prompt merely for promptness sake can backfire if you have insufficient information or if you are upset. In such instances, well timed could mean somewhat delayed.

- **Ensure understanding.** Is your feedback concise and complete enough that the receiver clearly and fully understands your communication? Remember that every successful communication requires both transference and understanding of meaning. If feedback is to be effective, you need to ensure that the receiver understands it. As suggested in our discussion of listening techniques, ask the receiver to rephrase the message to find out whether he or she fully captured the meaning you intended.

- **Direct negative feedback toward behavior that the receiver can control.** Little value comes from reminding a person of some shortcoming over which he or she has no control. Negative feedback should be directed toward behavior that the receiver can do something about. For instance, criticizing an employee who's late for work because she forgot to set her alarm clock is valid. Criticizing her for being late for work when the subway she takes to work every day had a power failure, stranding her for 90 minutes, is pointless. She was powerless to do anything to correct what happened—short of finding a different means of traveling to work, which may be unrealistic. In addition, when negative feedback is given concerning something that the receiver can control it might be a good idea to indicate specifically what can be done to improve the situation. Such suggestions take some of the sting out of the criticism and offer guidance to receivers who understand the problem but don't know how to resolve it.

Words and Expressions

ultimately	[ˈʌltəmɪtli]	ad.	最后，最终；基本上
competency	[ˈkɑmpɪtənsi]	n.	资格；能力
prerequisite	[prɪˈrɛkwɪzɪt]	n.	先决条件；前提；必要条件
stimuli	[ˈstɪmjəlai]	n.	刺激；刺激物
intensity	[ɪnˈtensɪti]	n.	强烈；（感情的）强烈程度
empathy	[ˈempəθi]	n.	（心）移情作用；同感，共鸣
precede	[prɪˈsid]	v.	在……之前发生；优于
flexibility	[ˌflɛksəˈbɪləti]	n.	柔韧性；灵活性
tendency	[ˈtendənsi]	n.	倾向，趋势
promptly	[ˈprɑmptli]	ad.	敏捷地；迅速地；毫不迟疑地
enthusiastically	[ɪnˌθjuːzɪˈæstɪkəli]	ad.	热心地；满腔热情地
substantially	[səbˈstænʃəli]	ad.	本质上，实质上；大体上
distort	[dɪˈstɔrt]	v.	歪曲；扭曲
vague	[veɪɡ]	a.	模糊的；（表达或感知）含糊的

descriptive	[dɪˈskrɪptɪv]	a. 描写的，描述的；分类的
counterproductive	[ˌkaʊntərprəˈdʌktɪv]	a. 使达不到预期目标的
deviation	[ˌdiviˈeʃən]	n. 背离，偏离
dump	[dʌmp]	v. 倾倒；卸下
elapse	[ɪˈlæps]	n. (时间的) 消逝
promptness	[ˈprɔmptnəs]	n. 敏捷，迅速
concise	[kənˈsaɪs]	a. 简明的；简洁的
strand	[strænd]	v. 滞留；搁浅

Text B   The Concept of "Face" in Chinese-American Interaction

Americans rarely speak about face, so you might suspect that concern for face is a Chinese (or Asian) preoccupation. But sociologists know that the concept exists among Americans as well as Chinese. Scholars who have examined the face concept have pronounced it a universal concern of human beings.

In all societies, each person (not including infants and small children or those suffering from serious mental illness) presents him- or herself as a certain type of human being to relatives, friends, colleagues, acquaintances, and even to strangers. This means that the person claims to be someone with certain characteristics and traits. One generally makes such claims by implicit means: dialect and accent, topics of discussion, attire and self-decoration, usual patterns of behavior, values and attitudes (inferred from behaviors), choice of companions, and so on. One might also make such claims by explicit (verbal) means: "I am such-and-such a type of person. I usually do thus-and-so when faced with a certain kind of situation.[(1)]"

Human characteristics and traits can vary enormously. Here are just six examples drawn from the dozens of parameters along which human differences can be described. Each is deliberately stated in terms of polar opposites, whereas, of course, any given human being can be described as existing anywhere on the continuum between those two opposites: (1) concern or lack of concern for attractive physical appearance; (2) preference for order or disorder in maintaining one's possessions; (3) concern or lack of concern for religious values and practices; (4) preference for self-restraint or self-indulgence; (5) tendency to be nurturing and kind, or stern and demanding, toward others; (6) tendency to be creative or conformist in thinking.

As people grow into adulthood, they gradually adopt certain claims regarding their own characteristics and traits, and they learn to make these claims, implicitly and sometimes explicitly, to others. People also learn to recognize other individuals' implicit claims about themselves and to accept (or in some case to appear to accept) those claims. One might say that people learn to accept "at face value" another person's "line" regarding the type of person that he or she is. This set of claims, or line, of each person is his or her face.

In every social situation, everyone present is putting forward a certain face. As long as each person's face, the social situation can proceed relatively smoothly in the sense that personal relationships can develop and business can be transacted. Mutual acceptance of another's face does not guarantee that people will agree about everything or will feel highly positive about one another. Personal relationships may develop toward friendship or enmity; business dealings may yield deals or disappointment. The point is that the focus of the social situation is the desires and concerns of its participants, not the implicit claims of those participants about their traits and characteristics.

It is entirely possible to call into question the claims of any person regarding his or her characteristics and traits. One may do this in an explicit manner, as occurs when someone cries out in anger to another, "You are a liar! You are a fraud!" In such a case, the focus of the social situation shifts abruptly from the desires and concerns of its participants to the image that one of the participants has been putting forward to the others. To be accused of lying of fraud is to have one's face called into question, to have one's apparent integrity impugned. The accusers are saying, in effect, "Your traits and characteristics are not what you want us to believe they are." For the accused, this is a most difficult and embarrassing moment, regardless of whether he or she is honest or deceitful.

It is also possible to call into question a person's face in an implicit manner. Doing so requires that one fail to accept at face value the traits and characteristics the other person is claiming. There are countless ways of doing this; here are two examples.

1. Suppose that a new graduate student, proud of her straight—A college record, behaving as a young adult professional should and wearing her dress-for-success suit, enters the office of her new academic adviser. In the course of their conversation, he refers to her as a "girl", talks down to her by explaining a simple point in her field, and questions her ability to complete the academic year successfully. The adviser has implicitly called into question the young woman's claims about herself, causing her to lose face.

2. Suppose that, during a school holiday, a father takes his ten-year-old daughter with him to his office. The father's supervisor appears and, in full view of the daughter, severely criticizes the father for some error[2]. In this case, the father's claims about himself to his supervisor are damaged; his claims about himself to his daughter are even more damaged. It is a supervisor's place to correct the errors of subordinates (though there are tactful as well as harsh ways of doing this). But the father feels deeply embarrassed in front of his daughter, since the validity of his face is likely to have been severely undermined from her point of view.

If you have ever told a white lie[3], you have a basis in your own experience for understanding face. The purpose of a white lie is to enable you to avoid calling into question the views that someone holds of him-or herself. It is, in other words, a face-saving[4] device. <u>The face that the white liar is saving may be his own as well as that of the person to whom the lie is told.</u>

Purposeful duplicity is hardly the only way to maintain one's own face and that of acquaintances. Personal qualities such as tact, diplomacy, and sensitivity, which are admired by Americans, are related to one's ability to recognize and preserve others' claims for themselves. So, even though people in the United States rarely talk about face, they do recognize its existence as well as its value in enabling all parties to a social interaction to maintain their claims.

The basic parameters of the face concept, then, are these.

Unit 7 Communication

(1) Each person's set of personal claims is socially vital as a pattern of characteristics that other people can recognize and expect to be more or less consistent. Other learns to interact with that person in order to transact business or develop a relationship.

(2) Each person's set of personal claims is psychologically vital as the pattern of characteristics that constitutes his or her identity, generating a sense of dignity, integrity, and self-respect.

(3) This set of claims about oneself is one's face, the sense of self that one puts forward to others which reasonable (if not perfect) consistency.

(4) In any type of social situation. Everyone present has a stake in preserving everyone else's face as well as his or her own; the mutual preservation of face enables social life to proceed. Tact, diplomacy, and sensitivity are among the admirable behavioral qualities that enable the parties to social interaction to do this successfully. White lying, perhaps less admirable, also enables people to preserve face.

(5) Loss of face occurs when a person's set of claims is implicitly or explicitly called into question by others. Loss of face creates embarrassment and perhaps anger in the person so questioned because, with or without justification, it threatens to unmask the individual, to strip away the role he or she has been taking with others.

(6) The person who has unintentionally caused another's loss of face is also likely to lose face, because he or she probably views him- or herself as someone who is sufficiently tactful to avoid causing such embarrassment.

(7) When anyone obviously loses face, the focus of the social situation quickly shifts, at least momentarily, to concern over what will be done about the situation by the person who lost face and by the person who caused the problem.

Words and Expressions

abruptly	[ə'brʌptli]	a.	突然地；莽撞地
acquaintance	[ə'kweɪntəns]	n.	熟人，相识
attire	[ə'taɪə]	n.	服装，盛装
conformist	[kən'fɔːmɪst]	n.	遵奉者
countless	['kauntləs]	a.	无数的，多得数不清的
deceitful	[dɪ'siːtfl]	a.	不讲究的，骗人的
dignity	['dɪgnəti]	n.	尊严，高贵
diplomacy	[dɪ'pləuməsiː]	n.	外交
duplicity	[djuː'plisəti]	n.	欺骗，表里不一
embarrass	[ɪm'bærəs]	v.	使尴尬，给…出难题
fraud	[frɔd]	n.	欺骗，诈骗
implicit	[ɪm'plɪsɪt]	a.	含蓄的；绝对的
impugn	[ɪm'pjuːn]	v.	非难，对……有怀疑
integrity	[ɪn'tegrəti]	n.	完整；正直

mutual	[ˈmjuːtʃuəl]	*a.*	共同的；相互的
parameter	[pəˈræmɪtə]	*n.*	参数；限制因素
polar	[ˈpəulə]	*a.*	极地的；完全相反的
preoccupation	[priˌɔːkjuˈpeɪʃn]	*n.*	入神，全神贯注
tact	[tækt]	*n.*	机智，机敏
unintentionally	[ˌʌnɪnˈtenʃənli]	*a.*	非故意的，非存心的
unmask	[ˌʌnˈmæsk]	*v.*	除去面具，揭露
self-indulgence			自我放纵，任性
self-restraint			自制
strip away			揭掉，去掉

Notes

(1) I am such-and-such a type of person. I usually do thus-and-so when faced with a certain kind of situation. such-and-such：*adj.* 某某的，如此这般的，这样那样的。
我是这种类型的人，当遇到某些特定情况的时候我会这么做。

(2) The father's supervisor appears and, in full view of the daughter, severely criticized the father for some error. in full view of：把……尽收眼底；完全在……视野之中。
父亲的主管出现了，他当着女儿的面，对父亲工作中的一些错误给予了严厉的批评。

(3) white lie：善意的谎言。

(4) face-saving *adj.* 保全面子的，顾全面子的

PART Ⅱ DIALOGUE

Dialogue 1 Customs Clearance

A：Customs Inspector；B：Passenger

A：Please show me your customs declaration form, sir.

B：Certainly. Here it is.

A：Do you have anything to declare?

B：I suppose no, except a carton of cigarettes. That's duty-free, isn't it?

A：Yes, one person can bring in one carton duty-free. Will you open your suitcase, please?

B：Certainly. These are for my personal use. And these are gifts for my friends.

A：Do you have any liquor or cigarettes?

B：Yes, I have five bottles of brandy.

A：You'll have to pay duty on that. Is that a new camera?

B：No, it's an old one.

A：May I see it, please?

B：Of course.

A：When did you buy it?

B：Last year. I've a receipt of it.

A：That would be good enough. Please give this declaration form to that official at the exit.

A：请出示您的海关申报表，先生。

B：当然，给您。

A：您有要申报的吗？

B：不，没有。除了一条香烟。这是免税的，不是吗？

A：是的，每个人可以带一条免税烟。请打开您的手提箱好吗？

B：这些都是我个人用的，那些是给我朋友的礼物。

A：您带有任何酒类或香烟吗？

B：是的，我带了五瓶白兰地。

A：这个您得支付关税。那是一个新的相机吗？

B：不，它是旧的。

A：请问我可以看一下吗？

B：当然。

A：您什么时候买的？

B：去年，有收条的。

A：那就没别的问题了。请把这个申报表给出口处的那位工作人员。

Dialogue 2　Reserving a Room

G：Guest；A：Attendant

G：Have you any vacant rooms?

A：Yes, sir. What kind of room would you want?

G：A single room with a bath. I'd prefer a room facing south, on the second floor.

A：Good. We have a room available.

G：What's the price?

A：280 RMB, but we don't have lunch.

G：Fine, I'll take it. Oh, by the way, would it be convenient to see the room now?

A：Of course. This way, please. This is the second floor. Here is your room.

G：Oh, this room is too dark. Are there any other rooms?

A：I'm afraid we don't have the same sort of room. They were all occupied.

G：Do you mean you still have some other sort of rooms?

A：Yes, but there are no bathroom and heating in those rooms, besides, they are on the top floor.

G：I don't mind that. Does it face south?

A：Yes, it's much brighter.

G：Can you show me the room?

A：Certainly. Would you like to follow me?

G：Fine.

A：Here we are.

旅游英语(修订版)

G：This room is better. How much is this room?

A：250 RMB for this room.

G：Good. I'll take this one.

G：有空房吗?

A：有的，先生。您要什么样的房间?

G：一个带浴室的单人房间。我想要一个二楼朝南的房间。

A：好的，我们有一间。

G：价格是多少?

A：280 元人民币，但不包括午餐。

G：行，我要一间。嗯，顺便问一下，现在方便去看房间吗?

A：当然可以。这边请。这是二楼，这是您的房间。

G：噢，这房间太暗了，还有其他房间吗?

A：这种房间恐怕没有了，都住满了。

G：你是说还有别的什么样子的房间?

A：是的，但那些房间不带浴室和暖气，而且在顶层。

G：这我不介意，朝南吗?

A：是的，光线要好多了。

G：您能带我去看一下吗?

A：当然可以，请随我来好吗?

G：可以。

A：这就是。

G：这个房间好多了。价格是多少?

A：这间 250 元。

G：行，我要这间。

PART Ⅲ　GOOD TO KNOW：Chinese Traditional Items

毛笔	brush pen；Chinese brush（pen）	砚台	ink stone；ink slab
景泰蓝	cloisonné（enamel）	拔火罐	cupping
中国结	Chinese knots	宣纸	rice paper
唐三彩	Tang tri-color pottery	帽筒	hat stand（s）
古瓷	old china	釉子	glaze
瓷	porcelain；china	釉陶	glazed pottery
卜卦	divination	十二地支	Twelve Earthly Branches
十天干	Ten Heavenly Stems	古董/玩物	antique；curio
国宝	national treasures	陵墓	mausoleum
玛瑙	agate	遗址	ruins；relics
贴金	gold-coated	甲胄	armor
文物	historical relics；cultural objects	弩	cross-bow

Communication Unit 7

古迹	historic site	盆景	potted scenery
穴位	acupuncture points (acupoints)	战车	chariot
祭器	sacrificial utensils	弓步	bow stance

四合院　courtyard houses; siheyuan (quadruple); courtyards; quadrangle-courtyard house

针灸　acupuncture and moxibustion

PART Ⅳ　EXERCISES

Ⅰ. Listening comprehension.

1. What is the speed of maglev rail train?
2. When will the first prototype be ready?
3. Totally, how long is the world's longest high-speed rail network?
4. What is the speed of the current high-speed rail line between Shanghai and Beijing?

Ⅱ. Put the following into Chinese.

1. folk art _____
2. string instrument _____
3. shadow puppet play _____
4. Chinese herb _____
5. Chinese martial art _____
6. the Terra-cotta Army of the First Qin Emperor _____
7. Shuttlecock kicking _____
8. bamboo flute _____
9. The Mongolian Horsemanship _____
10. cultural heritage _____

Ⅲ. Decide whether the following sentences are real conditional sentences or unreal conditional sentences.

1. If you heat ice, it melts.
2. If I make a promise, I will keep it.
3. If it rained, I went to work by car.
4. If we catch the 10 o'clock train, we shall get there on time.
5. If my father will give me permission, I shall spend a few months abroad.
6. If you would try, you would like it.
7. Set your alarm clock, and you won't oversleep.
8. Set your alarm clock, or you will oversleep.
9. If we caught the 10 o'clock train, we would (could, might, etc) get there on time.

10. If I had a lot of money, I would buy that car.

11. If I knew how it worked, I could tell you what to do.

12. If you were to miss the 10 o'clock train, we wouldn't get there on time.

13. If you would cook the dinner, I'd do the washing.

14. If you had told me, I would have paid him.

IV. **Reading comprehension.**

Housekeeping Department

The Front Office receptionist's prime duty is to sell accommodation, but without the housekeeping staff, there would be no accommodation fit to sell. Without the Housekeeping Department, a hotel cannot operate. To see to the cleanliness and good order of all rooms in the hotel is the main function of the housekeeping staff.

In order to allocate and supervise the work of the staff, a head housekeeper is appointed and is entirely responsible for the administration of this department, who ranks as one of the executive staff on a par with the head chef of the Food & Beverage Department.

Room maids have to be informed of which rooms are due to be vacated or relet. This information is obtained from the housekeeper's copy of the arrival and departure list complied by the Front Office receptionist.

It is generally the supervisors who check rooms to see if they are let or vacant and if they are properly cleaned and ready for letting and at the same time check if all furniture and furnishings are in good order and repair. As he/ she checks the rooms the supervisors complied a report called a bed occupancy list, sleeper's list or room status report. Once this list is completed, it is sent to the Front Office Reception Desk to be checked against the room board.

Such a list is complied two or three times each day. In this way, the receptionist is able to verify that the room board is accurate and agrees with the actual occupancy state of the rooms.

There is a linen-room under the control of a linen keeper, who is directly responsible to the head housekeeper. It is in the linen-room that all the linens and staff uniforms are stored, sorted, checked, issued and repaired. Needless to say, the laundry service is a must of the Housekeeping Department.

In all hotels room maids are employed to do the actual cleaning of the guest rooms. With regard to the cleaning of public areas, it is the PA cleaner's job, which includes the cleaning of all public rooms, lounges, corridors, halls, public toilets and the various offices of the hotel. But the cleaning of restaurant, banqueting rooms and bars is often the responsibility of the staff working in those areas and not the cleaners.

Since the Housekeeping Department is a predominantly female department, it is necessary to hire some housemen to deal with the heavy work, such as the moving of the furniture or heavy linen baskets and trolleys.

1. Match each word or phrase at the left with its meaning on the right.

(1) cozy   a. woman who cleans and tidies the bedrooms in a hotel

（2）receptionist b. comfortable and warm
（3）laundry c. interrupt
（4）tidy up d. untidy and dirty
（5）disturb e. a hotel employee whose job is to clean the clothes of hotel guests
（6）in a mess f. clothes need to be washed
（7）valet g. a person whose job is to book rooms for people and answer their questions
（8）chambermaid h. make a place clean and in order

2. Choose the best answer.

（1）Turn-down service is a kind of service done by the _____ Department.
A. Tourism B. Housekeeping C. Hospitality D. Laundry

（2）The housekeeping is responsible for _____ of all guestrooms in a hotel.
A. accommodating B. neatness and cleanliness
C. management D. serve

（3）In hotels the "DND" sign stands for _____.
A. Do Not Drop B. Do Not Diffuse C. Do Not Delay D. Do Not Disturb

（4）I'm sorry, we don't have any rooms _____ that weekend.
A. available B. rentable C. service D. servant

（5）Everything is in _____.
A. good B. order C. right D. place

（6）Hotels and restaurants are also known as the _____ industry.
A. tourism B. banquet C. hospitality D. food service

（7）Let me know if I can be of further _____.
A. service B. assess C. assistance D. assistant

（8）The concierge will _____ you to your room.
A. get B. take C. carry D. show

（9）This service is _____ as part of your room rate.
A. given B. provided C. seen D. regarded

（10）The room being "out of order" means the following EXCEPT the room _____.
A. is occupied B. is very dirty C. is untidy D. need repairing

V. Translate the following sentences into Chinese. They are underlined in the texts.

1. Managers ultimately get things done through others, competencies in leadership, communication, and other interpersonal skills are prerequisites to managerial effectiveness.

2. What it means is that you need to be aware of potential resistance and learn to use negative feedback in situations in which it's most likely to be accepted.

3. They are vague, and, although they provide information, they do not tell the receiver enough so that he or she can correct the "bad attitude," or on what basis you concluded that a good job has been done so the person knows what behaviors to repeat.

4. A new employee who makes a mistake is more likely to respond to his or her manager's

suggestions for improving right after the mistake or at the end of the work day rather than during a performance review session six months from now.

5. The face that the white liar is saving may be his own as well as that of the person to whom the lie is told.

VI. Write a letter of thanks in order to express your gratitude for the host's gracious invitation and hospitality.

1. Tell the host the specific reasons for your letter of thanks;
2. Your letter should be decent rather than gushing;
3. Invite the host to come to your dinner party next Wednesday.

Unit 8　Special Interest Tours

PART I　TEXT

Text A　Virtual Tourism

If the real economic value of virtual tourism[1] can be tapped effectively, it might be a new source of funds for wildlife conservation.

As a new era of Internet and broadcasting technologies emerges, the possibility of minimal impact mass tourism is nearing a reality. Through the use of powerful web servers, streaming video[2], broadcast-quality cameras, video compression, and satellite communications, it is increasingly possible to bring live wildlife images to huge numbers of virtual tourists.

The explosive growth of wildlife programs on cable television highlights the pent-up demand for virtual wildlife tourism. An average day of cable television now offers around 32 hours of animal-related shows.

This article looks at the nascent but rapidly evolving industry of virtual wildlife tourism and now it might offer park and reserve managers a new and significant source of revenue to help offset management costs.

Cutting out the Middle Man

Whereas in the past wildlife footage has been exclusively the domain of professional production companies, today's latest, relatively inexpensive technologies allow almost anyone to package and deliver live or edited wildlife footage to viewers around the world.

Traditionally, broadcast companies and production firms gain access to wildlife for free through national parks authorities, conversation site managers, or wildlife researchers. Though production costs are high, risks considerable, and margins thin, they make money through wide distribution, sales, and advertising. Seldom, if ever, do the park managers or researchers benefit financially. More often, they believe that the public relations value from viewers seeing "their" wildlife is sufficient compensation. Today, new media technologies not only open up unique wildlife viewing experiences for virtual tourists but also offer the potential for directly linking reverse managers and researchers to viewers. In its most interactive and expensive form, virtual tourists can remotely control a camera located thousands of miles away.

A For-profit Venture

One of the most popular sources for virtual wildlife tourism has been AfriCam, a for-profit

South African Internet and broadcasting company. It used all forms of wildlife content delivery to try to turn a profit. Despite early signs of success, it has recently suspended its web cam and streaming video services because they were not financially sustainable.

AfriCam's initial set-up was impressive. Free web cams of wildlife from over twenty locations attracted online shoppers and advertisers. Due to its early start in wildlife viewing on the Internet, it attracted a huge visitor base. At one time AfriCam boasted over 30 million visitors to its site per month and accounted for 48 percent of all of South Africa's Internet traffic, all this with very little promotion.

Eighty percent of AfriCam's original revenue came from "banner" advertisements[3]. It also has a number of other revenue-generating streams including an online outdoor shop, photography shop, travel service, music and art sales, and online wildlife courses. With some heavy investment, AfriCam has also turned to TV broadcasting and sold a weekly television program to the British Broadcasting Corporation and another to South African Broadcasting Corporation that captures the highlights of 8 hours of live wildlife recording around prime viewing spots such as Waterholes[4].

With costs covered from the sale of these shows, AfriCam tried to establish a live pay-per-view streaming video service for Internet users with high-speed connections. The charge per month was US $5 and the bandwidth cost AfriCam US $2 per user. As of April 2000 turnover was around seven million dollars and was expected to grow by 200-300 percent over the next year or two.

Although demand for virtual wildlife tourism seems to be growing as rapidly as the technology, its value remains ill-defined, and ownership rights are ambiguous. Here are some key points to bear in mind:

Can Wildlife Web Cams Generate Money?

So far, most virtual wildlife tourism on the web has been free. Though virtual tourists do not appear willing to pay for unedited wildlife footage, they may be wiling to pay for edited highlights. After all, cable television subscribers pay for wildlife programs such as *Crocodile Hunter*, *The Jeff Corwin Experience*, and Jack Hanna's *Animal Adventures*.[5]

But wildlife web cams have rarely, if ever, generated revenue. The "banner ad" model (advertising on websites so visitors can click through and purchase goods and services) has largely failed. And bandwidth charges for streaming video are still high, making video an unlikely tool for conservation. That said, the Internet adult entertainment industry made over one billion dollars last year, demonstrating that people are willing to pay for content over the web. So far, wildlife web cams and streaming video appear to be useful public relations, research, and awareness raising tools, but conservation managers have not yet found a way for them to generate revenue.

Wildlife Is a Commodity

Presently, television broadcasting has the best potential to generate money for conservation.

Yet to date, media production companies have treated wildlife as a public good, paying for access only in terms of publicity. However, as with any commodity, we need to regulate the supply of and access to wildlife and wildlands to prevent the market from being flooded and the material devalued. It is therefore important that park authorities, conservation organizations, and researchers do not underestimate the value of "their" wildlife and knowledge.

Control the Media Rights

Park authorities, managers, and researchers could, and probably should, license media rights rather than relinquish them. They should also take care not to sign away valuable rights by not reading the fine print. Moreover, conservation organizations and national park authorities (particularly in the developing world) need to work together to control access to sites and ensure that an equitable share of the proceeds contributes to the costs of conservation. Managers can retain control over their wildlife content is by owning the equipment and contracting the production and distribution.

Just as local communities and nations awoke to the pharmaceutical value of their natural resources and began to regulate bioprospecting, it is time that parks authorities and conservation organizations regulated access to valuable wildlife by hanging on to media rights, controlling access, and demanding a share of the proceeds. If this happens, virtual wildlife tourism may one day become a significant source of revenue for wildlife conservation.

What's on the Web?

There are a variety of virtual tourism approaches already on the worldwide web. While none are currently making money, most of them still believe that their cameras would help support the preserves—through education and awareness, even most of the set-ups are paid for by grants and donations.

Words and Expressions

bandwidth	[ˈbændwɪdθ]	n.	带宽
bioprospecting	[baɪəʊˈprɒspektɪŋ]	n.	生物勘探
compensation	[ˌkɒmpenˈseɪʃn]	n.	补偿（金）
compression	[kəmˈpreʃən]	n.	压缩；压紧
conservation	[ˌkɒnsəˈveɪʃn]	n.	保护；节约
devalue	[ˌdiːˈvæljuː]	v.	（使）贬值；降低价值
domain	[dəʊˈmeɪn]	n.	领地；领域；范围
equitable	[ˈekwɪtəbl]	a.	公平的；公正的；合理的
exclusively	[ɪkˈskluːsɪvli]	a.	专门地；唯一地；特定地
footage	[ˈfʊtɪdʒ]	n.	以尺计算长度；连续镜头
for-profit	[ˈfɔːˈprɒfɪt]	a.	以营利为目的的
margin	[ˈmɑːdʒɪn]	n.	边际

moratorium	[ˌmɔːrəˈtɔːriəm]	n.	暂停；延期偿付
nascent	[ˈnæsnt]	a.	新生的
remotely	[rɪˈməʊtli]	a.	轻微地，远离地，远程地
reverse	[rɪˈvɜːs]	a.	反面的，颠倒的；v. 逆转，倒退
pent-up	[ˌpentˈʌp]	a.	被抑制的
relinquish	[rɪˈlɪŋkwɪʃ]	vt.	放弃，放手
quetzal	[ketˈsɑːl]	n.	绿咬鹃，格查尔（危地马拉货币）
sponsorship	[ˈspɒnsəʃɪp]	n.	赞助，倡议
subscriber	[səbˈskraɪbə]	n.	捐款人，订阅者
suspend	[səˈspend]	v.	延缓，暂停
sustainable	[səˈsteɪnəbl]	a.	可持续的
underestimate	[ˌʌndərˈestɪmeɪt]	n.	低估
unedited	[ʌnˈedɪtɪd]	a.	未编辑的，未修订的
visitation	[ˌvɪzɪˈteɪʃn]	n.	访问，探视；天罚
ill-defined	[ˌɪldɪˈfaɪnd]	a.	不清楚的，欠明了的

Notes

（1）本文选自 *Winter 2002*（Vol. 3，No. 1），作者 Julia F. Carpenter, Daniel Zatz, Julia Mair, David S. Wilkie，有删减。

Virtual tourism：虚拟旅游是运用三维实景展示，将现实中的旅游场景制作成用于互联网、多媒体、触摸屏等多种载体进行展示的电子文件，可以按固定路线或自选路线从不同的角度观赏，获得身临其境的体验。根据临场参与感和交互方式的不同，虚拟显示系统主要可分为以下三类。

a. 桌面虚拟显示系统：主要是通过计算机显示器来显示虚拟世界，计算机图形技术在其中起着非常重要的作用。它的逼真程度较低，沉浸感较差，并不是严格意义上的虚拟现实系统。诸如 VRML 的一些三维游戏均为桌面虚拟现实系统。

b. 座舱式虚拟显示系统：使用这种系统时，用户置身于一个特制的座舱之中，舱内有一个可以向外看虚拟世界的屏幕，转动座舱就可以从不同的角度观察虚拟世界，用户不需要佩戴其他特殊装置，从而无负担地与虚拟世界交互。这类系统能达到的沉浸感也较差。

c. 沉浸式虚拟显示系统：这类系统有着较强的沉浸感，它往往配备头盔式显示器或是全方位的监视器，使用户能自由地变换虚拟空间。

（2）streaming video：视频流（即用影音串流媒体技术传送的录像）。

（3）"banner" advertisements：即横幅广告，可显示在网站中各个地方。

（4）Waterholes：这里指南非国家公园里的"水坑"，游客可以观看来喝水的野生动物。

（5）*Crocodile Hunter*, *The Jeff Corwin Experience*, and Jack Hanna's *Animal Adventures*：这里指有线电视 Discovery 付费频道播出的一些旅游探险节目。

Text B Adventure Tours in Antarctica

At 13.6 million square kilometres, Antarctica is the largest remaining wilderness on earth. It is covered by a sheet of ice which is on average 2.1 kilometres thick. While no humans live there permanently, the region is visited by hundreds of scientists each summer at one of 37 research stations operated by 18 different countries. Because of the unique location of Antarctica and its international significance, no one nation has sovereignty over any part of Antarctica. The region is governed by the Antarctic Treaty System of 1959 (came into effect in 1961), which provides for the conservation, research and management of Antarctic resources, and how these are to be used. As regards tourism, the Treaty in Recommendation VIII-9/1975 acknowledges that "tourism is a natural development in this Area and that it requires regulation."

The Argentinian ship, *Les Eclaireurs*, was the first to bring tourists to the Antarctica peninsula (the 1600-kilometer spine that juts from the Antarctica continent towards South America) in 1957—1958. In total, four cruises from Antarctica and Chile brought about 500 tourists in that season. *Lars-Eric Lindblad*, however, is generally acknowledged to be the first to run international adventure tours to Antarctica from New York (he chartered an Argentinian naval ship), starting in 1966. By the end of the 1900s, 84,173 ship-based passengers had visited Antarctica, with 14,623 alone visiting the region in 1999/2000, the most popular season ever. The importance of ship-based tourism remains today, with up to 90 percent of all tourists arriving this way.

Most trips to the Antarctica peninsula depart from Ushuaia, Punta Arenas, Chile, or Port Stanley in the Falkland Islands, with the trip from the South American continent to Antarctica talking approximately two days. Ships accommodate anywhere from 35 to 400 passengers. Itineraries to this region of Antarctica vary according to the type of vessel used. Trips beyond the Antarctica peninsula, for example, require an ice-breaker. Those travelling to the Ross Sea section of Antarctica depart from Hobart, Tasmania, Invercargill, New Zealand, or Christchurch, New Zealand, from late December to late February, with mid-January to mid-February reported to be the best time to view wildlife. Adventure-tour activities on such trips normally include activities such as viewing penguins (some ships have helicopters with which to visit certain penguin colonies), whales, seals, and sea birds; visiting historic sites, scientific and whaling stations; and appreciating the grand scenery of the region. Tourists typically spend about two hours on shore at a time walking around and photographing wildlife.

Due to the absence of legislation regarding tourism efforts in the Antarctica treaty, tourism operators, through the efforts of *Lars-Eric Lindblad*, took it upon themselves to codes of ethics for operators and tourists, called the International Association of Antarctica Tour Operators (IAATO), to help administer these guidelines. The Rules for Antarctic Visitors, as distributed by Marine Expeditions, are as follows:

- Do not leave footprints in fragile mosses, lichens or grasses.
- Do not dump plastic or other non-biodegradable garbage overboard or on the continent.
- Do not violate the seals', penguins' or seabirds' personal space.

- Start with a baseline distance of 5 metres from penguins, seabirds and true seals, and 18 metres from fur seals.
- Give animals the right of way.
- Stay on the edge of, and don't walk through, animal groups.
- Back off if necessary.
- Never touch the animals.
- Do not interfere with protected areas or scientific research.
- Do not take souvenirs.

Despite these guidelines, a researcher has put together a list of some ethical transgressions that he has observed in his polar travels over the course of many years. These include:

- A musician scaring away a group of penguins by giving his "first Antarctic flute concert."
- Passengers collecting stones, feather and bones for souvenirs.
- A passenger tossing stones at the foot of a penguin to improve a photographic opportunity.
- Visitors touching penguins.
- A tourist walking straight into a penguin rookery, despite warning, stating that he had "paid for the right to go as he pleased." The penguins were scared off, exposing chicks to predators and freezing temperatures.
- A captain positioning himself next to a seal for a better photo opportunity.
- A zodiac driver consuming alcohol before an excursion conducted after sunset.
- A crew member harassing juvenile penguins dying after having been abandoned by their parents.

The management of people in this type of wilderness is difficult probably because of the lack of sovereignty by any one country, and because of the differing cultural views on wilderness management philosophies. Tourists have consistently shown interest in the development of more facilities on the continent-like toilets, accommodation, post office, gift shop, and other activities such as diving, skiing and camping.

The fact that only 2 percent of the land is ice free leads to a tremendous amount of competition between humans and wildlife, the latter using this area for breeding. This is compounded by the fact that tourism season coincides with the peak breeding season. The constant human intervention is thought to cause behavioural changes in animals, denudation of habitat, and the spread of new organisms which might have the potential to spread animal and plant diseases. In 1997, for example, a poultry virus brought to the continent either by scientists or tourists, was found to have infected Antarctic penguins.

Like the Galapagos, Antarctica is truly one of the world's prime adventure tourism hotspots. How it comes to be managed is absolutely critical as a case study which might provide meaningful leadership in the management of other tourism regions around the world. In considering this region, the question of humankind's obsession with visiting every corner of the planet comes to mind. Some argue, as scientists in Antarctica might support, that tourists have no reason or purpose to be in Antarctica. Others suggest that it is our right as humans to go where there is opportunity to see and experience new lands. The question might become more important over time as we see tourism continually expand into the world's most pristine areas. The argument for tourism in these areas is the notion that it helps to support economically depressed communities. Antarctica is perhaps the only place in the world where this position does not hold true.

Words and Expressions

peninsula	[pəˈnɪnsələ]	n.	半岛
penguin	[ˈpeŋgwɪn]	n.	企鹅
fragile	[ˈfrædʒl]	a.	易碎的，脆的；虚弱的
moss	[mɔs]	n.	苔藓；藓沼
lichen	[ˈlaɪkən]	n.	[植] 地衣，苔藓
biodegradable	[ˌbaɪədɪˈgreɪdəbl]	a.	能进行生物降解的
violate	[ˈvaɪəlet]	v.	违反；侵犯
baseline	[ˈbeɪslaɪn]	n.	基线；零位线
transgression	[trænsˈgreʃn]	n.	违反
scare	[skɛr]	v.	使惊恐；惊吓
toss	[tɔs]	v.	扔；摇荡
rookery	[ˈrʊkəri]	n.	白嘴鸦的群栖地；海豹等的穴
zodiac	[ˈzoʊdɪæk]	n.	黄道带
juvenile	[ˈdʒuvənl]	a.	少年的；幼稚的
compound	[ˈkɑmpaʊnd]	v.	调和；使混合
denudation	[ˌdɪnjuˈdeɪʃən]	n.	裸露；滥伐
obsession	[əbˈseʃn]	n.	着魔；萦绕
pristine	[prɪˈstiːn]	a.	太古的；原始状态的

PART II   DIALOGUE

Dialogue 1   Arranging the Luggage

B: Bellman; S: Susan

B: Good morning, madam. I'm your bellman. I'll get the baggage up to your room.

S: Thank you very much.

B: Are these three pieces all yours?

S: Yes.

B: Let me carry them for you.

S: Thanks. I can take this briefcase.

B: Oh, leave it to me. I'll do that for you. This way, please. Here we are. Please take this elevator to the seventh floor. The floor attendant will meet you at your elevator entrance there and show you to Room 720. I'll take the baggage elevator and get your baggage up to your room.

S: Very good. See you then.

B: See you in a minute.

B: 早上好，夫人。我是行李员。我会把行李送到您的房间去的。

S: 非常感谢。

B: 这三件行李都是您的吗？

S: 是的。

B: 让我来搬。

S: 谢谢。我可以拿这个手提箱。

B: 哦，我来吧。我会替您搬的。请走这边。我们到了。请乘这部电梯上七楼。楼层服务员会在电梯门口迎接您，领您到720房间的。我乘行李电梯，把您的行李送到房间去。

S: 很好。一会儿见。

B: 一会儿见。

Dialogue 2 Tidying the Room

A: Attendant; B: Mrs. Black; M: Mr. Black

(The room attendant with a trolley meets the Blacks in the corridor.)

A: Good morning, Mr. and Mrs. Blacks. May I come through, please?

B: Good morning. It's almost 11 o'clock, and our room hasn't been made up yet.

A: I'm so sorry, madam. I was just coming along to your room. I'll be there as soon as I finish this one.

B: Really? Could you do our room first next time? We always seem to be the last.

A: Well. I have a section of fourteen rooms, and I always do the check-out rooms first unless there is a request.

M: Check-out rooms? What are they? Do you mean that the people who go out early get their rooms done first? If that is so, we were out 7:30 this morning.

A: A check-out room means a room which is being vacated at the end of a guest's stay. We have to get the room ready for reservations again by the front desk.

M: Well, we would like to take a nap after lunch.

A: Yes, I see. Your room will be ready in half an hour, Mr. and Mrs. Black.

B: Can you do this for us every day?

A: Certainly, Mrs. Black. We always try to have rooms made up early on request. Just let us know what you need.

B: Good. We do appreciate the favor of your putting our room first.

A: My pleasure. I hope you are enjoying your stay with us.

(客房服务员推着手推车遇见了走廊里的布莱克夫妇。)

A: 早上好，布莱克先生、布莱克夫人，我可以过去吗？

B: 早上好。快11点钟了，我们的房间还没有收拾。

A: 对不起，夫人。我正要去你们的房间，打扫完这间房我就去。

B: 是吗？下次能不能先打扫我们的房间？我们的房间好像总是最后一个打扫。

A：哦，我有 14 间房要打扫。我总是先清扫人走后空着的房间，除非您有什么要求。
M：人走后空着的房间？是什么意思？你是说你先收拾那些人早些出去的房间？如果是那样，今天早上我们 7:30 就出去了。
A：人走后空着的房间是指客人办理退房后的房间。我们必须把这些房间准备好，以便前台再安排客人入住。
M：嗯，午饭后我们想睡一会儿。
A：我知道了，布莱克先生、布莱克夫人，你们的房间半个小时后会收拾好。
B：你能不能每天都这样呢？
A：可以，布莱克夫人。我们总是尽力按要求早收拾房间。需要什么的话，尽管告诉我们。
B：好的，我们确实要谢谢你先把我们的房间收拾好。
A：我很乐意。希望你们住得愉快。

Word Service Station

| cozy | 舒适的，惬意的 | tidy up | 整理 |
| mess | 杂乱，脏乱 | hair dryer | 电吹风 |

PART Ⅲ　GOOD TO KNOW：Cashier's Terms

account	账户	blank check	空白支票
cashier	出纳	change	零钱
credit card	信用卡	debt	欠款
denomination	面值	treasurer's check	银行本票
fee, charge	费用	imprint	刷卡
payment	付款	peak time	高峰期
service charge	服务费	traveler's check	旅行支票
bad check	空头支票	cash	现金
certificate check	保付支票	debit	借方
debt notice	欠款通知	deposit	押金
discount	折扣	extra charge	附加费用
gift certificate	礼券	personal check	个人支票
rental	租金		

PART Ⅳ　EXERCISES

8-听力资源

Ⅰ．Listening comprehension.

It's 60 feet long, made of lightweight, fuel-efficient material and can 1 _____ eight people out of this world and back.

The first commercial spaceship was unveiled by Sir Richard Branson, who hopes to start passenger trips within 2 _____ years. The price tag: £ 130,000.

"In time we hope to get that price down and down and down so that, you know, one day, people can think: 'Shall I take my family on 3 _____ to the Caribbean or maybe we should try 4 _____ travel this year?' That's our aim."

Those that can pay will get the 5 _____ three-hour thrill ride. The 6 _____ rockets to 62 miles above the earth's surface. 7 _____ will feel weightless for up to five 8 _____ before heading down through the atmosphere and gliding back to earth.

Organizers say some 300 have already 9 _____ up. Space, as a tourist destination, may be one step 10 _____.

II. Translate the following words into Chinese.

1. curio _____
2. embroidery _____
3. hemp _____
4. silkworm _____
5. beverage _____
6. ginseng _____
7. jade _____
8. procelain _____
9. calligraphy _____
10. crystal _____

III. Combine each pair of simple sentences into one sentence, using subordination. If more than one subordinator is available, make more than one kind of sentence.

1. The rain stopped. The sun came out.
2. We left for the beach. We finished the work.
3. You are grown up. You must stop this childish behavior.
4. They put a couch at the corner. The chair had been there before.
5. Hold my arm. You don't fall.
6. I was so tired. I could hardly keep my eyes open.
7. My wife was using the vacuum cleaner. I was trying to listen to music.
8. You promise to behave yourself. You shall not go to the party this afternoon.
9. He will probably agree. You never know.
10. Air traffic is closely controlled. Flying is relatively safe.

IV. Reading comprehension.

Musée du Louvre

The **Musée du Louvre**[1], or officially the Grand Louvre—in English, the **Louvre**

Unit 8 Special Interest Tours

Museum or **Great Louvre**, or simply the **Louvre**— is the largest national museum of France, the most visited museum in the world, and a historic monument. It is a central landmark of Paris, located on the Right Bank of the Seine[2] in the 1st arrondissement[3] (neighborhood). Nearly 35,000 objects from prehistory to the 19th century are exhibited over an area of 60,600 square metres (652,300 square feet).

The museum is housed in the Louvre Palace (Palais du Louvre) which began as a fortress built in the late 12th century under Philip II. Remnants[4] of the fortress are still visible. The building was extended many times to form the present Louvre Palace. In 1672, Louis XIV chose the Palace of Versailles[5] for his household, leaving the Louvre primarily as a place to display the royal collection, including, from 1692, a collection of antique sculpture. In 1692, the building was occupied by the Académie des Inscriptions et Belles Lettres[6] and the Académie Royale de Peinture et de Sculpture[7], which in 1699 held the first of a series of salons. The Académie remained at the Louvre for 100 years. During the French Revolution, the National Assembly decreed that the Louvre should be used as a museum, to display the nation's masterpieces.

The museum opened on 10 August 1793 with an exhibition of 537 paintings, the majority of the works being confiscated[8] church and royal property. Because of structural problems with the building, the museum was closed in 1796 until 1801. The size of the collection increased under Napoleon when the museum was renamed the Musée Napoléon. After his defeat at Waterloo[9], many works seized by Napoléon armies were returned to their original owners. The collection was further increased during the reigns of Louis XVIII and Charles X, and during the Second French Empire[10] the museum gained 20,000 pieces. Holdings have grown steadily through donations and gifts since the Third Republic, except during the two World Wars. As of 2008, the collection is divided among eight curatorial departments[11]: Egyptian Antiquities; Near Eastern Antiquities; Greek, Etruscan, and Roman Antiquities; Islamic Art; Sculpture; Decorative Arts; Paintings; Prints and Drawings.

[1] Musée du Louvre: 卢浮宫
[2] Seine: 塞纳河
[3] arrondissement: 郡，县，区
[4] remnant: 遗迹
[5] the Palace of Versailles: 凡尔赛宫
[6] the Académie des Inscriptions et Belles Lettres: 法兰西铭文与美文学术院，简称"法兰西文学院"
[7] Académie Royale de Peinture et de Sculpture: 皇家绘画暨雕刻学院
[8] confiscate: 征用；没收；充公
[9] Waterloo: 滑铁卢
[10] Second French Empire: 法兰西第二帝国
[11] curatorial department: 馆部

Give answers to the following questions.

1. What is the specific location of the Louvre?

2. How many objects are exhibited in the Louvre?

3. What was the original usage of the Louvre?

4. When did the Louvre begin to display the national masterpiece?

5. How many curatorial departments are there in the Louvre? What are they?

V. Translate the following sentences into Chinese. They are underlined in the texts.

1. Traditionally, broadcast companies and production firms gain access to wildlife for free through national parks authorities, conversation site managers, or wildlife researchers. Though production costs are high, risks considerable, and margins thin, they make money through wide distribution, sales, and advertising.

2. At one time AfriCam boasted over 30 million visitors to its site per month and accounted for 48 percent of all of South Africa's Internet traffic, all this with very little promotion.

3. Park authorities, managers, and researchers could, and probably should, license media rights rather than relinquish them. They should also take care not to sign away valuable rights by not reading the fine print. Moreover, conservation organizations and national park authorities (particularly in the developing world) need to work together to control access to sites and ensure that an equitable share of the proceeds contributes to the costs of conservation.

4. The fact that only 2 percent of the land is ice free leads to a tremendous amount of competition between humans and wildlife, the latter using this area for breeding.

5. The argument for tourism in these areas is the notion that it helps to support economically depressed communities. Antarctica is perhaps the only place in the world where this position does not hold true.

VI. Writing.

Write an advertisement for a tourist attraction in your hometown, paying attention to the persuasive tone.

Activity 4: Freedom Trail

—Theme Trail Design based on the case study of Boston's Freedom Trail

Aim:

Based on team-work, students are assigned to study the Boston's Freedom Trail. Then, each team would be required to design a self-guided theme trail for a selected city and do a presentation on their planning at class. The presentation would be 10-15 minutes.

Background Materials:

The Freedom Trail is a red (mostly brick) path (also see http://www.thefreedomtrail.org/) through downtown Boston, Massachusetts, that leads to 16 significant historic sites. It is a 2.5-mile walk from Boston Common to Bunker Hill Monument in Charlestown. Simple ground markers explaining events, graveyards, notable churches and other buildings, and a historic naval frigate are stops along the way. Most sites are free; Old South Meeting House, Old State House, and Paul Revere House have small admission fees; while others suggest donations. The Freedom Trail is a unit of Boston National Historical Park and is overseen by The Freedom Trail Foundation.

The Freedom Trail was originally conceived by local journalist William Schofield, who since 1951 had promoted the idea of a pedestrian trail to link important local landmarks. John Hynes, the mayor of Boston, decided to put Schofield's idea into action. By 1953, 40,000 people annually were enjoying the sites and history on the Freedom Trail.

In 1974, Boston National Historical Park was established. The National Park Service opened a Visitor Center on State Street, where they give free maps of the Freedom Trail and other historic sites, as well as sell books about Boston and US history. Today, people walk on the red path of the Freedom Trail to learn about important events as the people worked to gain independence from Great Britain.

Unit 9   Sports and Outdoor Activities

PART I   TEXT

Text A   Backpacking

Backpacking[1] (in the US; tramping, trekking, or bushwalking in other countries) combines hiking and camping in a single trip. A backpacker hikes into the backcountry to spend one or more nights there, and carries supplies and equipment to satisfy sleeping and eating needs.

Definition

A backpacker packs all of his or her gear into a backpack. This gear must include food, water, and shelter, or the means to obtain them, but very little else, and often in a more compact and simpler form than one overnight stay in the wilderness (otherwise it is a day hike)[2]. Many backpacking trips last just a weekend (one or two nights), but long-distance expeditions may last weeks or months, sometimes aided by planned food and supply drops.

Backpacking camps are more Spartan than ordinary camps. In areas that experience a regular traffic of backpackers, a hike-in camp might have a fire ring and a small wooden bulletin board with a map and some warning or information signs. Many hike-in camps are no more than level patches of ground without scrub or underbrush. In very remote areas, established camps do not exist at all, and travelers must choose appropriate camps themselves.

In some places, backpackers have access to lodging that is more substantial than a tent. In the more remote parts of Great Britain, bothies[3] exist to provide simple (free) accommodation for backpackers. Another example is the High Sierra Camps in Yosemite National Park. Mountain huts provide similar accommodation in other countries, so being a member of a mountain hut organization is advantageous (perhaps required) to make use of their facilities. On other trails there are somewhat more established shelters of a sort that offer a place for weary hikers to spend the night without needing to set up a tent.

Most backpackers purposely try to avoid impacting on the land through which they travel. This includes following established trails as much as possible, not removing anything, and not leaving residue in the backcountry. The "Leave No Trace" movement offers a set of guidelines for low-impact backpacking (Leave nothing but footprints. Take nothing but photos. Kill nothing but time. Keep nothing but memories).

Motivation

People are drawn to backpacking primarily for recreation, to explore places that they consider beautiful and fascinating, many of which cannot be accessed in any other way. A backpacker can travel deeper into remote areas, away from people and their effects, than a day-hiker can. However, backpacking presents more advantages besides distance of travel. Many weekend trips cover routes that could be hiked in a single day, but people choose to backpack them anyway, for the experience of staying overnight.

These possibilities come with disadvantages. The weight of a pack, laden with supplies and gear, forces traditional backpackers to travel more slowly than day-hikers would, and it can become a nuisance and a distraction from enjoying the scenery. In addition, camp chores (such as pitching camp, breaking camp, and cooking) can easily consume several hours every day. However, with practice, much of this downtime can be purged from the day.

Backpackers face many risks, including adverse weather, difficult terrain, treacherous river crossings, and hungry or unpredictable animals (although the perceived danger from wild animals usually greatly exceeds the true risk). They are subject to illnesses, which run the gamut from simple dehydration to heart exhaustion, hypothermia, altitude sickness, and physical injury. The remoteness of backpacking locations exacerbates any mishap. However, these hazards do not deter backpackers who are properly prepared. Some simply accept danger as a risk that they must endure if they want to backpack; for others, the potential dangers actually enhance the allure of the wilderness.

Equipment

Almost all backpackers seek to minimize the weight and bulk of gear carried. A lighter pack causes less fatigue, injury and soreness, and allows the backpacker to travel longer distance. Every piece of equipment is evaluated for a balance of utility versus weight. Significant reductions in weight can usually be achieved with little sacrifice in equipment utility, though very lightweight equipment can be significantly more costly.

A large industry has developed to provide lightweight gear and food for backpackers. The gear includes the backpacks themselves, as well as ordinary camping equipment modified to reduce the weight, by either reducing the size, reducing the durability, or using lighter materials such as special plastics, alloys of aluminum, titanium, composite materials, impregnated fabrics and carbon fiber. Designers of portable stoves and tents have been particularly ingenious. Homemade gear is common too, such as the beverage-can stove.

Water

Backpackers often carry some water from the trailhead, to drink while walking. For short trips, they may carry enough to last the whole trip, but for long trips this is not practical. A backpack needs anywhere from 2 to 8 L (roughly 1/2 to 2 gallons) or more per day, depending on conditions, making a water supply for more than a few days prohibitively heavy. 1 litre (1.1 US qt) of water weights 1 kilogram (2.2 lb).

Backpackers may carry one to four litres of water, depending on conditions and availability.

Although some backpacking camps in heavily-used areas provide potable water, it must usually be obtained from lakes and streams or preferably springs.

According to health and medical experts, untreated water found in backcountry settings in the US and Canada is generally quite safe to drink. Yet despite this, many backpackers believe that drinking and cooking water nearly always needs treatment with a filter or chemical tablets to protect against bacteria and protozoa[4].

If water is unavailable, or if the only water available is irreparably filthy, backpackers may need to carry large amounts of water for long distances.

Water may be stored in bottles or in soft, collapsible hydration packs (bladders). Some backpackers store water in ordinary plastic beverage bottles, while others use special Lexan bottles or metal canteens. For accessibility they may be carried by a shoulder strap or attached to the outside of a pack. Bladders are typically made of plastic, rubber, and/or fabric. They are light, easily stored and collapsible. They may be equipped with drinking hoses for easy access while hiking. In spite of this convenience, bladders are more prone to leaking than bottles, particularly at the hose connections[5]. Hoses also allow the hiker to lose track of the water supply in the bladder and to deplete it prematurely.

Food

Some backpackers enjoy cooking elaborate meals with fresh ingredients, particularly on short trips, and others carry the gear and take the time to catch fish or hunt small game for food. However, especially for long expeditions, most backpackers' food criteria are roughly the same: high food energy content, with long shelf life and low mass and volume. An additional concern is weight; while Dutch oven and campfire cookery are historically popular, small liquid-fuel camp stoves and ultralight cooking pots made of aluminum or titanium are more common in modern usage due to weight limitations and fire restrictions in many locales.

Ordinary household foods used on backpacking trips include cheese, bread, sausage, fruit, peanut butter, and pasta. Popular snack foods include trail mix, easily prepared at home; convenient and nutritious energy bars, chocolate, and other forms of candy, which provide quick energy and flavor. Traditional outdoor food includes dried foodstuffs such as jerky or pemmican, and also products like oatmeal (which can also be consumed raw in emergency situations).

Most backpackers avoid canned food, except for meats or small delicacies. Metal cans and their contents are usually heavy, and, like all trash, the empties must be carried back out.

For dinners, many hikers use specially manufactured, pre-cooked food that can be eaten hot. It is often sold in large, stiff bags that double as eating vessels. One common variety of special backpacking food is freeze-dried food, which can be quickly reconstituted by adding hot water. One can also purchase a commercial food dehydrator which removes the majority of water from a pre-cooked meal. To eat, water is mixed in with the meal several hours before eating and allowed to rehydrate before heating. Some various distributors of this are Backpackers Pantry and Mountain Outfitters. Another kind of special backpacking food is UHT-packaged without dehydration, and can be reheated with a special, water-activated chemical heater. This technology originated with the US military's Meal Ready-to-Eat ("MRE"), but is now produced also for the commercial market. The small chemical heater obviates the need for a portable stove and fuel, however the added weight of the MRE's and their packing reduce the weight advantage.

As more and more "big box" retail stores carry pre-packaged dehydrated foods (such as Mountain House Brand) however, it is becoming increasingly easier to buy packed meals retail versus mail order, whereas MRE's are rarely carried in retail stores.

Words and Expressions

allure	[ə'ljʊə]	n.	诱惑力，吸引力；v. 诱惑，吸引
aluminium	[ˌæljʊ'mɪnɪəm]	n.	铝
backcountry	['bækkʌntri]	n.	边远地区
bulletin	['bʊlətɪn]	n.	公报，期刊，公示；vt. 发表，公告通知
chore	[tʃɔː]	n.	杂务，琐事
collapsible	[kə'læpsəbl]	a.	可折叠的
criteria	[kraɪ'tɪərɪə]	n.	标准，尺度，准则
deter	[dɪ'təː]	v.	阻止，威慑，威吓
distraction	[dɪ'strækʃən]	n.	分心，消遣，发狂
durability	[ˌdjʊərə'bɪləti]	n.	持久性，耐久性
exacerbate	[ɪɡ'zæsərbeɪt]	v.	(使) 加重，恶化，激怒
fabric	['fæbrɪk]	n.	纤维织物
fatigue	[fə'tiːɡ]	n.	疲劳，疲乏，劳务杂役；v. (使) 疲劳
filthy	['fɪlθi]	a.	肮脏的，卑劣的
gamut	['ɡæmət]	n.	全音阶，长音阶；n. 全部，整个范围
gear	[ɡɪə]	n.	小装备；衣服，齿轮；v. 调整，使适应于
hydration	[haɪ'dreɪʃn]	n.	水合作用
hypothermia	[ˌhaɪpə'θɜːmɪə]	n.	[医] 体温过低
impregnate	[ɪm'preɡneɪt]	v.	注入，使充满；使怀孕；a. 充满的；怀孕的
ingenious	[ɪn'dʒiːnɪəs]	a.	机灵的，精制的
irreparably	[ɪ'repərəbəli]	a.	不能挽回地
jerky	['dʒɜːki]	a.	急动的，颠簸的；n. 肉干
laden	['leɪdn]	a.	满载的，负担重的
mishap	['mɪshæp]	n.	不幸之事，灾祸，恶运
nuisance	['njuːsəns]	n.	讨厌的人，讨厌的东西
nutritious	[nuː'trɪʃəs]	a.	有营养的，滋养的
oatmeal	['əʊtmiːl]	n.	燕麦片，浅棕色
patch	[pætʃ]	n.	小片，补丁；vt. 修补，补缀
pemmican	['pemɪkən]	n.	干肉饼；摘要，要旨
plastics	['plæstɪks]	n.	塑料制品

prohibitively	[prə'hɪbətɪvli]	*a.* 禁止地，抑制地
purge	[pə:dʒ]	*n.* 整肃，清除，净化；*v.* 净化，清除
reconstitute	[rɪ:'kɔnstɪtju:t]	*v.* 再造；再组成
rehydrate	[ˌrɪ:'haɪdreɪt]	*v.* 补充体液
remote	[rɪ'məut]	*a.* 偏僻的，远程的；*n.* 远程操作
residue	['rezɪdu:]	*n.* 残渣，剩余物
scrub	[skrʌb]	*n.* 用力擦洗；渺小之物；*v.* 用力擦洗
titanium	[tɪ'teɪnɪəm]	*n.* 钛
trailhead	['treɪlhed]	*n.* 小道的起点
treacherous	['tretʃərəs]	*a.* 背叛的，危险的
ultralight	['ʌltrəlaɪt]	*a.* 超轻型的
underbrush	['ʌndərbrʌʃ]	*n.* 矮树丛

Notes

（1）本文选自 Wikipedia, the free encyclopedia，有删减。

（2）This gear must include food, water, and shelter, or the means to obtain them, but very little else, and often in a more compact and simpler form than one overnight stay in the wilderness (otherwise it is a day hike). 这里就是指一般的宿营、露营。这句意指背包旅行携带的物品比一般的露营所需物品更简单，装得更紧凑。

（3）bothy 是一种简单的房子，通常位于偏远的山间，不上锁，供守林员或路人免费使用，在英伦三岛较为常见。

（4）Yet despite this, many backpackers believe that drinking and cooking water nearly always needs treatment with a filter or chemical tablets to protect against bacteria and protozoa. 尽管如此，很多背包客仍然相信饮用水和烹饪用水需要用过滤器或者化学药品来处理，以避免细菌或原生动物污染。

（5）In spite of this convenience, bladders are more prone to leaking than bottles, particularly at the hose connections. 虽然袋装水有许多方便之处，但是，袋子本身比瓶子更容易漏水，尤其是在袋子与水管的连接之处。

be prone to，有……的倾向，易于。例如：People are more prone to making mistakes when they are tried. 人们在疲劳时更容易出差错。

Text B　Sport Tourism [1]

Overview of Sport and Tourism

Today vast numbers of people participate in or watch sports and almost everyone aspires to a holiday. Though the connections between sport and tourism have long been established, the relationship is now gaining global significance. Media attention has increased and people are becoming more and more aware of the health and recreational benefits that sport and tourism provide. Elliott has shown that the televised production of England's cricket tour to the West

Indies[2] increased ongoing package tourism to these islands by as much as 60 percent, an outcome also noted by Ritchie and Lyons in their study of the 1998 Calgary[3] Winter Olympics, where holiday visits to Calgary increased dramatically after the Games.

The growing number of travel companies that now produces brochures to advertise their sports and adventure holidays—for example, white water rafting through the Arctic, scuba diving in Kenya, or trekking in Nepal—testify to the increasing interest in sport tourism[4]. In travel-and-tourist magazines, resort advertising continues to emphasize the availability of sport facilities and opportunities. Spectator vacations are also increasingly popular with huge numbers of visitors attracted to various kinds of sports events. Le Tour, France's prestigious three-week cycle race, claims to be the world's largest annual sports spectating event, attracting several million spectators along its 2,500-mile route, while in Britain it is claimed that around 2.5 million people watch outdoor sport and another 1 million watch indoor sport while on holiday there.

Congresses, seminars, and workshops on sport and tourism have been documented as taking place since 1971 when the International Council for Sport Science and Physical Education (ICSSPE[5]) held a congress in Helsinki[6], Finland, on the topic "Activity Holiday-Making." The International Council for Sport Science and Physical Education and the International Council for Health, Physical Education and Recreation (ICHPER[7]) jointly sponsored the first congress that specifically addresses sport tourism which was held in Israel[8] in 1986. The first journal dedicated to sport tourism[9], The Journal of Sport Tourism International Council, this journal is now produced quarterly in the E-zine format with access through the Internet[10].

The relationship between sport and tourism in the modern world is symbiotic. It is not simply that sport furthers tourism by offering an ever-increasing range of valued visitor experiences; tourism also aids sport. This is illustrated in the following figure as an interdependent relationship[11]. The figure identifies sport as a special segment of the tourism industry. Our model illustrates the relationship between sport and tourism as interactive with tourism, which in turn influences sports participation and the sports infrastructure. Sport and tourism are now inextricably linked, and as globalization advances, new and exciting possibilities are opening up to enrich touristic experiences through sport and enhance sport development through tourism.

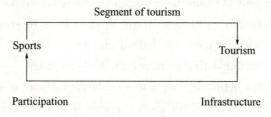

Figure Basic Model of Sport Tourism

Changes in the international travel market worldwide are leading to an increasing variety of tourist types, needs, and patterns. Adventure and activity holidays are a recognized and growing segment of the tourist industry, and sports training (e.g., the regular practice of sport) is acknowledged as an important and potentially health-enhancing activity for which tourism can be the catalyst.

Health care and training of the body have become an important part of the tourism industry. From the start, tourism was promoted for its health-improving functions. People used to go to seaside resorts because of the "presumed health-giving properties of sea bathing." Sea bathing led to sunbathing, but the risk of skin cancer has shifted emphasis toward a fit body, a body that is trained through exercise and sport. Sport as therapy is another growing segment of the tourism industry, with an estimated 15 million annual visits to spas in Europe alone, a figure that is similar to the markets in the United States and Asia.

Sport as part of business hospitality is big, profitable, and growing, with most of the clients spectating at events miles away from their place of work. Active sport associated with business tours is also increasingly widespread. However, due to space limitations and a stronger commitment to sporting holidays, we must treat this type of sport tourism cursorily.

Travel agents are always on the lookout for new markets as a way of broadening their business[12]. Jolley and Curphey (1994) reported that the six thousand agents who were at the American Society of Travel Agents' World Travel Congress in Portugal in 1994 identified the sports sector as a major growth market of niche travel: "Whatever the special interest a company somewhere will organize a holiday around it."

It has become almost impossible for professional sportsmen and sportswomen to pursue their careers without engaging in travel. Team tours are also popular with amateur clubs who engage agents to find matches and make accommodation and transport arrangements.

These examples provide an introduction to the sport tourism phenomenon, which we will now define.

Definition of Sport Tourism

As a concept, sport tourism is often seen as more recent origin than either sport or tourism. Yet what may be the earliest published work specifically linking sport and tourism can be traced to 1887. Victor Balck, the father of modern Swedish sport, included in a book dealing with different sports a chapter describing "Tourism and Sport." The term sport tourism or sport tourist is found increasingly in recent literature though few definitions are available.

Sport tourism falls into two categories, travel to participate in sport and travel to observe sport. Therefore, sport tourism may be defined as travel for non-commercial reasons, to participate in or observe sporting activities away from the home range.

Although we accept this definition, we also include the category of business and commercial tourism. That is, sport tourism can occur while a person is traveling for business or commercial reasons.

Word and Expressions

aspire	[əsˈpaɪə]	v.	热望
catalyst	[ˈkætlɪst]	n.	催化剂

Unit 9 Sports and Outdoor Activities

categorize	[ˈkætɪgəraɪz]	v.	分类
cricket	[ˈkrɪkɪt]	n.	蟋蟀；板球
cursorily	[ˈkəːsərəli]	a.	粗略地，不注意细节地
discriminating	[dɪˈskrɪməˌneɪtɪŋ]	a.	有辨别力的
enrich	[ɪnˈrɪtʃ]	v.	使丰富
globalization	[ˌgləubəlaɪˈzeɪʃn]	n.	全球一体化，世界一体化
inextricably	[ˌɪnɪkˈstrɪkəbli]	a.	解不开地
interactive	[ˌɪntəˈæktɪv]	a.	互相作用的
officiator	[əˈfɪʃɪˌeɪtə]	n.	裁判
ongoing	[ˈɔnˌgəuɪŋ]	a.	进行中的
prestigious	[preˈstɪːdʒəs]	a.	有声望的
presume	[prɪˈzjuːm]	v.	认为
profitable	[ˈprɔfɪtəbl]	a.	赚钱的；获利的
scuba	[ˈskuːbə]	n.	自携式水下呼吸器
symbiotic	[ˌsɪmbaɪˈɔtɪk]	a.	共栖的，共生的
Swedish	[ˈswiːdɪʃ]	a.	瑞典的
testify	[ˈtestɪfai]	v.	作证；提供证据
therapy	[ˈθerəpi]	n.	疗法
trek	[trek]	v.	做艰辛的长途旅行

Notes

（1）选自 *Sport Tourism*，edited by Joy Standeven and Paul De Knop, Human Kinetics，1998 年出版。

（2）the West Indies：西印度群岛。

（3）Calgary：卡尔加里（加拿大西南部城市）。

（4）white-water rafting in Arctic，scuba diving in Kenya，or trekking in Nepal-testify to the increasing interest in sport tourism：跨北冰洋乘筏漂流，在肯尼亚潜水，或是在尼泊尔长途跋涉——都是人们对体育旅游兴趣大增的证明。white-water rafting：清流漂筏。scuba diving：戴自携式水下呼吸器的潜水。

（5）ICSSPE：国际运动科学和体育教育理事会。

（6）Helsinki：芬兰首都赫尔辛基。

（7）ICHPER：国际卫生体育及娱乐理事会。

（8）Israel：以色列。

（9）sport tourism：以体育为主题的旅游，体育旅游。

（10）in the E-zine format with access through the Internet：以电子版出现，在互联网上可以看见。

（11）an interdependent relationship：一种相互依存的关系。

（12）Travel agents are always on the lookout for new markets as a way of broadening their business. 旅行社时刻关注着新市场，这是他们拓展业务的一种途径。

123

PART Ⅱ　DIALOGUE

Dialogue 1　Room Service

A：Head Waiter of the Room Service； B：Tourist

A：Room service. May I help you?

B：Yes. I'd like to have my breakfast in my room tomorrow morning. Could you send it here? I'm in Room 1512.

A：Certainly, ma'am. We provide very good room service. What would you like?

B：I'd like to have a full breakfast.

A：What kind of juice would you like?

B：Orange juice.

A：Would you like sausage, bacon or ham?

B：Sausage, please.

A：How would you like your eggs, fried or boiled?

B：Two fried eggs, sunny-side up.

A：Very well, ma'am. So that's orange juice, sausage and eggs, sunny-side up.

B：That's right. By the way, is there any other way to have room service?

A：Yes, ma'am. Just check the items you would like for breakfast in your doorknob menu, mark down the time and hang it outside your door before you go to bed.

B：But what should we do with the dishes when we finish our breakfast?

A：Please leave them outside your room. The waiter will go to collect them.

B：I see. Thank you very much for your service.

A：房餐服务。有什么可以帮助你的吗？

B：是的。我想明天早上在我的房间里吃早饭，你能把它送到这里吗？我在1512房间。

A：当然，夫人。我们提供很好的房餐服务。请问要点什么呢？

B：我想吃一顿丰盛的早餐。

A：您想要什么果汁？

B：橙汁。

A：您喜欢香肠、熏猪肉，还是火腿？

B：请给我香肠。

A：您喜欢什么样的鸡蛋，煎或煮？

B：两个煎鸡蛋，单煎一面、蛋黄朝上的。

A：很好，夫人。橙汁、香肠和两个煎鸡蛋，单煎一面、蛋黄朝上的。

B：对的。顺便问一下，还有其他方法叫房餐服务吗？

A：是的，女士。您在门把手上的菜单上选好自己想吃的早餐，写下时间，睡觉之前把它挂在门外面。

B：但是，吃完早餐时，我们应该怎么处理盘子呢？
A：请把它们放在您的房间外面，服务员会去收拾它们。
B：我知道了，非常感谢你的服务。

Dialogue 2　About the Use of Safe-Deposit Box

A：Attendant of the Service Center；B：Tour Leader；C：Tourist

A：Good morning, sir. May I help you?

B：Yes. Can you show me how to use safe-deposit box in my room? The gentleman would like to keep some documents in it while he is out.

A：Certainly, sir. If you want to use the safe, please go to the Service Center first and fill out a signature card, then the clerk there will give you an activation pin.

B：Activation pin? What's the use of it?

A：Once you get the pin, please plug in and open the door of the safe. Insert the pin, then "OPEN" will be indicated on the door.

C：How do I lock the box?

A：After "OPEN" is shown, you must input a six-digit cipher code and the safe will be locked when closed. And "LOCK" will be indicated. You can set the code arbitrarily.

C：How do I open it when I want my documents?

A：Just put in the cipher code and open the safe after it is decoded. If you keep the code unchanged, the safe will be locked automatically when the door is closed.

C：Can other people open it?

A：Unless they know the code. The safe will not unlock if a wrong code is put in, and it shows "Error".

C：Well, it's very safe.

A：I think so. But be sure not to forget the code you set. In that case, you have to contact the service center and ask the clerk to open it for you.

B：Oh, I know how to use it now. Thank you very much indeed.

A：It's my pleasure. One more thing, if you stop to use the safe, please remove the activation pin and return it to the service center.

B：Sure. Thank you for your information. Goodbye.

A：Goodbye. Wish you a pleasant stay.

A：早晨好，先生我能为您做些什么？
B：是的，你能教我一下如何使用我房间里的保险箱吗？这位先生想当他外出的时候保存一些文件。
A：当然，先生。如果您想使用保险箱，请先去服务中心，填写一张签名卡，然后服务员会给你一个激活识别码。
B：激活识别码？它的用途是什么？
A：一旦你得到了激活识别码，输入后，门上将会显示"打开"，就能打开保险箱。

C：我如何锁上保险箱呢？
A：在"打开"显示后，您必须输入一个六位数字密码。当它的门关上时保险箱将被锁定，"锁"将显示。您可以任意设置密码。
C：当我想要我的文件时，我怎么打开它？
A：只要输入密码，在它解码后，安全柜打开。如果您保持密码不变，当门关闭时，保险箱会自动锁定。
C：别人能打开它吗？
A：除非他们知道密码。如果输入一个错误密码，安全柜不会解锁，它会显示"错误"。
C：好，它很安全。
A：我也这么认为。但一定不要忘记您所设置的密码。在那种情况下（如果你忘记了密码），您必须联系服务中心，找店员为您打开它。
B：哦，我现在知道如何使用它了。真的很感谢你。
A：乐意为你效劳。还有一件事，如果您不再使用保险箱，请清除激活识别码并归还到服务中心。
B：当然，谢谢你提供的信息。再见。
A：再见。祝您们住得愉快。

PART Ⅲ　GOOD TO KNOW：Chinese Art

handicraft	手工艺，手工艺品	machine embroidery	机绣
cutwork embroidery	雕绣	hand embroidery	手工绣
double-sided embroidery	双面绣	plain embroidery	平绣
cloisonné	景泰蓝瓷器	cane products	藤制品
stone carving	石雕	floor screen	八扇屏风
wood figurine	木雕	mandarin fan	宫扇
jade carving	玉雕	silk fan	绢扇
color modeling	彩塑	folding fan	折扇
silk flower	绢花	silk painting	绢画
magic flower	翻花	landscape painting	山水画
traditional Chinese painting	国画	straw articles	草编织品
maize-leaf articles	玉米皮制品	classical painting	古典画

PART Ⅳ　EXERCISES

9-听力资源

Ⅰ. Listening comprehension.

In this section, you will hear a talk. You will hear the talk ONCE ONLY. While listening, you may look at Answer Sheet and write NO MORE THAN THREE WORDS for each gap. Make sure the word (s) you fill in is (are) both grammatically and semantically acceptable.

Differences Between Chinese Cultures and American Cultures

1. General differences

A. History

China: a traditional centuries-old country

America: a (n) (1) _____ nation

B. Cultural identity

China: long endured traditions and customs

America: a (n) (2) _____ of cultures

2. Specific differences

A. (3) _____

China: formal and hierarchical

America: loose and (4) _____

B. Confrontation/ Conflict

China: (5) _____ direct conflict or confrontation

America: direct conflict or confrontation over issues

C. Self

China: be willing to (6) _____ for greater good

America: look more at (7) _____

D. (8) _____ and reputation

China: avoid humiliating actions

America: getting the job done is more important

E. (9) _____

China: (10) _____ comes ahead of business

America: business is more important

II. Put the following words into Chinese.

1. Thanksgiving _____
2. outlet _____
3. ounce _____
4. refund _____
5. pharmaceuticals _____
6. accommodate _____
7. exchange _____
8. paradise _____
9. toiletry _____
10. pharmacy _____

III. Complete the sentences with the appropriate relative words.

1. Song birds are birds _____ sing.

2. I know someone else _____ mother teaches here.
3. He may be late, in _____ case we should wait for him.
4. I will give all _____ I have.
5. The book _____ you suggested is sold in the bookstore.
6. They have four children, all of _____ are now at school.
7. He _____ hesitates is lost.
8. Mr. Lee is the only dealer _____ I know _____ gives good prices.
9. I know a place _____ you can find beautiful wild flowers.
10. Is there anything _____ I can do for you?

IV. Reading comprehension.

How Social Media Is Changing the Way We Travel

Sleep in a stranger's house, join a dinner party where you know no one, hire a bike from a local... The boom in collaborative social travel continues apace, with locals catering directly for travellers wanting a more real (or cheaper) deal.

Leading the charge is *airbnb*, the phenomenally successful global lodging website that is now planning to branch out into city tours and other travel experiences.

Increasingly the middleman is being cut out of all areas of travel, as tourists enjoy peer-to-peer tours by locals, home-cooked meals, and equipment, car and even boat hire.

From January, Spanish start-up *Trip for Real*—which is partly bankrolled by Catalan superstar chef Ferran Adrià—plans to launch in London, with at least 150 hosts on its books. The competitor to *Voyable* already offers 2,500 activities across 50 Spanish cities and shows no sign of slowing down, with further expansion into other European cities—including Lisbon, Paris and Rome—to follow soon. "It's a magic combination of offering extra income to locals in difficult times and providing authentic experiences to travellers. It's not that the desire for authentic travel hasn't been there before, but big companies can't deliver it. We have a solution that can," said Emily Elwes, *Trip for Real*'s communications manager.

Over in the US, visitors to Boston, Los Angeles, San Francisco and Seattle are giving car-rental giants like *Hertz* and *Alamo* a miss and using traveller-to-traveller car hire service *Flightcar*, while for sailors in the US there's *Boatbound*, with over 13 million owners offsetting the cost of boat ownership by renting theirs out to "pre-screened, qualified" travellers. Meanwhile *Spinlister*, which provides bike and surf rentals from locals in more than 100 countries, has now added snow equipment rental.

Travellers wanting to join a dinner party or supper club with locals have more choice than ever. *Feastly*, in several major US cities, offers experiences such as an 11-course Pakistani Ramadan feast in Washington DC. *PlateCulture*, which launched last year and mostly arranges meals across Asia, continues to add new options. *EatWith*—founded in Tel Aviv in 2013—now offers meals in 90 cities of 32 countries (with more than 200 hosts in Barcelona alone). To ensure hosts offer a genuine hospitality experience and are not just in it for the money, *EatWith* implements a tight vetting process, with only 4% of applicants accepted to the site.

"The key to these experiences is that it's really a personal one-to-one transaction," says Bournemouth University tourism professor Stephen Page. "I thought *airbnb* was crazy at first, but the need for authentic experiences is there. It's a natural evolution facilitated, in part, by social media. Innovations are giving people more power and flexibility to get rid of the distribution chain. I think it's a trend that's going to last—and become ever more mainstream."

Questions:
1. List what services each social media offer.
   airbnb _____ ; Vayable _____ ;
   Flightcar _____ ; Boatbound _____ ;
   Spinlister _____ ; Feastly _____ ;
   PlateCulture _____ ; EatWith _____ .
2. What can social media offer to tourism?
3. What are the reasons that social media can boom tourism?
4. Can all people use these sites?

V. Translate the following sentences into Chinese. They are underlined in the texts.

1. The "Leave No Trace" movement offers a set of guidelines for low-impact backpacking (Leave nothing but footprints. Take nothing but photos. Kill nothing but time. Keep nothing but memories).

2. Backpackers face many risks, including adverse weather, difficult terrain, treacherous river crossings, and hungry or unpredictable animals (although the perceived danger from wild animals usually greatly exceeds the true risk). They are subject to illnesses, which run the gamut from simple dehydration to heart exhaustion, hypothermia, altitude sickness, and physical injury. The remoteness of backpacking locations exacerbates any mishap.

3. Significant reductions in weight can usually be achieved with little sacrifice in equipment utility, though very lightweight equipment can be significantly more costly.

4. The growing number of travel companies that now produces brochures to advertise their sports and adventure holidays—for example, while water rafting through the Arctic, scuba diving in Kenya, or trekking in Nepal—testify to the increasing interest in sport tourism.

5. Sport and tourism are now inextricably linked, and as globalization advances, new and exciting possibilities are opening up to enrich touristic experiences through sport and enhance sport development through tourism.

VI. Writing.

How to Write a Complaint Letter

Not every service or product meets our satisfaction. When we are dissatisfied, we should voice our dissatisfaction. In this way, we can have the seller or provider replace the defective goods, resupply the service, or refund our money. No seller likes to do any of these, but our carefully written letter of complaint may motivate him to do so.

When we write a letter of complaint, we will do well to keep these tips in mind: Firstly, be courteous though firm. We will not win the seller's cooperation by anger. Secondly, be reasonable. Show logically and factually that the responsibility lies with the seller. The seller should be impressed with our fairness and quiet grasp of the facts in the matter. Thirdly, be specific about what is wrong. Be equally specific about what we want to do about it. Lastly, tell how we have been hurt or inconvenienced by the problem. This strengthens our argument for compensation.

If we can follow these tips in writing our letters of complaint, chances are that we may succeed in what we intend.

<u>Simulate and create</u>: Draft a complaint letter about the poor service you received at a shopping center.

Unit 10   Leisure and Recreation

PART I   TEXT

Text A   Elephant Tourism in Laos

Most domesticated elephants in Laos are employed in the lucrative logging industry. While profitable for mahouts, the work is extremely hard going and elephants often become sick or injured. Worked to the point of exhaustion, these elephants are not reproducing, with life spans, birth ratios and quality of life considerably reduced as a result.

Being physically drained is only one reason why elephants are not reproducing. <u>Mahouts working their female elephants in the logging industry make sure they do not get pregnant, as they simply cannot afford to have an out-of-work elephant for such a long period (approx. 22 months)</u>. Understandingly, an elephant not financially contributing in any way can be an incredible burden to a mahout and his family. The same applies for the elephant's calf—they are not strong enough to work in the logging camps until they reach the age of 15. Reproduction is simply a too-costly exercise!

Tourism is a wonderful alternative industry to logging for the domesticated elephants of Laos. As long as there aren't 3 or 4 tourists on the back of the 1 elephant! Ecotourism supplies income for the mahout, while allowing female elephants to work while pregnant without any health risks to her unborn calf. Calves can also generate income as tourists can happily spend hours photographing and feeding them. Importantly, mahouts can use their knowledge of the forest when guiding tourists through their province. This way, mahouts can live close to their families (unlike logging) and still enjoy of working with their elephants. This is important if they want to ensure the next generation is interested in becoming mahouts themselves.

Cruelty-free and quality tourism[1] with elephants is an equitable species conservation plan for domesticated elephants.

Why Choosing Elephant Adventures?

Elephant Adventures Co. supports the conservation programme run by the National Animal Health Centre and ElefantAsia non-profit organization in Sayaboury Province[2], Laos 5% of

Elephant Adventure's total turnover is contributed towards the running of the Sayaboury Mobile Elephant Clinic. The unit supplies drugs and veterinary care to the elephants of Laos, free of charge.

The goal of ElefantAsia's "Lao Elephant Care and Management Programme" is to assist the Government and elephant keepers to improve the welfare of elephants.

ElefantAsia also contributes to the transfer of skills and technologies to the local Department of Livestock veterinarians through training and field missions. These activities are carried out to strengthen the ability and the understanding of the local veterinarians who are in charge of the health care of elephants at both province and district levels.

ElefantAsia operates a Mobile Elephant Clinic in Sayaboury province. The project aims at providing medical care for elephants in remote areas. It undertakes registration, provides information and preventive medicine, regular health care and general emergency medicine.

Here in Sayaboury, elephants are considered sacred. Since time immemorial they have served Lao people in the forest and played an integral role in Buddhist and animist beliefs. If the species was to become extinct, a fundamental part of the area's cultural heritage would also be lost.

The "Way of the Mahout" is a unique experience in the heart of Sayaboury jungle. Ride your elephant and learn the secrets of Laos' most experienced mahouts. Share their lifestyle during this incredible journey along rivers and lush untouched forests. By keeping elephants in their traditional environment, this initiative aims at conserving local elephant-lore and at supporting the reconversion of logging elephants into tourism in order to improve the living conditions of both mahouts and elephants.

Fair and environmentally friendly tourism can help preserve the last populations of Asian elephants and favour the development of sustainable solutions for letting people and elephants live side by side.

The essence of the trip:
- Contribute to the protection of the Asian elephant
- Discover the Lao forest on elephant back
- Meet the most experienced Mahouts in Laos and share their traditions
- Cruise downstream on the Mekong River[3]
- Experience life with Lao people issued from various ethnic groups

Tips for Elephant Adventure in Laos

COLLECTIVE PHARMACY: A collective pharmacy provided by Elephant Adventures and adapted to your expedition is placed under the responsibility of your guide.

PROTECTION OF THE SITES: The ecological balance of the area that you will cross is very precarious. The arrival of tourists, even in restricted groups, disturbs this balance. In the interest of all, each participant is responsible for minimizing their own environmental footprint.

CLIMATE: This varies greatly according to season; it is dry from November to March, with

Unit 10　Leisure and Recreation

some fog. It then becomes hotter and wet between April and October.

TIPS: Culturally, it is normal to give tips to the local guides and drivers, if you are satisfied of course! However, when tipping, take into account that most local people earn around 35 dollars per month. Ensure that your tip is in agreement with realities of the country, i.e. proportional to the standard of living.

HABITS AND CUSTOMS: Laos is a conservative country and it is therefore necessary to avoid being bare-chested. Always wear at least a T-shirt and shorts. Women should bring a sarong for river bathing.

LODGING: Accommodation is at local guesthouses and in tents.

FOOD: Food will often include rice, beef, fish, pork and chicken, pastes and noodles, chopped meat or green papaw salad.

TRAVELLING DOCUMENTATION:

Please ensure your passport has 6 months of validity beyond the date of return of your trip.

Words and Expressions

Buddhist	['budɪst]	a.	佛教的；n. 佛教徒
calf	[kæf]	n.	小牛，幼崽；小腿肚
compulsory	[kəm'pʌsəri]	a.	强制的，势在必行的；义务的
cruelty-free	[k'ruːəltɪː'frɪ]	a.	（消费品）无残酷性的
cruise	[kruːz]	v.	慢速行驶，乘船游览，游弋；n. 巡航，游轮
donate	[dəu'neɪt]	v.	捐赠，捐献
drain	[dreɪn]	v.	排出，排干，喝光，耗尽；n. 下水道；消耗
embassy	['embəsi]	n.	大使馆，大使馆全体人员
immemorial	[ɪmə'mɔːrɪəl]	a.	远古的，久远的
integral	['ɪntɪgrəl]	a.	完整的，构成整体所必需的
livestock	['laɪvstɔːk]	n.	家畜，牲畜
log	[lɔːg]	v.	砍伐，记入（日志）
lucrative	['luːkrətɪv]	a.	合算的，获利的
mahout	[mə'haut]	n.	象夫，管象的人
paste	[peɪst]	n.	面团，糊状物；vt. 裱糊，粘贴
papaw	[pə'pɔː]	n.	番木瓜，万寿果
picturesque	[ˌpɪktʃə'resk]	a.	生动的，窈丽的；别致的
portfolio	[pɔːt'fəuliəu]	n.	文件夹，公事包；作品集；（大臣或）部长职务
pharmacy	['fɑːməsi]	n.	药房，药剂学
precarious	[prɪ'keərɪəs]	a.	不稳定的，不安全的
pregnant	['pregnənt]	a.	怀孕的；意味深长的
ratio	['reɪʃɪəu]	n.	比率，比例
reconversion	[ˌriːkən'vəːʃən]	n.	完全恢复复原
registration	[ˌredʒɪ'streɪʃən]	n.	注册，登记，挂号

sacred	[ˈseikrid]	*a.* 神圣的，受尊重的
span	[spæn]	*v.* 延续，横跨，贯穿；弥补；*n.* 时期，跨度，间距
validity	[vəˈlidəti]	*n.* 合法性，有效性，正确性
veterinarian	[ˌvetəriˈneriən]	*n.* 兽医
out-of-work		不工作的，停止不用的

Notes

（1）quality tourism：品质旅游，是针对传统线路的混乱而创建的品牌旅游。

（2）Sayaboury province：沙耶武里省，老挝西北部的一个省，东界湄公河，西邻泰国，首府沙耶武里，下分10个县。

（3）Mekong River：湄公河，干流全长4909千米，是亚洲最重要的跨国水系，世界第七大河，东南亚第一长河。它发源于中国青海省玉树藏族自治州杂多县，流经中国、老挝、缅甸、泰国、柬埔寨和越南，于越南胡志明市流入南海。

Text B   Cruise

What Is a Cruise Ship?

A cruise ship or cruise liner is a passenger ship used for pleasure voyages, where the voyage itself and the ship's amenities are part of the experience[1]. Cruising has become a major part of the tourism industry, with millions of passengers each year. The industry's rapid growth has seen nine or more newly built ships catering to North American clientele added every year since 2001, as well as others servicing European clientele. Smaller markets such as the Asia-Pacific region are generally serviced by older tonnage displaced by new ships introduced into the high growth areas. Cruise ships operate mostly on routes that return passengers to their originating port. In contrast, dedicated transport oriented ocean liners do "line voyages" and typically transport passengers from one point to another, rather than on round trips. Some cruise ships also engage in longer ships which may not lead back to the same port for many months (longer round trips).

A typical vacation on a cruise ship starts when luggage is tagged for the ship at the airport. Upon arriving at the port of embarkation, passengers are ferried by air-conditioned buses to the ship for boarding, and luggage is delivered by the cruise ship staff to the passenger's cabin. <u>Waiters dot the ship, offering tropical drinks while the cruise staff orients passengers to the various decks, cabins, and public rooms.</u> In a few hours (most ships sail in the early morning), dinner is served in the main dining rooms, in which the wide selection rivals that of the finest restaurants, and the variety of main dishes are designed to suit every palate. Diners can always order double portions if they decide not to save room for the variety of desserts and after-dinner specialties.

After dinner, cruisers can choose between many forms of entertainment, including live music, dancing, nightclubs, and a selection of movies, or they can sleep through the midnight buffet until breakfast. (Most ships have five or more distinct nightclubs.) During the night, a daily program of activities arrives at the passengers' cabins. The biggest decisions to be made for the duration of the vacation will be what to do (or not to do), what to eat and when (usually eight separate serving times not including the 24-hour room service), and when to sleep. Service in all areas from dining to housekeeping is upscale and immediate. The service is so good that a common shipboard joke says that if you leave your bed during the night to visit the head, your cabin steward will have made the bed and placed chocolates on the pillow by the time you return.

After the cruise, passengers are transported back to the airport in air-conditioned buses for the flight home. Representatives of the cruise line are on hand at the airport to help cruisers in meeting their scheduled flights. When all amenities are considered, most vacation packages would be hard pressed to match cruise tour's per-diem prices that range from $112 to $250 per person per day, depending on accommodations. Occasional specials allow for even lower prices, and special suite accommodations can be had for an additional payment.

The History of Cruising

Early years the first vessel built exclusively for this purpose was the Prinzessin Victoria Louise, designed by Albert Ballin, general manager of Hamburg-America Line[2]. The ship was completed in 1900.

The practice of cruising grew gradually out of the transatlantic crossing tradition, which never took less than four days. In the competition for passengers, ocean liners added many luxuries—the Titanic being the most famous example—such as fine dining and well-appointed staterooms.

In the late 19th century, Albert Ballin, director of the Hamburg-America Line, was the first to send his transatlantic ships out on long southern cruises during the worst of the winter season of the North Atlantic. Other companies followed suit. Some of them built specialized ships designed for easy transformation between summer crossings and winter cruising.

Jet Age

With the advent of large passenger jet aircraft in the 1960s, intercontinental travelers largely switched from ships to planes, sending the ocean liner trade into a slow decline. Ocean liner services aimed at passengers ceased in 1986, with the notable exception of transatlantic crossings operated by the Cunard Line, catering to the niche market who enjoy the few days of luxury and enforced idleness that a liner voyage affords. In comparison to liner crossings, cruising voyages gained popularity; slowly at first but at an increased rate from the 1980s onwards. Initially the fledgling industry was serviced primarily by small redundant liners, and even the first purpose built cruise ships were small. This changed after the success of the SS Norway (originally the ocean liner SS France, which was converted to a cruise ship) as the Caribbean's first "supership". Since then the size of cruise ships has risen dramatically to become the largest passenger ships ever built.

Modern Days

The 1970s television show *The Love Boat*, featuring Princess Cruises' since-sold ship Pacific Princess, did much to raise awareness of cruises as a vacation option for ordinary people in the United States. Initially this growth was centered around the Caribbean, Alaska, and Mexico, but now encompasses all areas of the globe. Today, several hundred cruise ships ply routes worldwide. And even larger vessels are on the horizon. Plans are set for at least two cruise ships that will be 220,000 gross tons and hold 5,400 passengers each.

For certain destinations such as the Arctic and Antarctica, cruise ships are very nearly the only way to visit.

The largest passenger cruise ships are the Freedom class vessels owned and operated by Royal Caribbean International; these are MS Freedom of the Seas, MS Liberty of the Seas and MS Independence of the Seas. A fourth ship is expected by 2011. Freedom of the Seas is 1,112 feet (339m) long, sits 209 feet (64m) above the water line, and measures 160,000 gross tons. Royal Caribbean plans to continue offering the largest ships with the new Oasis class of ships. When complete, the MS Oasis of the Seas and MS Allure of the Seas will be 1,181 feet (360m) long, sit 213 feet (65m) above the water line, and measure 220,000 gross tons.

The Organization of Cruise Ships

Cruise ships are organized much like floating hotels, with a complete hospitality staff in addition to the usual ship's crew. It is not uncommon for the most luxurious ships to have more crew and staff than passengers.

As with any vessel, adequate provisioning is crucial, especially on a cruise ship serving several thousand meals at each seating. For example, passengers and crew on the Royal Caribbean International ship Mariner of the Seas consume 20,000 pounds (9,000kg) of beef, 28,000 eggs, 8,000 gallons (30,000L) of ice cream, and 18,000 slices of pizza in a week.

Regional Industries

The number of cruise tourists worldwide in 2005 was estimated at some 14 million. The main region for cruising was North America (70% of cruises), where the Caribbean islands were the most popular destinations. Next was Continental Europe (13%). The fastest growing segment is cruises in the Baltic Sea. The most visited Baltic ports are Copenhagen, St. Petersburg, Tallinn, Stockholm and Helsinki.

But according to 2008 CEMAR[3] statistics the Mediterranean cruise is going through a fast and fundamental change, Italy has won price position as a destination for European cruises, and destinations for the whole of the Mediterranean basin. The most visited ports in Mediterranean Sea are Barcelona (Spain), Civitavecchia (Italy), Palma (Spain) and Venice (Italy).

Words and Expressions

adequate   ['ædɪkwɪt]   a. 适当的；足够的

convert	[kən'vɜːt]	v.	使转变，转换
decline	[dɪ'klaɪn]	v.	下倾，下降，下垂；衰落
displace	[dɪs'pleɪs]	v.	取代，置换，转移
entail	[ɪn'teɪl]	v.	使必需，使蒙受，使承担
evacuee	[ɪˌvækjuː'iː]	n.	撤离者，被疏散者
fleet	[fliːt]	a.	快速的，敏捷的，浅的；n. 舰队，港湾
fledgling	['fledʒlɪŋ]	n.	无经验的人，初出茅庐的人
idleness	['aɪdlnɪs]	n.	闲散，懒惰，赋闲无事
initially	[ɪ'nɪʃəli]	a.	最初，开头
intercontinental	[ˌɪntəˌkɔntɪ'nentl]	a.	大陆间的，洲际的
livery	['lɪvəri]	n.	侍从
moor	[muə]	v.	停泊，固定，系住；n. 沼泽，荒野
slat	[slæt]	n.	板条，狭板
option	['ɔpʃn]	n.	选项；买卖的特权
ply	[plaɪ]	v.	（船、车等）定期地来往
popularity	[ˌpɔpju'lærɪti]	n.	普及，流行；声望
provisioning	[prə'vɪʒənɪŋ]	n.	供应，（一批）供应品，预备
redundant	[rɪ'dʌndənt]	a.	多余的
refit	[ˌriː'fɪt]	v. & n.	整修，改装
stateroom	['steɪtruːm]	n.	[火车]高级包厢；政府公寓；[船]特等客舱
tonnage	['tʌnɪdʒ]	n.	登记吨位，排水量
transoceanic	[ˌtrænzəuʃɪ'ænɪk]	a.	在海洋彼岸的，横越海洋的
withstand	[wɪð'stænd]	v.	抵挡，经受住
be centered around			以……为中心
cruise train			旅游列车
gross ton			1 英吨 = 2240 磅
in service			服役，在使用中
jet age			喷气机时代
ocean liner			远洋定期客轮
on the horizon			在地平线上

Notes

（1）A cruise ship or cruise liner is a passenger ship used for pleasure voyages, where the voyage itself and the ship's amenities are part of the experience.

游轮是一种用于游览航行的客船，航行过程和船上的设施一并成为旅行经历的组成部分。

（2）The first vessel built exclusively for this purpose was the Prinzessin Victoria Louise, designed by Albert Ballin, general manager of Hamburg-America Line.

第一艘专为这个目的建造的船只是邮轮"Prinzessin Victoria Luise"号，由 Hamburg-

旅游英语（修订版）

America Line 公司的总经理 Albert Ballin 设计。

（3）CEMAR（Center of Ecosystem Management and Restoration）：生态管理与维护中心。

PART Ⅱ　DIALOGUE

Dialogue 1　Additional Bed

A：Receptionist；B：Tour leader

A：Good evening. May I help you?

B：Good evening. I'm Fang Ting, the tour leader of Zhejiang Overseas Tourism Company. The Australia Bound Travel has made a reservation for us.

A：Just a moment, please. Let me check our list... Yes, you have made a reservation for 12 double rooms and 4 single rooms. Is there any change in the number of your group members?

B：Yes. There are 29 persons in our group now. Mr. and Mrs. Brown have brought their daughter with them. So we need one more single room.

A：I'm sorry, Mr. Fang. We don't have any vacancy at the moment.

B：What should we do now?

A：Can the Browns have an extra bed in their double room for their daughter? It's more convenient for them to take care of her.

B：That's a good idea. How much does an extra bed cost?

A：It costs 25 US dollars per night.

B：That is all right. Our company will make payment for it. Thank you very much.

A：With pleasure. Do you have a group visa?

B：Yes. Here you are.

A：All right. I'll make a copy of your group visa. Please wait a minute.

A：晚上好。我能为您做些什么？

B：晚上好。我是方婷，浙江海外旅游公司的领队。澳大利亚邦德旅行社为我们预订了房间。

A：请稍等。让我看看我们的名单……是的，您已经预订了 12 间双人房和 4 间单人房。您的团队人员数量有变化吗？

B：对，我们团队现在有 29 人。布朗先生和夫人带着他们的女儿。所以我们需要多一个单人房间。

A：对不起，方先生。我们现在没有任何空房。

B：我们现在应该怎么办？

A：可以在他们双人房里增加一张额外的床，更方便他们照顾女儿。

B：那是个好主意。一张额外的床多少钱？

A：它每晚花费 25 美元。

B：很好。我们公司将为它付款。非常感谢您。
A：乐意效劳。你们有团体签证吗？
B：是的，给你。
A：好的。我将复印下你们的团体签证。请稍等。

Dialogue 2　Laundry Service

L：Louise；A：Attendant

L：I'd like to ask the laundry service.
A：Well, just put your stuff in the laundry bag and put it outside your room.
L：How soon can I have them back?
A：Usually in a day. If you give it in the morning, maybe you'll get it by evening.
L：How much is it?
A：The rate chart is contained in the stationery folder in your dresser's drawer.
L：Oh, I see. Well, would you please send someone to Room 511 to pick up some laundry for me?
A：Yes, sir. The chambermaid will be there in a few minutes.
L：Thank you.
A：You are welcome.

L：我需要一个洗衣服务。
A：好的，请您把衣服放到洗衣袋内，然后把洗衣袋放到门外。
L：大概要多久才能洗好？
A：通常一天就可以洗好。如果您早上拿出来洗的话，或许傍晚就可以拿回去。
L：洗衣价格是多少？
A：价格表在梳妆台抽屉里的信件夹内。
L：哦，我知道了。嗯，你能派人到511房间来把我要洗的衣服拿走吗？
A：可以，先生。服务员一会儿就会去。
L：谢谢你。
A：不客气。

Word Service Station

laundering	洗烫（衣物）	stationery	文具，信笺
unstitch	拆线	chambermaid	女服务员
sew	缝	colorfast	不褪色的

PART Ⅲ　GOOD TO KNOW：Business Service

telephone directory	电话簿	Internet access	互联网接入
extension	分机电话	express	快递
receiver	听筒	special line	专线

wake-up call/ morning call	叫醒电话	telegram（cable）	电报
zip code/ postal code	邮编	wireless Internet	无线上网
word processing	文字处理	paper clip	回形针

PART Ⅳ EXERCISES

10-听力资源

Ⅰ. Listening comprehension.

Business-Travel Visas—A Strange Sort of Welcome

Governments are deterring business travelers and tourists with cumbersome visa requirements that do little to make their countries more secure. The rise of big 1 _____ like China and India, and the steady march of globalization, have led to a surge in the numbers of people wanting to travel abroad for business or tourism.

As a result, demand for visas is at unprecedented levels. In the fiscal year to the end of September 2014 the United States 2 _____ just under 10 million visa—up from around 6 million in 1997, despite blips in the wake of the terrorist attacks of September 11th 2001 and the global financial crisis of 2007-2008. 3 _____, Britain and some other rich countries can travel to most places without a visa. Chinese and Indian travelers are far more likely to have to apply for them. And citizens of a few benighted places, such as Iraq and Afghanistan, have to submit to the cost and bureaucracy and often 4 _____—of the visa-application process to get to most places.

The most sensible response to this surge in demand for short-term visas would be for governments to streamline the application process and scrap the most onerous requirements. But governments are often not sensible about such things. The 26 European countries with a common visa policy—the "Schengen group" require tourists from India and other developing countries to provide several months' worth of bank statements and pay slips. Visitors to Britain often have to fill in a ten-page application form, including details of every trip abroad for the past ten years. Business travelers to India must provide two 5 _____ Mexico has scrapped a rule requiring visa applicants (including women) to submit a description of their 6 _____. But in 2016 America will start requiring visas for some travelers who currently do not need them if, for example, they have visited Iran, Iraq, Syria or Sudan in the previous five years. In many cases, instead of simplifying the visa process, governments have offloaded it to private 7 _____.

Travelers may now have to pay a service fee to the company handling their application on top of the standard visa fee. The biggest firm in this growing business is VFS Global, which is part of Kuoni, a Swiss tourism company. Starting from a single premises in Mumbai in 2001, handling applications for American visas, VFS now has more than 1,900 visa centers in 8 _____ countries, processing paperwork for 48 governments. Of the 113 million visa applications made worldwide in 2013, one in three went through a contractor, reckons VFS, which has about half the market. Its main rivals are CSC, with around 9 _____ of the market, and TLS contact, with around 7%. Dozens of smaller firms make up the remainder of the market. The private contractors collect and verify the applicant's paperwork, ensure that forms are filled in properly, take fingerprints and other 10 _____ and collect the fees.

II. Look at the pictures below and identify each one. Use the words from the list.

| projector | recording pen | digital camcorder | flip chart |
| slide | microphone | function hall | whiteboard | hi-fi AV |

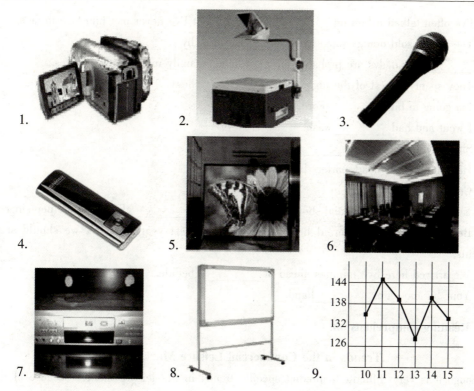

1. 2. 3. 4. 5. 6. 7. 8. 9.

III. Fill in the blanks with a, an or the. Put a " / " where no article is needed.

1. _____ hotel has _____ hot and cold running water in each room 24 hours.

2. _____ loss of pressure caused _____ speeding car to go into a skid.

3. Unless _____ crime, poverty, and other problems are dealt with there will be _____ widespread civil unrest.

4. This decision was _____ historic breakthrough; _____ first step towards _____ treaty on arms control.

5. In 1920 American women won _____ notable victory in their struggle for _____ equal rights.

6. I just can't lift these heavy boxes up the stairs. There is no point trying to do _____ impossible.

7. In 1609, Galileo improved _____ telescope and used it to study the stars and planets.

8. _____ dog likes to eat far more meat than _____ human being.

9. The police fired into _____ air to clear the demonstrators from the streets.

10. He had run away from home and gone to _____ sea when he was only sixteen years old.

11. Gradually _____ planet is getting warmer as a result of what is called the "greenhouse effect."

12. _____ Secretary General of the United Nations is making an important visit to the Middle East.

13. I've often talked o him on _____ telephone, but I've never met him face to face.

14. The grocer sold orange juice by _____ bottle or by _____ crate.

15. _____ Kennedys are probably the most famous family in the United States.

16. They spent the rest of the night playing _____ chess.

17. I'm going to buy _____ Ford.

18. I went and had _____ wash.

19. She is doing well in _____ school.

20. He contacted he headquarters by _____ radio.

21. Good nurses are always in _____ demand.

22. Everybody was pushing and shoving, trying to catch _____ glimpse of the pop singer.

23. Bearing in _____ mind how much we spent last year, I think we should start making cuts.

24. We arrived here five minutes ahead of _____ schedule.

25. Your big day is at _____ hand.

IV. Reading comprehension.

Trends in the Commercial Leisure Market

Although it is very difficult to predict specific trends in the leisure market because of the constantly evolving attitudes of the customers, it is believed that there are some trends that can be identified. Perhaps the most significant trend that is becoming evident is the expansion in the range of choices for leisure available to each person. We live in a society in which the use of information and its availability is increasing dramatically. We have moved from an industrial-based society where people have instantaneous access to diverse forms of leisure, a society where personal choice is the controlling variable. Leisure trends and ideas will develop from "bottom up" rather than the "top down." Thus, those commercial leisure service organizations that recognize the importance of individual choice will be successful.

High-Adventure and High-Risk Leisure Activities

Activities that provide opportunities for high-risk experiences are increasing. For example, in outdoor recreation, such activities as whitewater rafting, rappelling, spelunking, hang gliding, wind surfing, flying ultralight aircraft, and smaller adventures will probably increase in popularity.

Self-Improvement and Self-Development Programs

Many individuals desire the benefits that can be obtained from participation in programs orientated toward intellectual and spiritual self-improvement. The sales of books, periodicals, and products in this area have increased dramatically during the past decade.

Technological and Electronic Entertainment

Integrated computer/audio/video systems are increasing dramatically the number and diversity of leisure and entertainment services available. This will most likely result in a host of new forms of entertainment related to technology, including further expansion of activities such as video games, cable TV, video cassettes, and so on.

Entertainment and Eating Establishments

The fast food industry is likely to continue to expand. In addition, a greater number of dining establishments are being developed that have leisure entertainment as a draw-card for consumers. Pizza Time Theaters in San Francisco Bay area present an entire leisure experience via the use of audio-animatronics. The Magic restaurant chain creates a social environment focused on a "fantasy" dining experience.

Travel and Tourism

North Americans are travelling in record numbers. Not only are more Americans travelling internationally, but also in larger numbers domestically. This has direct implications for the hospitality industry and travel agencies as well as those locations (end destination points) visited by travelers.

Home Entertainment

Because of the increased availability of electronic hardware and software, people increasingly have access to such equipment in their homes for entertainment purposes. Thus, the home will become a focal point for many leisure pursuits and interests. The television today is a "hearth" around which families tend to congregate. Television has also provided the basis for the use of video cassettes, video games, computers and so on.

Fitness and Leisure

North Americans currently seem to be consumed by fitness and well-being. This leisure trend has tremendous implications not only for the delivery of services but also for the creation and distribution of goods. Running, jogging, aerobics, health clubs, squash, weightlifting and "health foods" are increasingly part of our popular culture. Information and services related to fitness, health, and well-being have increased dramatically and will probably continue to do so.

Complete the answers to the following questions with the information you get from the text.

(1) Why are trends in the leisure market said to be "very difficult to predict"?

Because customers constantly _____.

(2) What seems to be the most significant trend in the leisure market?

It is _____ available to each customer.

(3) What changes have been taken place in society?

Our society has switched from _____ to _____.

(4) What are some of the characteristics of an industrial-based society and an information-based society?

In an industrial-based society, people's lives are highly _____; while in an information-based society, _____ can be accommodated, people have immediate access to _____.

V. Translate the following sentences into Chinese. They are underlined in the texts.

1. Mahouts working their female elephants in the logging industry make sure they do not get pregnant, as they simply cannot afford to have an out-of-work elephant for such a long period (approx. 3–4 years).

2. These activities are carried out to strengthen the ability and the understanding of the local veterinarians who are in charge of the health care of elephants at both province and district levels.

3. By keeping elephants in their traditional environment, this initiative aims at conserving local elephant-lore and at supporting the reconversion of logging elephants into tourism in order to improve the living conditions of both mahouts and elephants.

4. Waiters dot the ship, offering tropical drinks while the cruise staff orients passengers to the various decks, cabins, and public rooms.

5. Ocean liner services aimed at passengers ceased in 1986, with the notable exception of transatlantic crossings operated by the Cunard Line, catering to the niche market who enjoy the few days of luxury and enforced idleness that a liner voyage affords.

VI. Discussion.

In May, 2016, Chinese tour guide Miss Ding got a Wechat message, from Mr. Meng, one of her group members who were travelling in Thailand, which reads, "Miss Ding, I am very sorry that, my wife and I left the group without telling you. Please don't try to look for us." Miss Ding tried to dial this guest, but the mobile phone was powered off.

If you were Miss Ding, what would you do? Please analyze the reasons and consequences of Mr. Meng's behavior.

Activity 5: The Ski Resort

Aim:

Based on team work, students are assigned to discuss the material, then to present a play of the village meeting on class; each student is required to play at least one role, and the play takes 10-15 minutes.

Meeting Agenda:

- Based on teamwork, students should be grouped into several teams to do the class discussion, each student would play one/several role (s) in the meeting.
- Total time – 30 minutes.
- First 5 minutes – Mayor is to open the meeting, be the chair of the meeting, control the discussion, invite people to talk, introduce Chairman of development consortium; Chairman is to put forward the motion, giving an overall statement of the plan, his/her reasons for wanting to develop, and the benefits/costs of the project.
- Next 15 minutes – To ascertain the overall opinion of residents and business people of Woomera – Mayor is to call on each person for his/her stance on the proposal. Allowance for discussion/debate.
- Final 10 minutes – To come to a conclusion regarding the development. Mayor is to call for a vote. Both mayor and Chairman of development consortium are to address the concerns. If group in terms of what will be done to make everyone happy. Till the end of the meeting, Chairman is to thank for the villages and promise necessary amendment to the plan for the sake of better environment protection.

(At the end of the activity—go through mistakes; suggest better phrases/meeting language)

- Students should study the development plan, outline the character and standpoint of the chosen role, discussing pros and cons with others in your group.
- Suggested teaching arrangement: 2 class hours.

Workshop material:

Tourism: The ski resort

The mountain village of Woomera has for a long time been off the beaten track (remote from populous or much-travelled regions) and only visited by a few tourists in the summer. Now a consortium (an association or a combination, as of businesses, financial institutions, or investors, for the purpose of engaging in a joint venture) of businessmen from a town in the valley has come up with a plan for the village to develop a ski resort. A tourist complex of hotels, apartments, boutiques, a swimming pool and other luxury facilities would be built to attract winter-sports enthusiasts. A public meeting to discuss the plans will take place tomorrow. Meanwhile, the pros & cons (advantages & disadvantages) of the plan are being discussed in the village inn, mayor's office, and private houses.

Mayor of the village: Supports the scheme – thinks development is good.

Chairman of the development consortium: Interested in making money.

Well Edecated Person – friend of mayor: Interested in business management.

Member of Local Councal: Is worried about the money the council will have to spend on roads, rail, waste disposal, etc.

Writer/Weekend Resident/Environmentalist: Enjoys rural peace and goes there to write, works in town on weekdays and gets away from it to his weekend cottage, angry that trees will be cut down, and wildlife will be killed/habitat destroyed and they will have to move.

Shopkeepep: Could make a lot of money by selling equipment, food, supplies, petrol, etc.

Bus Driver From Valley: Could get more business from tours, etc.

Doctor: Worried about diseases tourists might bring.

Local Labourer: Feels he will get more work and maybe a permanent job.

Farmer 1: Could sell more produce due to increased development/ Feels tourism will take his family better off.

Farmer 2: Does not like tourists/ Thinks the developers will want to take their land.

Teenager: Wants to meet tourists because he/she has a dream to travel.

Old Person: Doesn't like change/ May not like to see benefits of the scheme/ Thinks the scheme would destroy village life/ Worried about crimes.

Development plan:

The scheme will take 3 years to complete.

When construction is finished there will be:

- 400-bed hotels;
- 150 private apartments;
- 15 shops and boutiques;
- 1 supermarket;
- 1 bank;
- 7 ski-lifts with access to 150km of ski-run;
- improved road and rail access to the valley.

Unit 11   Ecotourism

PART I   TEXT

Text A   Ecotourism

Ceballos-Lascurain used to be regarded as the first to coin the term "ecotourism" in the early 1980s, who defined it as "travelling to relatively undisturbed or uncontaminated nature areas with the specific objective of studying, admiring, and enjoying the scenery and its wild plants and animals, as well as any existing cultural manifestations (both past and present) found in these areas" He illustrates that his initial reference to the term occurred in 1983, while he was in the process of developing PRONATURA, an NGO in Mexico. Recently, however, the term has been traced further back into 1965 to the work of Hetzer, who used it to explain the intricate relationship between tourists and the environments and cultures in which they interact. Hetzer identified four fundamental pillars that needed to be followed for a more responsible form of tourism which included: (1) minimum environmental impact, (2) minimum impact on—and maximum respect for—host cultures; (3) maximum economic benefits to the host country's grassroots; (4) maximum "recreational" satisfaction to participating tourists. The development of the concept of ecotourism grew, as a culmination of dissatisfaction with governments' and society's negative approach to development, especially from an ecological point of view.

There seems to be universal acceptance of the fact that ecotourism was viable long before the 1980s in practice, if not in name. [1] For example, Canadian government operated the "ecotours" during the mid-1970s which centred around the Trans-Canada Highway and were developed on basis of different ecological zones found along the course of the highway, despite the lack of a focused look at low impact, sustainability, community development, and the moral philosophy labels that are attached to ecotourism in the 1990s. The ecotours were developed at a time when the Canadian government felt it important to allow Canadian and foreign travelers to appreciate the human-land relationship in Canada, through the interpretation of the natural environment. Although a set definition of ecotourism was not provided, each of the ecotour guides contains the following foreword:

"Ecotours are prepared by the Canadian Forestry Service to help you, as a traveler, understand the features of the landscape you see as you cross the country. Both natural and human history are described and interpreted. The route covered by the Ecotours is divided into major landscape types, or Ecozones, and a map of each Ecozone shows the location of interesting features (identified by code numbers). While most features can be seen from your car, stops are suggested for some of them. Distances between points of interest are given in kilometers. Where side trips are described, distances are given to the turn off from the highway. You will derive the maximum value from this Ecotour if you keep a record of the distance travelled and read the information on each point of interest before reaching it."

Given the ambiguity associated with the historical origins of ecotourism, the purpose of the present study is to identify the key features, concepts, and principles of the term, especially the link between nature tourism or nature-oriented tourism and ecotourism, for the latter was often defined as a nature tourism in which the traveler is drawn to a destination because of his or her interest in one or more features of that destination's natural history. The visit combines education, recreation, and often adventure. In addition, nature tourism has hard and soft dimensions, based on the physical rigour of the experience and also the level of interest in natural history, similarly, some types of ecotourists, based on a more difficult or rigorous experience, and also on the dedication shown by the ecotourist relative to the interest in the activity, would be more willing to endure hardships than others in order to secure their experiences.

A subsequent definition identifies a conceptual difference between ecotourism and nature tourism. In recognizing the difficulties in defining nature tourism, both a narrow and broad scope to its definition were established. If nature tourism could be defined as tourism focused principally on natural resources such as relatively undisturbed parks and natural areas, wetlands, wildlife reserves, species, landscape, scenery and salt and fresh-water feature and other areas of protected flora, fauna, and habitats, it would narrowly refer to operators running nature-oriented tours, or, broadly apply to tourism's use of natural resources including beaches and country landscapes. Given this perspective, ecotourism is one part of a broader nature-based tourism or low impact nature tourism which contributes to the maintenance of species and habitats either directly through a contribution to conservation and/or indirectly by providing revenue to the local community sufficient for local people to value, and therefore protect, their wildlife heritage area as a source of income, besides, other key variable or principles that separate ecotourism from its more broad-based nature counterpart include an educative component and a sustainability component as well as the ethical nature of the experience.

More recently, the Quebec Declaration on Ecotourism[2] in 2002 suggested that five distinct criteria be used to define ecotourism, namely: nature-based product, minimal impact management, environmental education, contribution to conservation and contribution to community.

Words and Expressions

uncontaminated	[ˌʌnkənˈtæmɪneɪtɪd]	a. 未被污染的，未被玷污的
culmination	[ˌkʌlmɪˈneɪʃn]	n. 顶点，极点
viable	[ˈvaɪəbl]	a. 切实可行的；有望实现的
ambiguity	[ˌæmbɪˈjuːəti]	n. 含糊；意义不明确
rigour	[ˈrɪɡə]	n. 严厉；（气候等的）严酷
minimal	[ˈmɪnɪməl]	a. （正式）最小的，极少的，极小的

Notes

(1) There seems to be universal acceptance of the fact that ecotourism was viable long before the 1980s in practice, if not in name. 人们似乎普遍接受这样一个事实：虽然当时并未被称作生态旅游，但实际上，在20世纪80年代之前，生态旅游已经开始了。

(2) Quebec Declaration on Ecotourism：魁北克生态旅游宣言。根据联合国2002年国际生态旅游年的活动计划，由联合国环境署（UNEP）和世界旅游组织（WTO）发起、魁北克市旅游局和加拿大旅游委员会共同主办了世界生态旅游峰会，会后发表宣言，确认旅游有着重要且复杂的社会、经济和环境影响，考虑到人们对自然区域旅游的兴趣与日俱增，强调旅游应该通过增加东道主社区的经济收益、积极促进自然资源和东道主社区文化完整性的保护，以及通过增强旅游者对自然和文化遗产保护的意识来促进整个旅游业的可持续发展，承认与自然区域相关的文化多样性，尤其是由地方社区的历史遗存所形成的文化多样性，而其中许多是在数百年中已经被证实是可持续的。

Text B The Role of Ethics in Ecotourism

The basis of ethics' meaning relates to the study of what is good or right for human beings. So applied ethics has evolved both in business and in society as a whole to include a number of key areas related to human well-being and development, including business, the legal and medical professions, the biosphere and environment, and accordingly tourism.

Many regions of the world have been experiencing the most pressure from tourism, as a Hawaiian delegate of in a tourism conference uttered "We don't want tourism. We don't want you. We don't want to be degraded as servants and dancers. That is culture prostitution. I don't want to see a single one of you in Hawaii. There are no innocent tourists". Although this is an example of a social impact of tourism, more fundamentally it is a socially oriented ethical issue. In this case, tourism is an economic cornerstone of Hawaiian economy, however, to some people, its presence has contributed significantly to cultural dislocation within the region. There is a similar case among the aboriginal people in Canada who had been skeptical to tourism. In many cases, their scepticism was founded upon the fact that they were not players within the industry, and were therefore not realizing any of the potential economic behaviour that accrues from the industry.

The presence or absence of acceptable ethical behaviour in tourism setting is very much a function of how tourists, operators, and local people act and feel about each other and towards the resource base, so a balance must be struck between the various stakeholders of the tourism industry in ensuring that the goodwill of some stakeholders (e.g., tourists and local people) is not overridden by the misgivings of other stakeholder groups (e.g., government or industry). Obviously the sheer number of interactions between these different groups creates a myriad of cases where positive or negative impacts are generated.

Case 1：On a recent trip to the jungles of the Yucatan Peninsula in Mexico, our group was taken to a farmer's residence before venturing off to see some of the famous Mayan ruins. At this farm the operator took great joy in showing us three jaguars that were secured to a fence using four-foot chains. The operator's rationale for showing us the jaguars was that he was certain that we would be unable to see jaguars in the forest over the course of our tour. He knew that such a sighting would be highly valued by ecotourists. This was his way of guaranteeing that we saw these magnificent beasts. Clearly, the animals did not mean anything to the operator, and he was taken back by the suggestion of one of our party that he would have rather seen a picture of a jaguar in a book than a live animal under these circumstances.

Case 2: Another example involves tourists visiting the great Ayers Rock of central Australia. A well-visited attraction, Ayers Rock attracts many different kinds of tourists over the course of the year. While upon Ayers Rock, again some ten years ago, I witnessed two tourists in their early twenties chip away pieces of this monolith as souvenirs to take home. It led me to wonder what the implication of this behaviour would be if all tourists had done the same. It would not take long for such effects to become highly noticeable.

In many such cases the question relates to the discussion of human domination of the world. Should not all the planet's species have the opportunity to live in an untrammeled, unencumbered, natural state? Most people are concerned about issues like the disappearance of species, but not necessarily at the expense of other, more pressing matters such as population and pollution. Similarly, there are degrees of environmental ethics to which people submit. These range in philosophy from human-centred ethics, which advocate a stance whereby ethics are evaluated on the basis of how they affect humans; to ecological holism, where the biosphere and the major ecosystems of the planet are morally considerable. Plants, animals, rocks, etc. matter only inasmuch as they maintain the significant whole. Other intermediary ethics stance include animal-centred ethics, where individual members of a species are the focus; life-ethics, where all living things are valued (but not necessarily equally); and ethics which imply that all living and non-living things have intrinsic value, those with preservationist viewpoint adhere to more of a biocentric philosophy through the practice of little intervention, placing high value on natural resources, responsible use, and very small numbers of tourists.

Words and Expressions

biosphere	['baɪousfɪr]	n.	生物圈；生物界；生物层
prostitution	[ˌprɒstɪ'tuːʃn]	n.	才能的滥用；出卖灵魂
dislocation	[ˌdɪslə'keɪʃn]	n.	错位；混乱；紊乱
accrue	[ə'kru]	v.	增加；产生；获得
myriad	['mɪrɪəd]	a.	无数的；各式各样的
jaguar	['dʒæɡˌwɑr]	n.	（中、南美洲的）美洲虎
monolith	['mɑnəlɪθ]	n.	独块巨石，整体塑制品
untrammeled	[ʌn'træmld]	a.	自由自在的，无阻碍的
unencumbered	[ˌʌnɪn'kʌmbərd]	a.	没有阻碍的；无负担的
stance	[stæns]	n.	态度，立场
holism	['houlɪzəm]	n.	整体论
intrinsic	[ɪn'trɪnzɪk, -sɪk]	a.	固有的，内在的；本质的

Unit 11 Ecotourism

PART II DIALOGUE

Dialogue 1 Maintenance Service

A: Attendant of Service Center; B: Guest

A: Housekeeping. May I help you?

B: Yes. There are a lot of problems in Room 1512. Can you get someone up here?

A: What's wrong?

B: First, the air conditioner doesn't work. The room is very hot. Second, there is something wrong with the tap. It won't stop running. It's flooding the bathroom. Also, there is neither soap nor towels.

A: I am terribly sorry about it, sir. We'll send a repairman there immediately.

B: When he comes, would you tell him to bring a new bulb at the same time? The floor lamp just went out. What's more, the bath foam is also used up and the pillow cases are dirty.

A: That's too bad. I'm terribly sorry for all the inconveniences. Would you like to change rooms, sir?

B: No, I like this room because I can enjoy a wonderful view here. By the way, I think my wife needs more hangers for our clothes.

B: No problem. How many do you think will be enough?

A: Ten to twelve will do.

B: All right. Someone will go to your room with them right away.

A: 客房服务。请问有什么可以帮您的吗?

B: 是的。1512房间里有很多问题,你能找人来一下吗?

A: 怎么了?

B: 首先,空调不工作,房间很热;然后,水龙头有点问题,关不上,水快把浴室淹没了。另外,既没有肥皂,也没有毛巾。

A: 我真的很抱歉,先生。我们将马上派一个修理工来。

B: 当他来的时候,你能告诉他带一个新灯泡吗?落地灯刚熄灭了。还有,沐浴露也用完了,枕头脏兮兮的。

A: 太糟糕了,我为给您带来的不便感到非常抱歉,先生,您要换房间吗?

B: 不,我喜欢这个房间,因为我可以在这里欣赏到美丽的景色。对了,我想我妻子需要更多的衣架挂我们的衣服。

A: 没问题。您需要多少?

B: 十到十二个吧。

A: 好吧。马上会有人带着衣架去您的房间。

Dialogue 2 Lodging a Complaint at a Hotel

O: Operator; G: Guest; A: Attendant

O: Housekeeping. May I help you?

旅游英语(修订版)

G: Yes. I sent a sweater to the laundry but it comes back badly shrunk.

O: We're very sorry, madam. I'll send someone immediately.

(Five minutes later.)

A: Housekeeping. May I come in?

G: Yes. Look at this sweater. It's ruined.

A: We're very sorry, madam. Could you buy a replacement here and give us the receipt? We will refund the cost of the laundry and the new sweater.

G: I'm afraid I won't have time to buy a new one!

A: Could you buy a replacement in your hometown and send us the receipt? We will send you a bank draft for the amount.

G: Sounds reasonable.

A: Could you fill out this form with your name and forwarding address?

G: OK. Here you are.

A: We are very sorry for the inconvenience.

O: 客房服务。请问有什么可以帮您的吗?

G: 是的。我有一件毛衣拿去洗,但是送回来后严重缩水。

O: 女士,非常抱歉。我立刻派人过去。

(5分钟后)

A: 客房服务。我可以进来吗?

G: 可以。看看这件毛衣。它被毁了。

A: 女士,非常抱歉。您再买一件,并把收据交给我们好吗?我们会退还洗衣费并赔偿新毛衣的费用。

G: 恐怕我没有时间去买新的!

A: 您可以回去以后再买一件,然后把收据寄给我们吗?我们会用银行汇票把钱付给您。

G: 听起来很合理。

A: 请在表格上填写您的名字和邮寄地址,好吗?

G: 好的。给您。

A: 很抱歉给您带来不便。

Word Service Station

| refund | 退款 | draft | 汇票 |
| stain | 玷污 | replacement | 替换 |

PART Ⅲ GOOD TO KNOW: Traditional Chinese Architecture

zigzag bridge	曲桥	couplet	对联
pailou	牌楼	firecracker	鞭炮
winter solstice	冬至	animal zodiac	生肖
kiosk/pavilion	亭	garret	阁楼,顶楼

porch	门廊	canopy	天篷，华盖
lounge	大厅	fence/paling/railings	栅栏
glazed tile	琉璃瓦	dougong brackets	斗拱
cross beam	横梁	atrium	中庭，天井前厅
mansion	宅邸	pagoda/stupa	塔
patio	天井	pavilion	榭

PART Ⅳ EXERCISES

Ⅰ. Listening comprehension.

Primal Scream and Halloween Costume Catwalk

Primal Scream is a tradition at Harvard University. At midnight on the last night of 1 _____ period and before final exams begin, students streak through the Old Yard. The streakers begin in the north end of the Yard and generally make one 2 _____ around, but the more adventurous sometimes aim for more. This is done both 3 _____, even during New England winters.

Some of the streakers will "dress up" in capes and 4 _____, or top hat, but they are still totally naked. The walkways through which students run are lined with spectators and the Harvard University Band plays beforehand to excite the 5 _____.

Before it became a "night when the whole student body comes together to gawk (呆呆地看着) at just that," it was a night with a closer association to its name. 6 _____ in the 1960s students would congregate in the Yard or just open their windows and yell for 10 minutes. It was designed as a way to release stress. By the 1990s, the streaking aspect of the evening had become prominent. The transition from yelling to streaking is unclear. Old administrators that have been at Harvard since the 1970s speak of an earlier day of adventurous streakers.

Before the streaking in the Yard, there was the Quad Howl—streaking in what used to be old Radcliffe. These administrators of the Quad houses speculate that the change from the Quad to the Yard, which happened during their time, was because the narrow pathways of the Quad could not 7 _____ the increasing multitudes of people with an 8 _____ to get naked in public. The natural choice was to go join those in the Yard, giving them something to get excited about.

While Primal Scream is a "naked" tradition, Costume Catwalk is a "dressed-up" tradition at Harvard. It's a Harvard tradition for a group of 9 _____ to be named to the First-Year Social Committee (FYSC). The FYSC will be responsible for planning special events throughout the year. Every year, FYSC will host the Costume Catwalk. Scores of students turn out in clever costumes. They cheer on their classmates in a costume contest, and do a little stuff-strutting themselves. Freshmen dress as everything from attention-hungry male prostitutes to desperately attention-hungry female strippers, and in between, some good, wholesome 10 _____ as well. Anyway, all are ready to compete for glory.

Ⅱ. Match the two columns.

1. 遵守   A. calligraphy strokes
2. 甲骨文   B. conform to
3. 篆书   C. shell script
4. 行书   D. seal style
5. 隶书   E. official style
6. 楷书   F. regular style
7. 笔画   G. running style
8. 草书   H. swift style

Ⅲ. Fill in the blanks with some, or any, all, both, or either, no, little, few, a little, the little, the few, a few, each, every, other, another.

1. _____ man at the door is asking to see you.
2. _____ big tin container will do.
3. I'll go to _____ restaurant but that one.
4. They must _____ be answered.
5. There is a staircase at _____ end of the corridor.
6. He is blind in _____ eyes.
7. Not _____ water is suitable for drinking.
8. Unfortunately I was sitting at the table with smokers on _____ side of me.
9. _____ dogs in the restaurant.
10. The game wasn't very exciting, and _____ team played well.
11. I like _____ of that music.
12. _____ bicycles against this wall, by order.
13. The government has done _____ or nothing to help the poorest in this country.
14. He was a man of _____ words, but when he spoke it was worth listening to.
15. There was no one on the streets this early except for _____ lonely hurrying figures.
16. He gave two to _____.
17. The buses go _____ ten minutes.
18. Are there any _____ problems?
19. Would you like _____ cup of tea?
20. These shoes don't fit—have you got any _____?
21. Can I meet you _____ time?
22. There must be _____ other way of doing it.
23. There are five leaflets—please take one of _____.
24. She has _____ reason to be unhappy after losing her job and her home.
25. She is cleverer than _____ girls in her class.

IV. Reading comprehension.

The average consumer visits 3.6 sites when shopping for an airline ticket online, according to PhoCusWright, a Sherman, CT-based travel technology firm. Yahoo claims 76% of all online travel purchases are preceded by some sort of search function, according to Malcolmson, director of product development for Yahoo Travel. The 2004 Travel Consumer Survey published by Jupiter Research reported that "nearly two in five online travel consumers say they believe that no one site has the lowest rates or fares." Thus a niche has existed for aggregate travel search to find the lowest rates from multiple travel sites, obviating the need for consumers to cross-shop from site to site, with traveling searching occurring quite frequently.

Metasearch engines are so named as they conduct searches across multiple independent search engines. Metasearch engines often make use of "screen scraping" to get live availability of flights. Screen scraping is a way of crawling through the airline websites, getting content from those sites by extracting data from the same HTML feed used by consumers for browsing (rather than using a Semantic Web or database feed designed to be machine-readable). Metasearch engines usually process incoming data to eliminate duplicate entries, but may not expose "advanced search" options in the underlying databases (because not all databases support the same options).

Fare aggregators redirect the users to an airline, cruise, hotel, or car rental site or Online Travel Agent for the final purchase of a ticket. Aggregators' business models include getting feeds from major OTAs, then displaying to the users all of the results on one screen. The OTA then fulfills the ticket. Aggregators generate revenues through advertising and charging OTAs for referring clients. Examples of aggregate sites are Bravofly, Cheapflights, Priceline, Expedia, Reservations.com, Kayak.com, Momondo, LowEndTicket, FareBuzz and CheapOair. Kayak.com is unusual in linking to online travel agencies and hotel web sites alike, allowing the customer to choose whether to book directly on the hotel web site or through an online travel agency. Google Hotel Finder is an experiment that allows to find hotel prices with Google, however it does not offer to book hotels, merely to compare rates.

The difference between a "fare aggregator" and "metasearch engine" is unclear, though different terms may imply different levels of cooperation between the companies involved.

In 2008, Ryanair threatened to cancel all bookings made on Ryanair flights made through metasearch engines, but later allowed the sites to operate as long as they did not resell tickets or overload Ryanair's servers.

In 2015, Lufthansa Group (including Lufthansa, Austrian Airlines, Brussels Airlines and Swiss) announced adding surcharge for flights booked on other sites.

Questions:

1. Why do consumers visit different sites for shopping an airline ticket?
2. How do Metasearch engines do to find the lowest rates from travel sites?
3. Do fare aggregators earn money directly from the consumers?

V. Translate the following sentences into Chinese. They are underlined in the text.

1. Travelling to relatively undisturbed or uncontaminated nature areas with the specific objective of studying, admiring, and enjoying the scenery and its wild plants and animals, as well as any existing cultural manifestations (both past and present) found in these areas.

2. Canadian government operated the "ecotours" during the mid-1970s which centred around the Trans-Canada Highway and were developed on basis of different ecological zones found along the course of the highway, despite the lack of a focused look at low impact, sustainability, community development, and the moral philosophy labels that are attached to ecotourism in the 1990s.

3. Given the ambiguity associated with the historical origins of ecotourism, the purpose of the present study is to identify the key features, concepts, and principles of the term, especially the link between nature tourism or nature-oriented tourism and ecotourism, for the latter was often defined as a nature tourism in which the traveler is drawn to a destination because of his or her interest in one or more features of that destination's natural history.

4. If nature tourism could be defined as tourism focused principally resources such as relatively undisturbed parks and natural areas, wetlands, wildlife reserves, species, landscape, scenery and salt and fresh-water feature and other areas of protected flora, fauna, and habitats, it would narrowly refer to operators running nature-oriented tours, or broadly apply to tourism's use of natural resources including beaches and country landscapes.

5. The presence or absence of acceptable ethical behaviour in tourism setting is very much a function of how tourists, operators, and local people act and feel about each other and towards the resource base, so a balance must be struck between the various stakeholders of the tourism industry in ensuring that the goodwill of some stakeholders (e. g., tourists and local people) is not overridden by the misgivings of other stakeholder groups (e. g., government or industry).

VI. Discussion.

Your group is travelling to Perth in Western Australia and after being handed customs declaration forms to fill in on board the plane some of your group members have mistakenly ticked the box that says they have no food. After arriving their bags were X-rayed and several are found to be carrying food. There has been some confusion amongst your group as to what things they should declare as food. For example, the following items are included under the label of food and may not be allowed into Australia. Dried fruit, spices, herbs, honey, sugar, candy, sunflower seeds and chocolates of any kind. Travelers are regularly caught and fined between 200 and 400 dollars for not declaring that they were carrying food.

What will you do to ensure that your group understand these requirements clearly?

Unit 12 Tourism Culture

PART I TEXT

Text A What Is Religion?

Originating from almost every corner of the globe, the world's religions are as diverse as its cultures. This makes religion difficult to define, especially as it deals with intangible concepts: God, the purpose of life, the afterlife, and so on. Nevertheless there are several threads common to all faiths the world over that make religion what it is.

Virtually every culture that we know of has some kind of religion. In fact, worship of God or the gods is so common that archaeologists, when they come upon some ancient objects or structure that they do not understand, they usually ascribe to it ritual or religious purposes. Not only is religion almost universal, it has also had a huge impact on human culture. For example, many of the world's greatest buildings, from medieval cathedrals to Mayan temples, are religious. And a great deal of literature, from Dante's *Divine Comedy* to the works of the great Sufi poet Rumi[1], not to mention the sacred scriptures of the world's great faiths, is religious in inspiration.

Enduring Relevance

Religion, because it deals with the big issues in life—good and evil, first causes and last things—is important to people. Believers cling to their faith and prepared to die for it. In cultures where the state has tried to wipe out religion or to discourage it, people carried on worshipping, even if they risked falling foul of a ruthless state. Even today, when, for many, science offers a more rigorous and hopeful set of answers to life's problems, people persist in their faith. Many of the major religions, including Christianity in the developing world and Islam worldwide are expanding and winning more converts. Religion is playing as prominent a role in life today as it has ever done.

Religious Diversity

For centuries, people have looked at the phenomenon of faith and tried to answer the question "What is religion?" They have come up with a striking variety of answers. The 19th century English writer Matthew Arnold described religion as "morality touched with emotion." Around the same time, German theologian Friedrich Schleiermacher called it "a feeling of absolute dependence," while the English cardinal John Henry Newman found its essence in "authority and obedience." English anthropologist Sir James Frazer, who was most famous for his text on comparative religion, *The Golden Bough* (1890), spoke of it as a way to appease the powers that "control the course of nature or of human life." The 19th century German social and political theorist Karl Marx was suspicious of religions, called it "the opium of the people," but he also saw something positive in it when he called it "the heart of the heartless world."

In many cultures, the essence of religion is the relationship between humanity and one or more gods. But not all of the belief systems that we call religions have gods. Many Buddhists do not worship a deity, and Jainism (an important and influential Indian religion) does not have a God. Another common thread in much religion is morality: teaching people to be good. But some religions, such as that of the Ancient Greeks, are centered on amoral deities, and other faiths, such as many primal religions, place more emphasis on honoring the gods in the right way than on living a moral life. Most religions have authority figures or ritual leaders who provide guidance and instruction. But some groups, including certain Protestant Christians such as the Quakers, reject the idea of the priesthood and insist that all believers can have access to the divine.

On close inspection, though, the world's religions are sometimes less dissimilar than they at first seem. There appears to be a sharp division between the monotheistic faiths (Christianity, Islam, and Judaism especially) and those, like Hinduism, that recognize many gods. But Hindus see their multitude of gods as aspects of one supreme reality, and even the Chinese have a supreme deity, the Jade Emperor or ruler of Heaven. Even so, it is difficult to generalize about belief systems. To understand why, we need only compare Shinto, with its countless spirits or Kami, and Judaism, with its one God; or Islam, with its proscription of images of God, and Hinduism, with its use of deity images for worship.

The Common Themes

Rather than settle on one phrase that tries to sum up all religions, students of religion today try for a more broadly descriptive approach. They speak of religions as belief systems that display seven or eight key features that are combined in each faith. The seven elements here are based on the key features listed by the British philosopher and theologian Ninian Smart in books such as *The Religious Experience of Mankind* (1969). The first feature is doctrine, a body of basic principles and teachings. The second, mythology, comprises the stories about the gods and the history of the religion. Next comes the concept of religious experience, the way in which humans can encounter the divine, often in heightened states of consciousness. The fourth feature is the religious institution, which can be a vast global organization such as the Catholic Church or a small but organized body such as a Buddhist monastery. The next feature is the ethical content of the religion—the set of practical instructions that tell followers how to live their lives—which covers both Matthew Arnold's emotional dimension to religion and broader guidance about the correct way to do things. The sixth feature is ritual, the gamut of ceremony from solemn sacrifice to the joyous outpouring of religious festivals. Finally comes the sacred objects and places: inanimate items, buildings, or natural settings that have some spiritual significance. Together, these seven features describe what is common to the varied religions of the world.

Big Questions

Through its various common elements, religion addresses some of humanity's biggest questions. These issues are big in the cosmic sense, encompassing the creation of the world, the meaning of life, the significance of suffering and pain, and the realm of the supernatural . They are also big in the sense that they affect everyone, dealing with behavior and ethics. The beliefs of followers of primal religions touch day-to-day life and survival-worshipping the gods may be said to help the crops grow, or lead to success in the hunt. Highly developed belief systems, with their scriptures and sophisticated theological arguments, may seem remote from these primal faiths, but they are not. Every faith looks to the absolute in the hope of making life better on Earth.

Religious Communities

All faiths are also, in one way or another, both individual and collective. The believer may pray or worship at home, or may take part in solitary meditation. For the Buddhist, solitary meditation may be the most important of all religious activities, and some Christians see private prayer as the activity that brings them closest to God. But there is usually also a coming together— in collective worship, religious instruction, or work for the community—which allows people to share their faith. Most religions offer regular opportunities for followers to join together and many pay special attention to the notion of the religious community. Terms such as "church" or "synagogue" refer as much to groups of worshippers as they do to the buildings in which they worship. Religious people acting collectively have often been a powerful force for good in the world, helping the sick and the needy, taking part in education, and providing community services that, even today, are not provided by governments in many parts of the world. The collective aspects of religion are particularly emphasized at key times in the year, such as major calendar festivals, or at key times of life—for example, at birth, coming of age, marriage, and, when the time comes, death.

The Spread Of Faiths

The faiths that have the most widespread influence began in various parts of Asia before spreading around the world. Western Asia, the Indian subcontinent, China, and Japan have all been fertile seed-grounds for major religions. Each of these areas has produced faiths with distinctive themes, from the emphasis on monotheism in western Asia to the development of the concept of Karma in India.

A number of different factors led to the foundation of the major world religions. One was the presence of a rich indigenous religious tradition that was able to develop beyond the tribe or area where it first evolved. Hinduism, for example, trace its roots back to concepts that evolved thousands of years ago in what is now Pakistan—for example, belief in a number of different gods, and practices centering on the use of water for ritual cleansing. Elaborated and combined with other Indian deities and ideas, these grew into the sophisticated belief system known today as Hinduism.

Roots In Antiquity

China also had an ancient polytheistic system that eventually influenced Daoism, Buddhism, and Chinese popular religion. And in Japan, Shinto had its roots in traditional beliefs in a multitude of spirits. Another early factor that allowed religions to develop was the emergence of religious leaders, prophets, and teachers who became revered as mouthpieces of the words of God or interpreters of sacred texts and ideas. The teachings of Jesus Christ or the words of God as revealed to the prophet Muhammad, inspired followers in western Asia and the Arabian peninsula.

The Written Word

A final factor was the growth of literacy, because once ideas and doctrines could be written down, a religion was no longer reliant on one group for leadership or teaching, but could spread as sacred texts were carried and distributed by travelers. The followers of the founding fathers of the world's religions soon began converting others in their own regions and beyond. Religious ideas could also be spread by missionaries, migrants, teachers, soldiers, or merchants. The spread of religious teachings was further encouraged by educational developments, by political conquests, and by the growth of global trade. All of these carried Christianity and Islam far beyond the place where they first took hold. Trade routes also helped to spread Buddhism. Other faiths, such as Judaism and Sikhism, have been spread not by missionary work, but by the often forced migrations of persecuted people. The process continues to this day. In our modern era of mass communication, the spread of religious ideas and the creation of networks of faith has a new impetus.

Words and Expressions

intangible	[ɪnˈtændʒəbəl]	a.	触不到的；难以理解的
virtually	[ˈvɜːtʃuəli]	adv.	实际上；无形中
ascribe	[əˈskraɪb]	v.	把……归因于；认为……是由于
medieval	[ˌmediˈiːvl]	a.	中古的，中世纪的
Mayan	[ˈmɑjən]	a.	玛雅人的，玛雅语的
Sufi	[ˈsuːfi]	n.	（伊斯兰）苏菲派信徒
relevance	[ˈreləvəns]	n.	相关性，关联；实用性
foul	[faʊl]	n.	犯规；缠结；碰撞
ruthless	[ˈruːθləs]	a.	残酷；无情的；残忍的
rigorous	[ˈrɪgərəs]	a.	严厉的；缜密的
striking	[ˈstraɪkɪŋ]	a.	显著的；引人注目的
morality	[məˈræləti]	n.	道德；道德准则
theologian	[ˌθiːəˈləʊdʒən]	n.	神学家，神学研究者
cardinal	[ˈkɑːdɪnl]	n.	基数；枢机主教
obedience	[əˈbɪdɪəns]	v.	遵守；顺从；（教会的）权威，管辖

anthropologist	[ˌænθrəˈpɒlədʒɪst]	n.	人类学家
appease	[əˈpiːz]	v.	安抚，抚慰；绥靖（满足另一国的要求以避免战争）
theorist	[ˈθɪərɪst]	n.	理论家；学说创立人；空论家
suspicious	[səˈspɪʃəs]	a.	可疑的，怀疑的
opium	[ˈəʊpiəm]	n.	鸦片；麻醉剂
humanity	[hjuːˈmænəti]	n.	人类；人文学科
deity	[ˈdeɪəti]	n.	神，女神；上帝
Jainism	[ˈdʒeɪnɪzəm]	n.	耆那教
amoral	[ˌeɪˈmɒrəl]	a.	无道德原则的
primal	[ˈpraɪml]	a.	主要的；原始的
priesthood	[ˈpriːsthʊd]	n.	祭司职；神职
dissimilar	[dɪˈsɪmələ]	a.	不同的，不相似的
monotheistic	[ˌmɒnəʊθɪˈɪstɪk]	a.	一神论的
multitude	[ˈmʌltɪtud]	n.	许多；大众，人群
proscription	[prəˈskrɪpʃən]	n.	禁止，剥夺权利
descriptive	[dɪˈskrɪptɪv]	a.	描述的；分类的
doctrine	[ˈdɑktrɪn]	n.	教条，教义
mythology	[mɪˈθɑlədʒi]	n.	神话学；神话（总称）
ethical	[ˈeθɪkl]	a.	伦理学的；道德的
gamut	[ˈgæmət]	n.	全范围，全部
inanimate	[ɪnˈænəmɪt]	a.	无生命的；无生气的
cosmic	[ˈkɑzmɪk]	a.	宇宙的；极广阔的
realm	[rɛlm]	n.	领域，范围；王国
solitary	[ˈsɑlətri]	a.	独自的；独立的
meditation	[ˌmedɪˈteɪʃn]	n.	默想；默念；沉思；冥想
collective	[kəˈlektɪv]	a.	集体的；共同的
Hinduism	[ˈhɪnduˌɪzəm]	n.	印度教
polytheistic	[ˌpɒlɪθɪˈɪstɪk]	a.	多神崇拜的
Shinto	[ˈʃɪntoʊ]	n.	（日本的）神道教
prophet	[ˈprɑfɪt]	n.	预言家；先知
literacy	[ˈlɪtərəsi]	n.	识字；精通文学
reliant	[rɪˈlaɪənt]	a.	依赖的；信任的
Sikhism	[ˈsɪkˌɪzəm]	n.	锡克教
impetus	[ˈɪmpɪtəs]	n.	动力；促进

Notes

（1）Rumi：古波斯著名诗人、神学家，全名是莫拉维·贾拉鲁丁·鲁米（Molana Jalaluddin Rumi），原名叫穆罕默德，贾拉鲁丁则是他的称号，意思是宗教圣人；鲁米出生于

1207年9月30日，1252年创立了莫拉维教派，也即西方所熟知的"旋转的苦修僧"（Whirling Dervishes），他的诗歌巨作——《玛斯那维》（*Mathnawi*），被誉为"波斯语的《古兰经》"。

Text B Films in Contemporary China

The history of film in China is almost as long as it in the West. China's film production began in 1890 with the filming of a stage play of a famous Beijing opera. In the 1920s to 1940s a lively film industry developed in Shanghai. After 1949, the film industry experienced steady growth, but the Cultural Revolution was a disastrous setback for the cinema.

In the 1980s a new group of filmmakers emerged, often referred to as the Fifth Generation, since they were graduates of the fifth class (1982) to come out of Beijing Film Academy. The Fifth Generation filmmakers have celebrated the human experience in all its particulars. Their films are distinguished by stunning visual effects and by story lines which take the viewer—even the foreign viewer-deep into the reality of daily existence. We see expanses of green millet fields, double takes of figures behind sheets of flame, aerial views of the sea stretching from a diminutive wharf past cliffs and craggy little islands into an unfathomable distance, and quiet, intimate glimpses of old stone houses in Beijing alleys. There is much to delight the eye and draw viewers into the lives of the people-sunsets, wine, fire, opera costumes; there are blazes of color everywhere, and then dim night and lurking violence. In scenes of cruelty and extreme misfortune, a sense of fatalistic inevitability is heightened by the sheer ordinariness of everyday Chinese speech, an aspect that tends to be lost in the English captions.

Beginning with *Yellow Earth* (1984), directed by Chen Kaige and filmed by Zhang Yimou, the Fifth Generation has produced a series of sumptuous films, many starring Zhang's then partner, Gong Li, combining a strong historical sense with high drama.

All the members of this new generation were deeply affected by the Cultural Revolution. Chen Kaige spent eight years doing farm work in Yunnan; Zhang Yimou worked as a laborer in a spinning mill, like the character in his film *Ju Dou*. They have set their films in the recent past, enabling the directors to confront social traumas that were too powerful to be treated directly. Crude and brutal scenes may allegorically evoke memories that are personal or political: in *Red Sorghum* a bully urinates into the wine vats to demonstrate his power and contempt, and on the other hand the depiction of ordinary life can be redemptive. In Wu Yigong's *My Memories of Old Beijing* there are water sellers wheeling up their barrows with buckets to get water at the street well, visually effective as a regular punctuation in the life of the neighborhood. The lead character, a little girl, goes through all the experiences of growing up without ever leaving the quiet alleys where she lives. Chen Kaige's *Farewell My Concubine* shows how the Cultural Revolution led friends into betraying one another.

In the 1990s, infected by a new fatalism stemming from the amorality of the economic boom, a Sixth Generation of filmmakers appeared. Their films are usually set in the immediate present, often against gritty, urban landscapes.

With the advent of reforms in 1978, China let go of old moorings and set off into the unknown. In the quarter century that has followed, the country has changed to a degree that is unprecedented and breathtaking. China is now hurtling down a road where there are at least hints of greater openness, more access to information, and opportunities for individual initiative, and she is becoming a respected participant in the global order. Economically, a rationalized commercial system is emerging that is gaining influence in the region and the world. An expending middle class of businesspeople and intellectuals, many trained abroad, is achieving material success and new status as part of an international professional elite. Better communications by road, rail, and air, reduce the chances that the mass famines that scarred China's past will ever return. Culturally, in the fields of literature, art, music, and film, Chinese are breaking down the barriers between the categories of "Chinese" and "western" in ways that no one could have predicted only two decades ago. There is a thriving creativity here, consistent with a great cultural heritage, which signals hope for China's future.

Words and Expressions

disastrous	[dɪˈzæstrəs]	a. 灾难性的
setback	[ˈsetˌbæk]	n. 挫折；阻碍；逆流
ideologically	[ˌaɪdɪrˈlɔdʒɪkli]	adv. 思想体系上；意识形态上
stun	[stʌn]	v. 使目瞪口呆；使昏迷
diminutive	[dɪˈmɪnjətɪv]	a. 小的，小型的
wharf	[wɔrf]	n. 码头，停泊处
craggy	[ˈkrægi]	a. 陡峭的，崎岖的
unfathomable	[ʌnˈfæðəməbl]	a. 深不可测的
alley	[ˈæli]	n. 胡同，小巷
cruelty	[ˈkruəlti]	n. 残忍；残忍的行为
inevitability	[ɪnˌevɪtəˈbɪləti]	n. 必然性；不可避免性
sheer	[ʃɪr]	v. 完全的；全然的；绝对的
caption	[ˈkæpʃn]	n. 标题；说明文字；字幕
sumptuous	[ˈsʌmptʃuəs]	a. 豪华的；美轮美奂
veil	[vel]	v. 掩饰；用帷幕分隔；隐匿
rage	[reɪdʒ]	n. 愤怒；猛烈；渴望
spin	[spɪn]	v. (使)快速旋转；纺(线)
confront	[kənˈfrʌnt]	v. 面对；碰到
trauma	[ˈtraʊmə]	n. (心理或精神)创伤
allegorically	[ˌæləˈgɔrɪkli]	adv. 寓言地；比喻地
bully	[ˈbʊli]	n. 仗势欺人者，横行霸道者
urinate	[ˈjʊrəneɪt]	v. 排尿，撒尿
vat	[væt]	n. (酿造、制革等用的)大桶，大缸
contempt	[kənˈtempt]	n. 轻视；轻蔑
depiction	[dɪˈpɪkʃn]	n. 描写；叙述

redemptive	[ri'demptiv]	a.	赎回的，挽回的；用于补偿的
barrow	['bærou]	n.	独轮车；双轮手推车
punctuation	[ˌpʌŋktʃu'eiʃn]	n.	标点法；标点符号
fatalism	['fetlizəm]	n.	宿命论；天数
stem	[stem]	n.	干，茎；v. 起源于
amorality	[ˌeimə'ræləti]	n.	超道德，非道德
gritty	['ɡriti]	a.	含砂的；逼真的，活生生的
advent	['ædvent]	n.	出现；到来
unprecedented	[ʌn'presiˌdentid]	a.	前所未有的，无前例的

PART Ⅱ   DIALOGUE

Dialogue 1   Booking a Table

O: Operator; G: Guest

O: Good morning, Banquet Reservations. What can I do for you?

G: Yes, I'd like to book a banquet in a private room at 6:00 p.m. the day after tomorrow.

O: Would you like Chinese, Western, Japanese or Korean cuisine?

G: Chinese food, please.

O: For how many people?

G: Let me see. 12 people.

O: Yes, sir, 12 persons. How much for food per person? The minimum charge for a private room is 100 yuan per person.

G: 150 yuan per person.

O: 150 yuan. And what drinks are you going to have?

G: Just get ready some Hennessy XO. We're going to order other drinks at the dinner time. All the drinks are on consumption basis?

O: Yes, sir. May I have your name, please?

G: James, John James.

O: How do you spell it?

G: J-O-H-N, J-A-M-E-S.

O: J-O-H-N, J-A-M-E-S. Yes, and your telephone number?

G: 6605-3818. By the way, could you fax the menu with the name of the banquet room? My fax number is 6605-3819.

O: Yes, 6605-3819. We'll be sure to fax you the menu with the name of the banquet room. Is there anything else I can do for you, Mr. James?

G: No. Thanks.

O: So, allow me to confirm the reservation: The reservation is made by Mr. James, a Chinese banquet for 12 people at 6:00 p.m. the day after tomorrow evening. The price is 150 yuan per person excluding drinks. We'll prepare Hennessey XO.

G：That's fine. Thank you.

O：My pleasure. We look forward to seeing you soon, Mr. James.

O：早上好。这是宴席预订部。需要我为您效劳吗？

G：是的。我想预订后天晚上 6 点的一个包间。

O：饭菜需要中式、西式、日式还是韩式？

G：来中餐吧。

O：有多少人？

G：我想一下，12 个人。

O：12 个人，明白了。那么每个人用餐的价位是多少？我们包间的每人最低消费是 100 元。

G：我们要的是每人 150 元的价位。

O：150 元。那么您需要什么样的酒水？

G：现在就定轩尼诗 XO 吧。至于其他饮品，到吃饭的时候再说吧。所有这些酒水也算消费吧？

O：是的，先生。请问您贵姓？

G：詹姆斯，约翰·詹姆斯。

O：请问怎么拼写？

G：J-O-H-N，J-A-M-E-S。

O：J-O-H-N，J-A-M-E-S。明白了，请问您的电话号码？

G：6605 3818。顺便问下，能否帮我将宴会房间名字和菜单一起传真过来？我的传真号码是 6605 3819。

O：明白，是 6605 3819。我们会将宴会房间名字和菜单一起传真过去的。詹姆斯先生，还需要我为您做点什么吗？

G：不用了，谢谢。

O：那么请允许我确认一下您的预订：您是詹姆斯先生，预订了一个包间，宴会是中餐，12 个人，时间是后天晚上 6 点，价位是每人 150 元，不包含饮品，我们会准备妥当轩尼诗 XO 的。

G：很好，谢谢你。

O：很荣幸。我们期待着早点见到您，詹姆斯先生。

Word Service Station

peak	高峰期	banquet	宴会
excluding	不包括	cuisine	菜肴
minimum	最低的	consumption	消费

Dialogue 2　Having Western Food

S：Susan；L：Lily

S：I'm sorry to have Western food with Tom tomorrow night, and I'm pretty worried.

旅游英语(修订版)

L：Why?

S：I'm not sure of my etiquette at the dinner table.

L：Well, just imitate your hosts and remember not to make any noise. Especially with soup, coffee, water, and other liquids.

S：Of course, I know that. But I'm afraid I'll drop a spoon or fork on the floor or something.

L：Don't worry about that. If you do, just pick it up.

S：Is there anything else I should be careful of?

L：Yes. Don't pick your teeth.

S：I see. Thank you.

L：You are welcome.

S：明天晚上要和汤姆去吃西餐，我有些担心。

L：为什么？

S：我对餐桌上的礼仪不够了解。

L：嗯，只要模仿主人并记住吃饭时不要有响声，特别是喝汤、咖啡、水和其他流质饮料时。

S：当然，我知道那些，但我怕万一掉一只汤匙或叉子在地上或出现其他的事情。

L：不用担心，如果万一你掉了东西，捡起来就行了。

S：还有没有其他我应该注意的事？

L：还有就是不要剔牙。

S：我知道了。谢谢。

L：不用客气。

Word Service Station

etiquette	礼仪，礼节	imitate	模仿
liquid	液体	pick teeth	剔牙
cocktail	鸡尾酒	appetite	胃口，食欲
à la carte	照菜单点	steak	牛排
impolite	无礼的，粗鲁的	pretty	相当的
tasty	美味的，可口的	butter	黄油
chop	排骨		

PART Ⅲ　GOOD TO KNOW：Sports Items

Aquatic Sports

swimming	游泳	freestyle	自由泳
backstroke	仰泳	breaststroke	蛙泳
butterfly	蝶泳	water polo	水球
diving	跳水	synchronized swimming	花样游泳

Track and Field Athletics

track	赛道	jumping	跳跃
high jump	跳高	long jump	跳远
triple jump	三级跳远	throwing	投掷
shot put	推铅球	discus	掷铁饼
javelin	标枪	marathon	马拉松

Ball Game

badminton	羽毛球	baseball	棒球
basketball	篮球	football	足球
handball	手球	hockey/field hockey	曲棍球
softball	垒球	table tennis	乒乓球
tennis	网球	volleyball	排球

Cycle Racing

road cycling	公路自行车赛	track cycling	场地自行车赛
mountain cycling	山地自行车赛		

Mountaining

BC (base camp)	大本营	ABC (Attack Base Camp)	前进营地
C1 (camp one)	1号营地	AC (Attack Camp)	突击营地
hidden crevasse	暗裂缝	plateau	平台
gully	岩沟	crevasse	明裂缝
icerack	冰塔	ice fall	冰瀑布
couloir	雪沟	pinnacle	尖峰
knife ridge	刃状山脊	col	山坳部
hanging glacier	悬冰川	snow face/wall	雪壁
ice face/wall	冰壁	traverse	横切
avalanche	雪崩	cornice	雪檐
glacier	冰川	ice field	冰原
ice tongue	冰舌	moraine	冰碛
cooking equipment	炊具	lighter	打火机
gas lamp	煤气灯	gas range	煤气炉
cotton glove	棉手套	climbing shoes	攀岩鞋

Golf

approach shot	轻击球，打近球	arc	飞行弧线
attest	证明，成绩	average golfer	一般水平选手
baby golf	小型高尔夫球赛	back spin	下旋球
back tee	发球区	pin	旗杆
baffy 5	5号球杆	balance point	（球杆）平衡点
ball mark	球迹	bang	撞击
bent grass	常绿草	Bermuda grass	百慕大草

birdie	小鸟球，三击入穴	bottle golf	儿童高尔夫球
carried honor	优先开球权	close stance	预备姿势
club house	会馆	grass bunker	绿草洼地
course	高尔夫球场	cup up	打高球
cup	球穴，球洞	fluff	击球失误
ladies' tee	女用球座	follow wind	顺风
gloves	手套	shot	击球
golf dom	高尔夫球界	golf links	高尔夫球场

Playground

stadium	体育馆	football field	足球场
Yoga gym	瑜伽馆	basketball court/gym	篮球馆
track and field ground	赛车场	golf course	高尔夫球场
archery range	射箭场	gymnasium	体操馆
bowling alley	保龄球场	billiard hall	台球室

PART Ⅳ EXERCISES

Ⅰ. Listening comprehension.

Business-Office Communication—The Slack Generation

How could workplace messaging replace other missives?

STEWART BUTTERFIELD, the boss of Slack, a messaging company, has been wonderfully unlucky in certain ventures. In 2002 he and a band of colleagues created an 1 _____ called Game Neverending. It never took off, but the tools they used to design it turned into Flickr, the web's first popular 2 _____ website. Yahoo bought it in 2005 for a reported 3 _____ dollars. Four years later Mr. Butterfield tried to create another online game, called Glitch. It flopped as well.

But Mr. Butterfield and his team developed an internal messaging system to 4 _____ on it, which became the basis for Slack.

In Silicon Valley, such a change in strategy is called a pivot; anywhere else it is called good fortune. Today Slack is one of the fastest-rising startups around, with 540 million dollars in funding and a valuation of around 5 _____ dollars. "I guess the lesson should be, pursue your dream and 6 _____ so you can do something else," says Cal Henderson, Slack's chief technology officer.

It is rare for business software to arouse emotion besides annoyance. But some positively gush about how Slack has simplified 7 _____. Instead of individual e-mails arriving in a central inbox and requiring attention, Slack structures 8 _____ within threads (called channels) where groups within firms can update each other in real time. It is casual and reflects how people actually communicate, eschewing e-mail's outdated formalities, says Chris Becherer of Pandora, an 9 _____ firm that uses Slack. Its other 10 _____ is efficiency.

Ⅱ. Put the following into Chinese.

1. customs luggage declaration _____
2. unaccompanied baggage _____
3. luggage check-in counter _____
4. parking area _____
5. transfer passenger _____
6. airport inquiries _____
7. tour leader _____
8. time difference _____
9. non-smoking _____
10. reception program _____

Ⅲ. Fill in the blanks with the proper forms of the given words.

1. I _____ (declare) the meeting open.
2. Harper _____ (pass) the ball to Jennings; Jennings _____ (shoot). (解说词)
3. I bet it _____ (rain) tomorrow.
4. Will you go to help me when the task _____ (be) given?
5. If it _____ (be) fine tomorrow, we will go to the country side.
6. Alice _____ (tell) me you are entering college next year.
7. —Did you want me?
   —Yes, I _____ (wonder) if you could give me some help.
8. Suppose they _____ (not believe) it, how should we convince them?
9. Jane is _____ (study) law while her sister is doing physics.
10. She is always _____ (borrow) money and _____ (forget) to pay me back.
11. —You don't believe it?
    —I _____ (tell) the truth.
12. I _____ (hope) you will give us some advice.
13. Patience _____ (wear) out stones.
14. Facts _____ (speak) louder than words.
15. Water _____ (not exist) on the moon.
16. It is the first time I _____ (be) here.
17. It was the first time she _____ (be) at a summer school.
18. She told me that she _____ (come) to see me when she _____ (visit) China again.

Ⅳ. Reading comprehension.

As is the case in many cultures, the degree to which a minority group was seen as different from the characteristics of the dominant majority determined the extent of that group's acceptance. Immigrants who were like the earlier settlers were accepted. The large numbers of immigrants with significantly different characteristics tended to be viewed as a threat to basic American values and the American way of life.

This was particularly true of the immigrants who arrived by the millions during the late nineteenth and early twentieth centuries. Most of them came from poverty-stricken nations of southern and eastern Europe. They spoke languages other than English, and large numbers of them were Catholics or Jews.

Americans at the time were very fearful of this new flood of immigrants. They were afraid that these people were so accustomed to lives of poverty and dependence that they would not understand such basic American values as freedom, self-reliance and competition. There were so many new immigrants that they might even change the basic values of the nation in undesirable ways.

Americans tried to meet what they saw as a threat to their values by offering English instruction for the new immigrants and citizenship classes to teach them basic American beliefs. The immigrants, however, often felt that their American teachers disapproved of the traditions of their homeland. Moreover, learning about American values gave them little help in meeting their most important needs such as employment, food, and a place to live.

Far more helpful to the new immigrants were the "political bosses" of the larger cities of the northeastern United States, where most of the immigrants first arrived. Those bosses saw to many of the practical needs of the immigrants and were more accepting of the different homeland traditions. In exchange for their help, the political bosses expected the immigrants to keep them in power by voting for them in elections.

In spite of this, many scholars believe that the political bosses performed an important function in the late nineteenth and early twentieth centuries. They helped to assimilate large numbers of disadvantaged white immigrants into the larger American culture. The fact that the United States had a rapidly expanding economy at the turn of the century made it possible for these new immigrants, often with the help of the bosses, to better their standard of living in the United States. As a result of these new opportunities and new rewards, immigrants came to accept most of the values of the larger American culture and were in turn accepted by the great majority of Americans. For white ethnic groups, therefore, it is generally true that their feeling of being a part of the larger culture, which is "American" is much stronger than their feeling of belonging to a separate ethnic group – Irish, Italian, Polish, etc.

1. A minority group's acceptance to the country was determined by _____.
A. the difference they showed from the majority
B. the time when they arrived at the new land
C. the background conditions they came from
D. the religious group to which they belonged

2. The immigrants' flooding in was considered a threat to American value mainly because they _____.

A. came from poverty-stricken nations of southern and eastern Europe
B. had been accustomed to poverty and dependence
C. had different homeland traditions and other particular characteristics
D. did not speak English

3. "citizenship classes" (Para. 4) were offered because Americans _____.
A. wanted to help the immigrants to solve their practical needs
B. would not accept any groups with different traditions
C. wanted the immigrants to deal with the threat to the American values
D. wanted the immigrants to learn about and to keep the American values

4. The political bosses helped the new immigrants for the main purpose of _____.
A. showing off their political powers and advantages
B. getting support in elections
C. assimilating the minority into the majority
D. showing their generosity

5. The living standards of the new immigrants were improved in the late nineteenth and early twentieth centuries mainly because _____.
A. they kept the political bosses in power
B. the political bosses gave them a lot of practical help
C. they had a much stronger feeling of being a part of the larger culture
D. there was a rapid growth in American economy at that time

V. Translate the following sentences into Chinese. They are underlined in the texts.

1. In cultures where the state has tried to wipe out religion or to discourage it, people carried on worshipping, even if they risked falling foul of a ruthless state.

2. The 19th century English writer Matthew Arnold described religion as "morality touched with emotion." Around the same time, German theologian Friedrich Schleiermacher called it "a feeling of absolute dependence," while the English cardinal John Henry Newman found its essence in "authority and obedience." English anthropologist Sir James Frazer, who was most famous for his text on comparative religion, *The Golden Bough* (1890), spoke of it as a way to appease the powers that "control the course of nature or of human life." The 19th century German social and political theorist Karl Marx was suspicious of religious, called it "the opium of the people," but he also saw something positive in it when he called it "the heart of the heartless world."

3. Terms such as "church" or "synagogue" refer as much to groups of worshippers as they do to the buildings in which they worship.

4. Another early factor that allowed religions to develop was the emergence of religious leaders, prophets, and teachers who became revered as mouthpieces of the words of God or interpreters of sacred texts and ideas.

VI. Writing.

How to Establish a Healthy Living Style?

1. 越来越多的人开始崇尚简单、健康的生活方式；
2. 造成现在这种现象的原因；
3. 我们可以……

Activity 6: Museum Visitors' Survey

Aim:

Based on team work, each student team is required to **RE-DESIGN** the questionnaire according to the museum at which the team would intend to do the survey, then collect at least 10 questionnaires; afterwards each team is supposed to spend 10-15 minutes sharing their findings based on the statistics of the survey.

Notes: **RE-DESIGN**ing the questionnaire is not just change the name of the museum, almost every item needs deliberating.

Agenda:

- Total time – 20 minutes/each group on class.
- For each group, do the on-site survey before the class presentation.
- Based on the results of the collected questionnaires, each group should work out a report concerning the analysis of the questionnaires and suggestions to the museum/gallery, then to share their findings through the class presentation, the presentation would last 10-15 minutes. The teacher would host the meeting and give comments on the performance of each group.
- Suggested teaching arrangement: 2 class hours.

The questionnaire is as shown in the next 4 pages and needs re-designing.

Museum Visitors' Survey

1. First of all, are you an xxx Museum member? At what level of membership do you currently belong?

    a. Not an xxx Museum member
    b. Student membership
    c. Individual membership
    d. Dual membership
    e. Family membership
    f. Fellow membership
    g. Supporting membership
    h. Sustaining membership
    i. Patron membership
    j. Benefactor membership

2. Are you a member of any other museums or cultural institutions?

   a. Not a member of other museums or cultural institutions

   b. Local art museum where you live

   c. Local natural history museum where you live

   d. Local conservatory or botanical gardens where you live

   e. Local public library where you live

   f. Other：

3. Frequency：

How often do you visit xxx Museum?

   a. Visit xxx Museum several times a year

   b. Visit xxx Museum a few times a year

   c. Visit xxx Museum about once a year

   d. Visited xxx Museum several times over the years

   e. Visited xxx Museum once or twice before

   f. This was my first visit to xxx Museum

4. Which art museums do you visit?

   a. Local art museum where you live

   b. Local conservatory or botanical gardens where you live

   c. Local natural history museum where you live

   d. Local history museum where you live

   e. Other：

5. Frequency of Gallery：

How often do you visit art galleries on an annual basis?

   a. Several times a month

   b. About once a month

   c. Several times a year

   d. Once or twice a year

   e. Almost never

6. Economic Impact 1：

How has the current economic situation affected your spending on various personal activities?

   a. Spending less money attending museums

   b. Spending less money attending theatre performances

   c. Spending less money attending musical concerts

   d. Spending less money attending movies

   e. Spending less money attending sporting events

   f. Spending less money attending charitable functions

   g. Spending less money on vacations

   h. Spending on these personal activities not impacted by current economic situation

7. Economic Impact 2：

Museum Visitors' Survey — Activity 6

And how has the current economic situation affected how frequently you do the following personal activities?

Check any that apply.

    a. Attending museums less frequently

    b. Attending theatre performances less frequently

    c. Attending musical concerts less frequently

    d. Attending movies less frequently

    e. Attending sporting events less frequently

    f. Attending charitable functions less frequently

    g. Going on vacations less frequently

    h. My frequency of doing these personal activities has not been impacted by current economic situation

8. Did you make your recent visit...

    a. Alone

    b. With spouse or significant other

    c. With adult friend (s) or family

    d. With your own children under age 18

    e. With friend (s) or family under age 18

    f. As part of a tour group

9. How much time did you spend at xxx Museum during your recent visit?

Choose one of the following answers.

    a. One day, 1-2 hours total

    b. One day, 3-4 hours total

    c. One day, 5 + hours total

    d. Two or more days, 1-4 hours total

    e. Two or more days, 5-8 hours total

    f. Two or more days, 9 + hours total

10. What was the primary reason for your recent visit to xxx Museum?

Choose one of the following answers.

    a. General interest in the museum

    b. Special exhibitions

    c. Permanent collection

    d. Lecture, film, or special program

    e. Other

11. What sections of the museum did you visit during your recent visit to xxx Museum?

Check any that apply.

    a. General interest in the museum

    b. Special exhibitions

    c. Permanent collection

d. Lecture, film, or special program

f. Theaters

e. Cafe

f. Shop

g. Don't remember

12. Overall, how would you rate your recent visit to xxx Museum on a scale of 0–10, with 10 meaning you were extremely satisfied with your experience and zero meaning you were extremely dissatisfied?

0. 1. 2-Extremely dissatisfied 3456-Basically satisfied   8910-Extremely satisfied

13. In your own words, how would you describe ×××Museum to someone who is not familiar with the Museum?

14. Was your decision to recently visit ×××Museum influenced at all by an advertisement or an article that you read?

Check any that apply.

a. Newspaper advertisement

b. Magazine advertisement

c. Radio advertisement

d. Online advertisement

e. Newspaper article

f. Magazine article

g. Online article

h. Blog posting

i. Advertisement on the subway

j. Decision to visit not influenced by advertisement or article

k. Other: recent ×××Museum visit

15. Attributes:

Thinking about ×××Museum and your recent experience at the Museum, please tell us whether, in your opinion, each of the following words or phrases describes ×××Museum very well, well, not very well, or not at all...

	very well	well	not very well	not at all	don't know
Represents Chinese history					
Met my expectations					
Comprehensive					
Friendly and helpful staff and volunteers					
Easy to navigate					
Worth the price of admission					
Open and collaborative					
Inspiring					
Educational and informative					

Museum Visitors' Survey —— Activity 6

16. After visiting the Museum, are you now interested in any of the following activities or actions?

Check any that apply.
   a. Return to the Museum again for future visits
   b. Visit the xxx Museum website to learn more about exhibitions or modern art
   c. Become a member of ×××Museum
   d. Receive a regular newsletter from ×××Museum
   e. Attend other events at the Museum
   f. Read xxx Museum publications
   g. Not interested in any further activities related to ×××Museum
   h. Other?

17. Next, we would like you to rate various aspects of the Museum experience at xxx Museum. For each, please rate your own experience during your recent visit to ×××Museum on a scale of 0-10, with 10 meaning you were extremely satisfied with your experience and zero meaning you were extremely dissatisfied. You can use any number from zero to ten, the higher the number the more satisfied you were with this aspect of your recent visit to ×××Museum. If you did not utilize this service or resource, please indicate whether you knew about it and chose not to use it, or you did not know it was available.

	0-Not at all useful	1	2	3	4	5	6	7	8	9	10-Extremely useful	Did not use if, but knew about if	I didn't know this was available
Audio guide													
An xxx Museum floor plan or map													
Information kiosks													
Volunteer desks													
Museum staff and security guards													

18. ×××Museum currently opens each day at 8:30 a.m. and closes at 5:30 p.m., except on Fridays and on one Monday per month when it remains open later in the evening. xxx Museum is now considering opening earlier in the morning or remaining open later in the evening in order to accommodate visitors who wish to visit the museum in the morning or at night. Would you be more likely to visit ×××Museum if it opened earlier in the morning or if it remained open later in the evening?

Choose one of the following answers.
   a. Morning, before 10:30 a.m.
   b. Evening, after 5:30 p.m.

c. I would not be more likely to visit during these extended hours

19. Which of the following steps could ×××Museum take that would cause you to visit the Museum more frequently than you currently visit?

Check any that apply.

a. Discounted admission price for return visitors

b. Special access to local artists and their exhibitions

c. Ability to bring a guest to the Museum at a reduced admission price

d. More contemporary exhibitions

e. More modern classic exhibitions

f. More exchange exhibitions

g. Special video exhibitions

h. Performance related exhibitions

i. Unlikely to visit ×××Museum more frequently

j. Other?

20. Which of the following personal interests do you participate in or follow on a regular basis?

Check any that apply.

a. Antiques

b. Astronomy

c. Automobiles

d. Aviation

e. Baking / cooking

f. Books

g. Camping

h. Card games

i. Computer or video games

j. Cycling

k. Dance

l. Drama / theater

m. Fashion design

n. Film / cinema

o. Fishing

p. Gardening

q. Genealogy

r. Golf

s. Hiking / outdoor activities

t. History

u. Hunting

v. Interior design

w. Metal working

x. Motorcycles

y. Music-writing and/or playing

z. Painting

aa. Photography

bb. Poetry

cc. Running

dd. Sculpture

ee. Skiing

ff. Tennis

gg. Wine

hh. Wood working

ii. Writing

jj. Yoga

21. On average, how many hours per day do you spend online—that is, actively using the internet?

Choose one of the following answers.

a. Less than 1 hour per day

Museum Visitors' Survey — Activity 6

b. 1-2 hours per day

c. 2-3 hours per day

d. 3-4 hours per day

e. 4 or more hours per day

22. Finally, a few questions for statistical purposes. First, what is your gender?

a. Female

b. Male

23. What is the last year of schooling that you have completed?

Choose one of the following answers.

a. 1-11th grade

b. High school graduate

c. Non-college post H. S.

d. Some college/Associate's degree

e. College graduate-4 year College

f. Post-graduate school-Master's, JD, PhD, etc.

24. In what year were you born?

25. Are you married, single, separated, divorced, or widowed?

Choose one of the following answers.

a. Married

b. Domestic Partnership

c. Single

d. Separated

e. Divorced

f. Widowed

Unit 13　Tourism Impact

PART I　TEXT

Text A　Social Impacts of Tourism

One of the most persuasive socially oriented frameworks developed to analyse the impact that tourism has on local people and their environment is based on the evolving sentiment that local people express as tourism expands and occupies greater proportions of a local economy over time. There are essentially four main stages to consider in the assessment of local feeling toward the tourism industry. These include:

1. Euphoria. Tourists are welcomed, with little control or planning.

2. Apathy. Tourists are taken for granted, with the relationship between both group becoming more formal or commercialized. Planning is concerned mostly with the marketing of the tourism product.

3. Annoyance. As saturation in the industry is experienced, local people have misgivings about the place of tourism. Planners increase infrastructure rather than limit growth.

4. Antagonism. Irritations are openly displayed towards tourists and tourism. Planning is remedial, yet promotion is increased to offset the deteriorating reputation of the destination.

There are myriad examples of regions that have been subject to this form of cycle within tourism. As a case in point, Bermuda experienced visitor numbers of some ten times its local population in 1980 (some 600,000 people) in an area approximately 21 square miles in size. This type of tourist-to-local ratio is indicative of the conditions that have led to social conflict. Although such a proliferation of visitation no doubt has its economic rewards, what the host country gives up to attract tourism dollars cannot be measured simply in economic term. It is no accident that the most vital and creative parts of the Caribbean, for example, have been precisely those that have been most touched by tourism. The often-quoted claim of Evan Hyde, a Black Power leader in Belize in the early 1970s, that "Tourism is whorism" reflects the frequent claims that tourism leads to conflict between locals and hosts.

A notable impact of tourism on traditional values is the demonstration effect, where local patterns of consumption change to imitate those of the tourists, even though local people only get to see a side of tourists that is often not representative of their values displayed at home (e.g., spending patterns). Alien commodities are rarely desired prior to their introduction into host communities and, for most residents of destination areas in the developing world, such commodities remain tantalizingly beyond reach. The process of commercialization and commodification[1] may ultimately erode the local goodwill and authenticity of products, cultural expressions are bastardized in order to be more comprehensible and therefore saleable to mass tourism. As local folk art becomes dilute, local interest in it declines.

Such a fragmentation of culture has been found to occur on many levels within destinations, most notably from the standpoint of prostitution; crime; the erosion of language in favour of more international dialects; the erosion of traditions, either forgotten or modified for tourists; changes to local music and other art forms; food, in the form of a more international cuisine; architecture; dress; family relationships; and in some cases, religion. Some key points that may be used as indicators or determinants of social impact within a tourist region are as follows:

1. the number of tourists;
2. the type of tourists;
3. the stage of tourist development;
4. the differential in economic development between tourist-generating and tourist-receiving zones;
5. the difference in cultural norms between tourist-generating and tourist-receiving zones;
6. the physical size of the area, which affects the densities of the tourist population;
7. the extent to which tourism is serviced by an immigrant worker population;
8. the degree to which incoming tourists purchase properties;
9. the degree to which local people retain ownership of properties and tourist facilities;
10. the attitudes of governmental bodies;
11. the beliefs of host communities, and the strengths of those beliefs;
12. the degree of exposure to other forces of technological, social, and economic change;
13. the policies adopted with respect to tourist dispersal;
14. the marketing of the tourist destination and the images that are created of that destination;
15. the homogeneity of the host society;
16. the accessibility to the tourist destination;
17. the original strength of artistic and folkloric practices, and the nature of those traditions.

As tourism continues to diversify and exploit relatively untouched regions and culture, there is the danger that a similar cycle of events will occur. The lessons from the Caribbean model of tourism development, for example, are that the industry must tread lightly in securing an equitable relationship between how the industry is planned and developed and the needs of local people. The small-scale, local architecture, tourism zoning, gradual growth, reliance on locally produced goods, joint ventures, and a diversification in the market, are all indicative of the alternative tourism development paradigm to which tourism must subscribe.

Words and Expressions

persuasive	[pərˈsweɪsɪv]	a.	有说服力的
euphoria	[juˈfɔrɪə]	n.	精神欢快；幸福感

apathy	[ˈæpəθi]	n. 漠然；冷淡
saturation	[ˌsætʃəˈreɪʃən]	n. （达到）饱和状态；浸透
antagonism	[ænˈtæɡəˌnɪzəm]	n. 对立；敌意
remedial	[rɪˈmɪdɪəl]	a. 治疗的；补救的，挽回的
deteriorate	[dɪˈtɪrɪəreɪt]	v. 恶化
myriad	[ˈmɪrɪəd]	a. 无数的；n. 极大数量
indicative	[ɪnˈdɪkətɪv]	a. 象征的；指示的
proliferation	[prəˌlɪfəˈreɪʃn]	n. 增殖，分芽繁殖
whorism	[ˈhɔrɪzm]	n. 娼妓化
tantalizingly	[ˈtæntəlaɪzɪŋli]	a. ……得令人着急
commercialisation	[kəˌmɜʃəlaɪˈzeɪʃən]	n. 商业化
bastardize	[ˈbæstərdaɪz]	v. 腐败，败坏
dilute	[daɪˈlut]	v. 稀释，冲淡
differential	[ˌdɪfəˈrenʃl]	a. 差别的
dispersal	[dɪˈspɜrsl]	n. 散布；分散
homogeneity	[ˌhɑmədʒəˈnɪəti]	n. 同种，同质；一致性
paradigm	[ˈpærəˌdaɪm]	n. 范例，样式
subscribe	[səbˈskraɪb]	n. 认购；订阅

Notes

（1）commercialization and commodification，商业化和商品化。

Text B Ecological Impacts of Tourism

Tourism industry has the capability of either moderately altering or completely transforming destination regions in adverse ways, because except the economic benefits of tourism, there was also a tremendous negative impact, including pollution, crowding and congestion, fire, land use loss, damage/destruction of heritage, damage to soil and vegetation, loss of flora and fauna and increased urbanization. For example, <u>in 1967, the Balearic Islands and the Costa Brava in Spain observed some of the stress caused by a high concentration of tourism and discussed employing regional development strategies designed to promote other areas that were as yet undeveloped</u>; in 1971, Tanzania felt it the vital necessity for game conservation in the interests of ecology, tourism, game farming and ranching, and for moral, aesthetic, philosophical and other reasons both at national and international levels; also in the cities, the unregulated development of hotels in the 1970s in London threatened the quality of life. In one word, while tourism has transformed much of the world's natural beauty into gold, the industry may have planted the seeds of its own destruction.

Tourism's expansion might result in unavoidable effect on the resources upon which it relied. There was indeed a distinct difference between development for purposes of improvement and aesthetic appeal versus the vulgar, undesirable, and irreparable damage created by modern tourism, so sound planning, dispersion of tourists, are means by which to minimize the negative impacts.

A framework to analyze the environmental stress was developed as ecological carrying capacity, a concept of determining ecological disturbance from tourism use and can be loosely defined on the basis of the following four interrelated elements: (1) the amount of use of a given kind; (2) a particular environment can endure; (3) over time; (4) without degradation of its suitability for that use.

Such framework is based on recognizing the dangers inherent in accommodating an increasing number and diversity of experiences for a growing consumer-based society. The diversity of experiences is due to the broad range of different user groups (non-recreational and recreational including consumptive and non-consumptive) in a setting and their various needs. Over time, managers have begun to learn to ensure the safety of the resource base first, even over the needs and expectations of participants.

In the strictest ecological sense, species maintain a balance between birth and death, and predator-prey relationships within an ecosystem. It is the human factor and the manipulation and exploitation of resources that offset this balance. However, it was quickly discovered that the resource-oriented point of view must be augmented by consideration of human values.

This prompted a new sense to try to balance the importance of both environmental impacts and human activities. Environmental impacts can be objectively measured through an analysis of ecological conditions. Concern lies in understanding the type, amount, and rate of impact on the resource base through recreational use. A campsite, for example, may be severely impacted over time by accommodating high levels of use. Significant changes may occur to the ecology of the site as evident through the compaction of soil (e.g., exposing roots and increasing erosion), vegetation (e.g., using both dead and live tree limbs for the construction of fires, and trampling saplings), wildlife (e.g., habitat modification, and animal harassment), and water (e.g., the addition of human waste and chemical toxins to the aquatic environment). The heaviest impact to a campsite, however, occurs during the first couple of years of use, and impact subsides over time as the site becomes harder and harder.

There are three different states in tourism's relationship with environmental conservation: conflict, coexistence and symbiosis. The satisfaction of tourism requirements must not be prejudicial to the social and economic interests of the population in tourist areas, to the environment and above all to natural resources which are the fundamental attractions of tourism and historical and cultural sites. All tourism resources are part of the heritage of mankind.

Words and Expressions

adverse	[ˈædvɜrs]	a.	不利的；有害的；相反的
congestion	[kənˈdʒestʃən]	n.	拥挤，堵车；阻塞
aesthetic	[esˈθetɪk]	a.	美学的；审美的
vulgar	[ˈvʌlgɚ]	a.	庸俗的；粗俗的；一般大众的

irreparable	[ɪˈrepərəbl]	a.	不可弥补的；无可补救的
predator-prey	[ˈpredətɚpre]	a.	捕食者-猎物的
manipulation	[məˌnɪpjʊˈleɪʃn]	n.	操纵；控制
augment	[ɔgˈment]	v.	加强；增加；扩张；扩大
severely	[səˈvɪrli]	a.	严格地；严重地
compaction	[kəmˈpækʃn]	n.	压紧；压实
trample	[ˈtræmpl]	v.	踩；践踏；无视
sapling	[ˈsæplɪŋ]	n.	幼树，树苗
toxin	[ˈtɑksɪn]	n.	毒素
aquatic	[əˈkwætɪk]	a.	水上的；水生的
subside	[səbˈsaɪd]	v.	减弱，平息；退去
coexistence	[ˌkoʊɪgˈzɪstəns]	n.	共存
symbiosis	[ˌsɪmbaɪˈoʊsɪs]	n.	共生；互利关系
prejudicial	[ˌpredʒəˈdɪʃl]	a.	引起偏见的；有损害的

PART Ⅱ　DIALOGUE

Dialogue 1　Booking Tickets for Shows

A：Local Guide；B：Tour Leader

A：Hello, Mr. Liu. There is a musical on at the Opera House. Do your group members want to watch it?

B：Sure. Most of us would like to see a musical while we are here. What is on at the Opera House?

A：It's *Miss Saigon*. It's the most popular musical on right now. It's a tragedy actually. However, the music is so beautiful and the story is so sad that I have seen it three times so far. There is a popular saying, "you are not really visiting New York without seeing a musical at the Opera House".

B：How is the comment about the performance?

A：The leading actress is quite famous. Her performance is so popular that the tickets are usually sold out in three days.

B：How much does a ticket cost?

A：$100 dollars each. The performance starts at 7:30 and lasts about two hours.

B：When shall we plan to go?

A：Maybe the day after tomorrow.

B：Please reserve the tickets for us.

A：No problem.

B：What should we dress when we go to the musical, formally or casually?

A：Formally is preferable.

A：你好，刘先生。歌剧院有一个音乐剧，你们的成员想看吗？
B：当然，我们大多数人都想在这里去看一场音乐剧。演的是什么？
A：是《西贡小姐》。它是现在最流行的音乐剧，实际上这是一个悲剧。然而，音乐是如此的美丽，故事是如此的悲伤，到目前为止我已经看过三遍了。有一种流行的说法"没有去歌剧院看音乐剧，就是没有真正拜访纽约。"
B：表演的评价如何？
A：女主角很有名，她的表演很受欢迎，票通常在三天内就卖完了。
B：一张票多少钱？
A：100美元一张，演出7：30开始，持续约两个小时。
B：我们应该什么时候过去呢？
A：也许后天。
B：请帮我们订一下票。
A：没问题。
B：我们去看音乐剧时应该穿什么呢？正式还是随便的？
A：正式的更好。

Dialogue 2　In the Fitness Center

C：Clerk；G：Guest

C：Good afternoon, Madam. Can I help you?

G：Oh, yes. I want to do some exercises. Would you introduce your facilities to me?

C：My pleasure. Let me show you around. We have a well-equipped gymnasium with the latest recreational sports apparatus. As you can see, we have bar bells, dumb bells, race apparatus, rowing machines, stationary bikes, muscle builder sets, chest expanders and spring-grips.

G：So many! Are they safe?

C：No problem. They are made by the famous sports apparatus company.

G：Good. I wander how to use these machines.

C：Our coach will tell you how to use them and he will supervise all your exercises.

G：That's great.

C：Would you like to have a try, Madam?

G：OK. But my clothes are not suitable. Are there any other exercises?

C：Yes, we have Yoga lessons, Qigong lessons and Taiji lessons from 6：00 p. m. to 7：00 p. m. every afternoon.

G：Do you have any ball sports rooms?

C：Well, we have a ping-pong room on the third floor. We have a bowling center and a game center on the fourth floor.

G：Is there a swimming pool?

C：The swimming pool is on the second floor under ground. It's 25 meters long and 2 meters deep, with security men on the pool side.

G: Very good. Thank you for your introduction. I will go swimming first.
C: Have a good time.
C: 下午好，夫人，我能为您做什么？
G: 哦，是的。我想做些运动。你能给我介绍一下你们的健身器材吗？
C: 我很荣幸。我带您转转。我们有很棒的健身房和最先进的娱乐健身器材。正如您所看到的，我们有棒铃、哑铃、跑步机、划艇机、固定自行车、肌肉训练器械、扩胸器和弹力器。
G: 这么多！它们安全吗？
C: 没问题。它们是著名的运动器材公司制造的。
G: 不错。我想知道如何使用这些器材。
C: 我们的教练会告诉您如何使用器材，而且他会指导您进行练习。
G: 很棒。
C: 您想试一下吗，夫人？
G: 好的。但是我的衣服不合适。还有其他运动吗？
C: 是的。我们每天下午6点到7点有瑜伽课程、气功课程和太极课程。
G: 你们有没有球类运动室？
C: 是的，我们在三层有乒乓球室，四层有保龄球中心和游戏中心。
G: 有游泳池吗？
C: 游泳池在地下二层。它有25米长，两米深。有救生员在周围。
G: 非常好。谢谢你的介绍。我要先去游泳。
C: 祝您过得愉快！

Word Service Station

sit-up	仰卧起坐	hip hop	街舞
push-up	俯卧撑	jump rope	跳绳
exercise bike	健身车	aerobics	有氧运动
step aerobics	踏板操	treadmill	跑步机
calisthenics	柔软体操	fitness ball	健身球
jogging	慢跑		

PART Ⅲ   GOOD TO KNOW: Public Transportation

cord	（公交车）拉线	transfer	（公交车）转车车票
fare box	（公交车）投币箱	strap	（公交车）吊环
track	轨道	platform	月台
turnstile	十字转门	ticket booth	售票亭
commuter train	通勤车	fare	车费
meter	计价器	taxi stand	出租车泊位
streetcar	有轨电车	aerial tramway	高架电车道

| cable car | 电缆车 | monorail | 单轨火车 |

PART Ⅳ EXERCISES

Ⅰ. Listening comprehension.

United States—Environmental Policy—Reefer Madness

Turning oil rigs into reefs（珊瑚礁）saves money and marine life. Yet many greens oppose it. When an offshore well stops producing oil, what should be done with the rig（钻井平台）. One option is to haul it ashore, break it up and 1 _____ it. This is expensive. For a big, deep-water oil or gas platform, it can cost $200 million dollars. Just hiring a derrick barge massive enough to do the job can cost $700,000 dollars a day. But there is an 2 _____: simply leave most of the structure where it is.

That is what you would expect a greedy oil firm to do: 3 _____ the ocean just to save a lousy few million dollars. The surprise is, the cheap option may actually be 4 _____. For a start, it takes a lot of energy to move a rig. The ships that would be needed to shift California's largest one would emit 29,400 tons of carbon dioxide, by one estimate. And moving a rig disturbs the 5 _____ that have attached themselves to its underside, or jacket. Far better, some say, to turn old rigs into coral reefs.

6 _____ typically involves bringing a platform's above-water parts ashore and cropping the lower parts to leave at least 26 meters of clearance: deep enough for ships to 7 _____, yet shallow enough for photosynthesis to nourish organisms on its upper reaches. Oil-rig reefs may 8 _____ and feed up to eight tons of fish. In 2009, Shell moved a jacket in the Gulf of Mexico ten kilometers (six miles) away. The fish followed.

More than 9 _____ platforms in American waters have become reefs in the past three decades. The Bureau of Safety and Environmental Enforcement urges states to 10 _____ reefing permits.

Ⅱ. Put the following into English.

1. 观光旅行
2. 抵/离时间
3. 办手续
4. 合单结账
5. 储存贵重物品
6. 外币兑换
7. 问询部
8. 值班经理
9. 前台收银员
10. 兑换限额

III. Fill in the blanks with appropriate prepositions.

1. I've got to get up _____ six tomorrow.
2. She left _____ the night of Friday 13 June.
3. She got in _____ the side door.
4. He has been _____ the bank longer than anyone else.
5. He is blind _____ one eye.
6. I have always put quality _____ quantity.
7. A van was parked right _____ my car.
8. No one _____ Bill knew the way.
9. He saved up money _____ giving up smoking.
10. Write your exercise _____ ink, not _____ pencil.
11. She made the evening dress _____ hand.
12. I am speaking _____ your friend, not _____ your employer.
13. There was a bridge _____ the river.
14. Can you finish the work _____ tomorrow?
15. She says that she's leaving the country _____ good.
16. I have always had a taste _____ 19th century literature.
17. She is crazy _____ dancing.
18. He was jealous _____ Tom's success.
19. We are delighted _____ our new house.
20. Please refrain _____ smoking.

IV. Reading comprehension.

The Duties of Receptionists and Reservation Clerks

Hotel Receptionist

A receptionist is the first person that hotel guests see or talk to when they arrive or ring to make a booking. A hotel receptionist needs to be welcoming, friendly and helpful, efficient and professional, well-organized and able to handle several tasks at once. In the larger hotels, the front office job is often split into three—that of receptionist, cashier and reservation clerk. In smaller hotels, however, the receptionist could be performing the duties of all three. So the front desk receptionist has to play a very important role in a hotel. Besides, the receptionist even has to deal with some complaints from the angry guests. The receptionist should listen to them, apologize for the trouble, clarify what the exact problem is and let them know you understand.

When checking in guests, you should perform these tasks:
- Welcoming guests as they arrive.
- Assign rooms, introduce services for the guests and issue room keys.
- Check with the housekeeping departments that rooms are ready for occupation.

Unit 13
Tourism Impact

- Liaise with the bell desk to deliver luggage to the rooms.
- Note requests for wake-up calls, transport arrangements and other general enquiries.
- Settle guests' complaints tack and diplomacy.
- Put together the guests' bill, take payment and help guests with any special requests.
- Communicate with other departments regarding group and VIP check-ins.
- Order taxis for guests and book excursions on request.

Main duties:

- Keep a record of guests' arrival, day and time of check-in, length of stay, and their special needs and preferences.
- Liaise with other departments such as housekeeping, restaurant and security, regarding VIP and group check-ins.
- Manage the booking of rooms.

1. Test your vocabulary of hotel reception. (Fill in the blanks with words from the box.)

payment	obligation	destination	the other	hotel occupancy
signature	cashiers	registration card	passport	receptionists
prior reservation checks				

Reception

The reception in a hotel is the desk or office that arranges to stay in a hotel or __(1)__ in for people and answers their questions. Hotel __(2)__ are found in or near hotel entrance halls, close to the center of activity. __(3)__ have to maintain accurate account balances for hotel expenses and collect payment from guests. When performing reservation and cashier duties, they may be working in the back office.

Registration

It is important for the hotel receptionist to make sure that guests are registered correctly. A __(4)__ is used to record the full name, nationality, home address, and __(5)__ of each guest. Foreign visitors must provide additional information such as __(6)__ number and its place of issues, and their next __(7)__. Many hotels use the registration card to find out more about their customers and ask questions about occupation, method of __(8)__, and purpose of visit.

Walk-in guest

In hospitality sector, a walk-in guest refers to that one person who has come to hotel without any __(9)__. Hotels do not have any sorts of __(10)__ to provide proper accommodation to walk-in guest if there is no available room. On the other hand, accommodating walk-in guest can enhance sales and daily __(11)__ if it is managed properly. If the agent cannot accommodate a guest then he should refer him to __(12)__ of that hotel group or any nearby hotel. By this way, if hotels of a locality maintain good relationship with each then high percentage of such guests can be accommodated.

2. Choose the best answer.

(1) The room at that hotel cost $300 a night, and that is a little _____ for me. There's no way I could pay for that.

A. reasonable   B. expensive   C. cheap   D. realistic

(2) Do you have any rooms with a _____ where I can prepare basic meals?

A. kitchenette   B. cooking   C. suite   D. pool

(3) Let me _____ to see if we have any rooms available.

A. view   B. check   C. test   D. look

(4) This hotel is one of the best in the city, and the employees try to roll out the _____ carpet for special guests.

A. blue   B. green   C. red   D. black

(5) I'd like to _____ an executive room for April 21st.

A. check in   B. schedule   C. make   D. order

(6) The _____ at the place I always go does a great job at perming your hair.

A. hair salon   B. barber shop   C. hair-stylist   D. barber's

(7) It's a must to _____ in the pool.

A. wear caps   B. wear sports shoes
C. take a shower before swimming   D. wear swimming glasses

(8) The _____ is the place where a woman can have her hair done.

A. barber's   B. hairdresser's   C. front desk   D. lobby

(9) If you want to _____ your straight hair, why not try a long wave style?

A. charge   B. dye   C. wash   D. change

(10) I want to _____ my hair cut and dyed.

A. take   B. need   C. had   D. have

V. Translate the following sentences into Chinese. They are underlined in the texts.

1. One of the most persuasive socially oriented frameworks developed to analyses the impact that tourism has on local people and their environment is based on the evolving sentiment that local people express as tourism expands and occupies greater proportions of a local economy over time.

2. Although such a proliferation of visitation no doubt has its economic rewards, what the host country gives up to attract tourism dollars cannot be measured simply in economic term. It is no accident that the most vital and creative parts of the Caribbean, for example, have been precisely those that have been most touched by tourism.

3. A notable impact of tourism on traditional values is the demonstration effect, where local patterns of consumption change to imitate those of the tourists, even though local people only get to see a side of tourists that is often not representative of their values displayed at home (e.g., spending patterns).

4. The Balearic Islands and the Costa Brava in Spain observed some of the stress caused by a high concentration of tourism and discussed employing regional development strategies designed to

promote other areas that were as yet undeveloped.

5. The satisfaction of tourism requirements must not be prejudicial to the social and economic interests of the population in tourist areas, to the environment and above all to natural resources which are the fundamental attractions of tourism and historical and cultural sites.

VI. Writing.

How to Prepare a Welcome Speech

A welcome speech marks the start of any special event or occasion requiring a formal opening. It could be a meeting, a lecture, a workshop, or a celebration.

The focus of the speech is always the audience and the goal is to make them look forward to whatever is coming next. You are uniting and bringing them together in the common purpose at the heart of the occasion.

To strike the right tone in the language you use, consider the audience and the event. Is it fun? Is it serious? Think about the common interest everybody shares. This will give you clues to guide your language choice.

The essential elements to cover in your welcome speech are:

- to specifically acknowledge an important guests;
- to generally welcome all the guests, stating the name of the event and host and thank them for coming;
- to give a brief introduction of the host;
- to give a brief introduction of the occasion;
- to give any especial welcomes i.e. to the important guests;
- to introduce the next speaker if appropriate.
- to conclude.

Simulate and create: Write a welcome speech using the content that you are most familiar with. Be sure you have covered all the seven essential parts above.

Unit 14　Tourism Sustainability

PART I　TEXT

Tourism Development in Cyprus Needs to Be Sustained

The tourism development strategy for the Republic of Cyprus[1] reflects the approach of aiming for sustainable development of an already substantially developed tourist destination, while still expanding tourism as a major economic sector of the country.

Cyprus is situated in the eastern Mediterranean Sea[2], south of Turkey. The population of the Republic is close to 600,000. It has an extensive coastline with numerous beaches and coastal plains. Much of the southern interior is occupied by the scenic, forested Troodos Mountains[3]. There are flanked by the central plains, where the capital city Nicosia[4] is located, and the coastal lowlands.

The country has a long history of prehistoric development, followed by successive periods of Classical and Hellenistic Greek, Roman, Byzantine[5], Frankish, Turkish and British occupation, and now independence. This history has left a rich heritage of archaeological and historic sites, picturesque villages and cultural traditions. The mild climate of Cyprus is one of the major general attractions for tourists.

Tourism in Cyprus in the twentieth century has undergone several changes. Before independence in 1960, tourism was small scale and based on the cool mountain environment. During the early post-independence years, there was greater emphasis on coastal tourism, appealing to a wider international market. Following partition of the island in 1974[6], coastal tourism experienced dramatic growth, making the country a mass tourism destination by the early 1980s. By then, concern was being expressed about the future direction of tourism, and the emphasis shifted somewhat away from quantitative to more qualitative development.

Expansion of tourism has been considerable since the early 1980s, with annual tourist arrivals reaching almost 1 million in 1987 and 1.7 million in 1990. The great majority of tourists are from Western Europe, with much smaller numbers from the Middle East and North America. Domestic tourism, mostly day trips, is also substantial in the country.

By the mid-1980s, there was still concern about the direction that tourism was taking. Environment degradation was commencing in the more developed tourism areas, and coastal tourism, focused on the beaches, was by far the dominant form.

Most tourism development has taken place in five main coastal regions. The typical forms of development are the higher-class multi-storied hotels, occupying prime sites adjacent to the best beaches. Lower category accommodation in the form of smaller hotels and hotel apartments are situated on the less desirable sites, often with poor access to the views of the beaches. There is very limited tourism in the mountains despite their scenic beauty, interesting historic villages and cool temperatures. The central plain area attracts few holiday tourists, although conference tourism is being developed in Nicosia. Although visited by tourists, the archaeological and historic sites are no longer primary attractions, not appealing to tourists who do not have special interest in Cypriot history and culture.

Words and Expressions

commence	[kə'mens]	v.	开始
Cyprus	['saɪprəs]	n.	塞浦路斯
flank	[flæŋk]	v.	从两侧包抄
frankish	['fræŋkɪʃ]	a.	法兰克的
prehistoric	[ˌpriːhɪ'stɔːrɪk]	a.	史前的；陈腐的
qualitative	['kwɔlɪtətɪv]	a.	质量的
quantitative	['kwɔntɪˌtətɪv]	a.	数量的，定量的
Nicosia	[ˌnɪkoʊ'sɪə]	n.	（塞浦路斯首都）尼科西亚

Notes

（1）Cyprus：塞浦路斯，希腊语中意为"产铜之岛"，位于地中海东部，是地中海地区最热门的旅游地之一。

（2）Mediterranean Sea：地中海，地中海被北面的欧洲大陆、南面的非洲大陆和东面的亚洲大陆包围着，东西共长约4 000千米，南北最宽处大约为1 800千米，面积约为251.2万平方千米。

（3）Troodos Mountains：特罗多斯山，塞浦路斯西南部山地，面积近3 200平方千米，约占全国面积的1/3。主峰奥林匹斯山海拔1 951米，为全国最高峰，峰顶冬季覆雪。

（4）Nicosia：尼科西亚，是塞浦路斯的首都，位于塞浦路斯岛梅索里亚平原中部，北依横跨岛国北岸的凯里尼亚山脉，西南同青松苍翠的特罗多斯山遥遥相望，面积约50平方千米，人口约23万（2016年），是塞浦路斯政治、经济和文化的中心。

（5）Byzantine：拜占庭的。公元395年，罗马帝国分裂为东西两部，东罗马帝国以巴尔干半岛为中心，领属包括叙利亚、巴勒斯坦、埃及和南高加索的一部分，首都君士坦丁堡，是古希腊移民城市拜占庭旧址，故又称"拜占庭帝国"。

（6）1974年4月20日，塞浦路斯发生政变。这场政变最终使塞国分裂，北部在1983年成立了"北塞浦路斯土耳其斯坦共和国"。

PART II DIALOGUE

Dialogue 1 Hairdressing

C：Clerk；G：Guest

C: Good morning, madam.

旅游英语(修订版)

G：Good morning. I would like a shampoo and set.

C：Yes, madam. What style do you want?

G：I'd like to try a new hair style. Could you show me some pictures of hair styles?

C：Sure. We have various models: bobbed hair, sweptback hair style, chaplet hair style, shoulder-length hair style, and hair done in a bun. Please have a look at them, madam.

G：Thanks. Please give me the style in this picture here but make the wave longer. I would like hair spray, please.

C：Yes, madam.

G：Oh, your hair dryer is too hot. Would you adjust it, please?

C：Sorry, madam. I'll adjust it right away. Is that all right now?

G：Yes, thanks.

C：Please have a look.

G：Perfectly done. Please trim my eyebrows and darken them.

C：All right, madam. And would you like a manicure?

G：Yes. Use a light nail varnish, please.

C：上午好，太太。

G：上午好。我想洗头并做发型。

C：好的，太太。您想做什么式样的?

G：我想换个新发型。你能不能给我看些发型样式的照片?

C：可以。我们有各种各样的发型，如剪短发、后掠式、盘花冠式、齐肩式，还有把头发挽成发髻。太太，您请看。

G：谢谢。请你按这张照片上的发型烫发，波浪大些，再喷些发胶。

C：好的，太太。

G：啊，吹风机太热了，请调整一下，好吗?

C：对不起，太太。我马上调整。现在可以了吗?

G：可以了，谢谢。

C：请您看一看。

G：做得好极了。请帮我修一下眉毛，再画深一点。

C：好的，太太。您想修一下指甲吗?

G：要的。请用浅色指甲油。

Word Service Station

moisturize	给……增加水分	tonic	滋补的
cleanse	使清洁，清洗	bob	剪短（头发）
sweptback	向后倾斜的	chaplet	花冠
spray	喷，洒	adjust	调整
manicure	修指甲	varnish	清漆，油

Dialogue 2 Booking Facilities and Personnel

C: Clerk; G: Guest

C: Good morning. What can I do for you?

G: Good morning. We're going to hold a seminar next Friday. I'd like to book some facilities and personnel for it.

C: Next Friday... that's December 16th, isn't it?

G: Yes. We need a conference hall for 100 people and four smaller rooms for discussion.

C: I see. We have a multi-function hall that can accommodate 100 to 400 guests for the meeting or cocktail parties. And we also have several smaller meeting rooms which can seat about 30 people.

G: Sounds good. What about the basic equipment for the hall?

C: We provide basic equipment such as recorders, microphones, loudspeakers.

G: And what about the technical equipment?

C: All the rooms are fully equipped with the things like computer, slides, overhead projectors. We will arrange the technicians to take care of the facilities running smoothly.

G: Thanks. The last but not the least, please make sure that there will be enough hands to serve the seminar, such as receiving guests, taking registration, carting, so on and so forth.

C: Don't worry. Everything will be ready by next Wednesday. And you can come and check it then.

G: Sure. Thanks.

C: 早上好。我能帮您什么？

G: 早上好。我们要在下周五举行一个研讨会。我想预订一些设备和请一些工作人员。

C: 下个星期五……那是12月16号，对吗？

G: 对。我们需要一个能容纳100人的会议厅，还要4个用作讨论的小房间。

C: 明白了。我们有一个多功能厅，可以供100到400人的会议或鸡尾酒会，我们还有能坐30人左右的小会议室。

G: 听起来不错。大厅的基本设施如何？

C: 我们提供基本的设施，例如录音机、麦克风、音箱。

G: 技术性的设备有什么？

C: 所有的房间都配有诸如电脑、幻灯、投影仪等设备。我们会安排技术人员保证设备正常运行。

G: 谢谢。最后重要的一点，请确保有足够的人手为研讨会服务，比如接待来宾，注册，运送，等等。

C: 不用担心。所有的一切会在下周三之前准备好。到时候您来检查。

G: 好的。谢谢。

Word Service Station

ground floor	（英）底层，一楼	switch	开关
venetian blind	百叶窗帘	curtain	窗帘
mattress	床垫	folding screen	屏风
first floor	（英）二楼，（美）一楼	socket	插座，插口
hanger	挂钩	drawer	抽屉
bedclothes	床上用品	cushion	靠垫，垫子

PART Ⅲ GOOD TO KNOW：Toursit Attractions

tourist attraction	景区	theme park	主题公园
natural/nature reserve	保护区	ruins	遗址
forest park	森林公园	observation deck/viewing platform	观景台
Geo park	地质公园	scenic spots and historical sites	名胜古迹
former resident	故居	art gallery	美术馆
memorial hall	纪念堂/馆	wildlife/safari park	野生动物园
marine/ocean park	海洋公园	amusement park	游乐园
pedestrian street/zone	步行街	resort	度假村
1st grade cultural relic	一级文物	ticket office	售票处
free admission	免门票	roller toaster	过山车
World Cultural Heritage Site	世界文化遗产地		
patriotism education base	爱国主义教育基地		

PART Ⅳ EXERCISES

14-听力资源

Ⅰ. Listening comprehension.

1. The unlicensed tour guides' job is _____.
2. Washington requires _____ for being a tour guide.
3. Mr. Main believes that the requirement violates his right to _____, but the city defends the licence as an _____.
4. Do all people think all jobs need strict controls? Why?

Ⅱ. Put the following into Chinese or English.

1. 精选路线 _____
2. 附加旅游项目 _____
3. 自由活动时间 _____
4. 特别服务要求 _____
5. 组团人数 _____

6. folk custom tour _____
7. trade observation tour _____
8. itinerary map _____
9. guest night _____
10. extension _____

III. Choose the right answer from the two choices given in brackets.

1. All foreign residents _____ (shall, could) have reported to the nearest police station by September 20.

2. The notice stated that visitors _____ (would, might) not take photographs inside the building.

3. This information _____ (can, must) in no circumstances be given to the general public.

4. You _____ (wouldn't, mustn't) tell anyone about his; it's a secret.

5. It's a very kind offer, but I really _____ (may not, can't) accept it.

6. You _____ (couldn't, shouldn't) leave your keys in the car.

7. You _____ (must, will) taste this cake. It's simply delicious.

8. _____ (Wouldn't, Shan't) you care to join us for dinner tonight?

9. Glad to meet you, Mrs. Swanson. _____ (Won't, Can't) you take off your coat?

10. We _____ (must, could) go for a drink after work tomorrow, if you like.

11. _____ (Shouldn't, Mustn't) we at least give him a chance?

12. You _____ (would, could) always try painting the wall a paler color and see if that looks any better.

13. You _____ (must, shall) have the money as soon as I get it.

14. I _____ (will not, cannot) have you talking indecently before the children.

15. Accept his offer now. He _____ (might have changed, could change) his mind.

16. She _____ (may as well refuse, may well refuse) to speak to you, because she's in a very bad mood.

17. Peter _____ (might phone, can phone). If he does, could you please ask him to ring later?

18. Our team has been players, so we _____ (ought to, must) win but you never know.

19. We _____ (should be, could be) able to move into our new house at the end of the month.

20. They _____ (must have arrived, ought to have arrived) at lunchtime, but the flight was delayed.

IV. Reading comprehension.

The Tourism Industry Faces Dilemma

Yogyakarta（城市名，汉译"日惹"）, an ancient university city in Central Java,

Indonesia, is at the heart of one of the regions selected by Indonesian tourism authorities to entice visitors beyond the small island of Bali, which is suffering from tourist overload. Those who rely on tourism for a living say they are especially concerned with the survival of Bali's local culture and fragile natural environment. "Indonesia has a wonderfully old and rich culture," says Jack Daniels, general manager of Bali-based Spice Island Cruises, "When cows were grazing on the fields in Paris outside Notre Dame（巴黎圣母院）, Indonesia had already built the Borobudur Temple（婆罗门教的浮屠庙）. The tourism industry must be the guardians of this quality."

Indonesia's rulers have set demanding and possibly unsustainable targets for tourism: 11 million international visitors per year by 2005, more than triple the current number. Tourism would become the largest sector of the country's economy, worth about US＄15 billion annually, overtaking the current foreign exchange pacesetters: oil and gas（US＄9.4 billion in 1995）and textiles（US＄5.5 billion）.

Consequently, Indonesia is expected to switch from a net energy exporter to a net energy importer by 2005. The government is hoping the shortfall in the country's accounts will be made up by extra revenue from tourism, which in 1995 reached US＄5.2 billion.

However, the road ahead may be rocky. The country's tourism leaders complain that the government does not understand how to market to tourists. Tour operators worry that the country's road, water and sewerage systems will not be able to sustain the extra visitors.

There are also concerns that street crime, in areas like Kuta in Bali（巴厘）, will proliferate with the increase of easy-target tourists. And hotel managers wonder where they will find the trained and qualified managerial staff to serve the additional international travelers.

Currently, many parts of the archipelago lack the infrastructure for any tourist other than those seeking "soft adventure" —action or activity holidays, like white-water rafting and rock climbing. But easier vehicular access to Bali from Jakarta could turn Bali into a little Bangkok, says Ida Bagus Lolec, managing director of Bali Tours and Travel. "People come to Bali for a culture jam, not a traffic jam," says Lolec. "Promoting the whole of Indonesia has its difficulties." Indonesia is the size of the United States from San Francisco to New York. And about the same distance as London is from Moscow. The government has so much else to think about—things like schools and hospitals—that there's not that much money left to spend on tourism marketing and promotion.

1. What problem is Bali suffering from at present?

2. What are the locals of Bali concerned about?

3. What would happen in 2005 if the government's targets for tourism industry were met?

4. What are tourism leaders worried about?

V. Translate the following sentences into Chinese. They are underlined in the texts.

1. The tourism development strategy for the Republic of Cyprus reflects the approach of aiming for sustainable development of an already substantially developed tourist destination, while still expanding tourism as a major economic sector of the country.

2. By then, concern was being expressed about the future direction of tourism, and the emphasis shifted somewhat away from quantitative to more qualitative development.

3. In this way, terrorist attacks on tourism can also be used to punish nationals of a country which supports the government which the terrorists are trying to overthrow or which is in opposition to their own activities.

4. Events which are used by governments to enhance their legitimacy can also be utilized by opposition groups to undermine support for government and to focus attention on government activities.

VI. Writing.

Application Letters

Knowing how to write a job application letter is often of great importance in getting a job because the purpose of the letter of application that goes with your resume is to introduce yourself briefly and to try and make the employer interested in you. The following are some of the things you have to observe in writing your job application letter.

In the first paragraph, state that you are an applicant for the job and note the source through which you learned about the job. In the second paragraph, state briefly your qualifications for the job and refer the reader to your resume. In the last paragraph, state your willingness to come for an interview. If you can be available for an interview at only certain times, indicate this.

Skip two spaces between the inside address and the salutation. Use a colon after the salutation. Sign your name at the bottom, in addition to typing it. As with the resume, neatness is crucial. Type the letter on good quality paper. Proofread very carefully for sentence correctness and spelling mistakes. Be brief and to the point: use no more than one page.

If you can follow these rules, the job application letter you have written is sure to be a good one.

<u>Simulate and create</u>: Follow the rules mentioned and write a job application letter.

Activity 7: Sherpa

Aim:

After watching the BBC documentary film—*Sherpa*, students are supposed to discuss, but not limited to, the following questions.

Agenda:

- Total time – 100-120 minutes in class;
- First 80 minutes, the teacher would guide the students to watch the films—*Sherpa*, which could be downloaded at...
- The last 20-40 minutes, the students would have a discussion on, but not limited by the questions below;
- It's recommended that, for the 1st group of questions, students sould give his /her own opinions, for the 2nd part, teamwork would be applied.

Questions A:

1. Phurba Tashi's wife, mother and his kids are against him going to climb the mountain. What are their reasons respectively?

2. Puhrba Tashi insists on mountain climbing, although he promised that he would not. Why?

3. In what ways tourism industry or careers, do people in the village of Khumjung benefit from mountain climbing tourism?

4. What are the different views concerned with Mount Everest held by Sherpa and Western mountain climbers?

5. What were the primary impressions of Sherpas in western people's view?

6. What are the changes concerned with western climbers' behavior in Mountain climbing tourism from year 1960 to 2010?

7. How does the mountain climbing industry contribute to the economy in Nepal and Khumjung?

8. What is the work that Sherpas undertake in the mountain climbing tourism industry?

9. In the film, Douglas asked "What is the moral justification for that?" after the avalanche. How would you answer this question?

10. How are Sherpas now treated differently from the time when Tenzing Norbay lived? What has caused the changes in the way they are now treated? What are the things that influence the interaction between Sherpa and Western climbers? How are these things relevant to the clash in 2013?

11. What are the measures taken by Sherpas so to reduce the risks associated with mountain climbing?

12. What are the reasons for the disaster on 18th April, 2014? How was the rescue carried out by the Nepalese government?

13. After the disaster, what were the demands that Sherpas gave to Western climbers and the Nepalese government?

14. From the perspective of tourism politics, what are reflected by the argument of continuing the mountain climbing or stopping the mountain climbing?

15. At the end of the film, Phurba Tashi gave up mountain climbing, which means he stopped creating new world records. Do you think this was the best solution for him? Are there any better possible solutions?

Questions B:

1. Please use a diagram to show the chain of relationships between the Nepalese government, mountain climbing organizers, the Sherpa leader, the other Sherpas, Western mountain climbers, and others concerned with the mountain climbing industry and how their relationships influenced what happened on the south side of Himalayas? What were their different views regarding the Himilayas as a tourism centre? Using the film as an example, please analyze how to balance the profits of the different stake holders involved in the industry?

2. What are the positions of Russell Brice (from amountain climbing company), Phurba Tashi (top guide among Sherpa, working for Russell Brice's company) and other Sherpas in the mountain climbing industry? How are their relationships? What is the role of Khumjung in Nepal?

3. Generally, the local people's attitude towards tourism has developed in 4 stages: welcoming tourists—indifference towards tourists—being annoyed with tourists and, finally rejection of tourists. Among these stages, the cold business and commercialization of tourism will eventually corrode the kindness of locals and the authenticity of the tourism goods. This will also damage the tourists' cultural experience. In this process, many elements might speed up or slow down the stages in the process. Examples that impact on these processes would be the quantity and types of tourists, the stage of development of tourism in the area, the cultural and economic difference between the destination and tourists homeland, the destination's physical terrain and the biological fragility of the area, the reliability of the local services to provide tourists with what they need, the difficulty in reaching the destination involved, the attitudes and policies held by the local government towards this kind of tourism. Please try to analyze which of these elements exist in this film. If they exist, please analyze in what form these elements exist and how they have affected the tourism industry.

References

[1] 姚宝荣，魏周，张煜，2004. 实用旅游英语[M]. 西安：陕西旅游出版社.
[2] 魏国富，2002. 实用旅游英语教程[M]. 上海：复旦大学出版社.
[3] 教育部《旅游英语》教材编写组，2017. 旅游英语[M]. 北京：高等教育出版社.
[4] 于立新，2008. 酒店实用英语[M]. 北京：电子工业出版社.
[5] 王迎新，2010. 酒店英语[M]. 北京：北京大学出版社.